THE BRIDGE AT REMAGEN

The Amazing Story of March 7, 1945— The Day the Rhine River was Crossed

KEN HECHLER

Foreword by Brig. Gen. S. L. A. Marshall

PICTORIAL HISTORIES PUBLISHING COMPANY
MISSOULA, MONTANA

LIBRARY OF CONGRESS
CATALOG CARD NO. 57-14677

ISBN 0-929521-79-X

First Printing 1957
First Revised Printing 1993
Second Revised Printing June 1995
Third Revised Printing April 1998

TYPOGRAPHY Arrow Graphics
COVER GRAPHICS Mike Egeler
PUBLISHING COORDINATOR Stan Cohen

The quotation on pages 132–33 is reprinted by permission of the publishers from *A Soldier's Story,* by Omar Bradley, Copyright 1951, by Henry Holt & Company, Inc. The quotations on pages iii and 134 are reprinted by permission of the publishers from *Crusade in Europe,* by Dwight D. Eisenhower, Copyright, 1948 by Doubleday & Company, Inc. The quotation on page 157 is reprinted by permission of the publishers from *Kesselring: A Soldier's Record,* by Albert Kesselring, Copyright, 1953, 1954 by William Morrow and Company, Inc.

All photos are courtesy of the author unless otherwise noted.

Cover poster courtesy Department of the Army, Office of the Chief of Public Relations.

PICTORIAL HISTORIES PUBLISHING COMPANY, INC.
713 South Third Street West
Missoula, Montana 59801

"Broad success in war is usually foreseen by days or weeks, with the result that when it actually arrives higher commanders and staffs have discounted it and are immersed in plans for the future. This was completely unforeseen. We were across the Rhine, on a permanent bridge; the traditional defensive barrier to the heart of Germany was pierced. The final defeat of the enemy, which we had long calculated would be accomplished in the spring and summer campaign of 1945, was suddenly, now, just around the corner."

—GENERAL DWIGHT D. EISENHOWER
Crusade in Europe

"For me it always typified one thing: the dash, the ingenuity, the readiness at the first opportunity that characterizes the American soldier."

—PRESIDENT DWIGHT D. EINSENHOWER
remarks at tenth anniversary reunion of Remagen heroes, The White House, March 7, 1955

By Ken Hechler

INSURGENCY: PERSONALITIES AND POLITICS OF THE TAFT ERA

THE BRIDGE AT REMAGEN

WEST VIRGINIA MEMORIES OF PRESIDENT KENNEDY

WORKING WITH TRUMAN

TOWARD THE ENDLESS FRONTIER

TOWARD THE SPACE FRONTIER

About Ken Hechler

Dr. Charles Moffat,
KEN HECHLER: MAVERICK PUBLIC SERVANT

PUBLISHER'S NOTE: If you like this book and care to comment on it, the author would appreciate hearing from you at 917 5th Ave., Huntington, West Virginia 25701. The author's telephone number at the Secretary of State's office in Charleston, West Virginia, is 304-558-6000, and he is available for talks at military reunions if travel expenses can be reimbursed.

Contents

The Charleston Daily Mail

VOLUME 104—No. 58   THE ASSOCIATED PRESS / THE UNITED PRESS   CHARLESTON, WEST VIRGINIA, FRIDAY EVENING, MARCH 9, 1945   14 PAGES   FIVE CENTS

FINAL EDITION

THE WEATHER
Fair tonight and Saturday.
Warmer Saturday.

Dismay Grips Germany as Yanks Widen Bridgehead; Hodges Pouring Thousands Over Rhine at Remagen

House Votes To Let Clubs Sell Liquors

Conferees End Work On Budget Measure; Jobless Pay Hiked

By Associated Press

In the first action of its kind since the first repealed prohibition in 1934, the West Virginia house of delegates moved to the senate Friday the question of whether citizens should be permitted to buy liquor by the drink in certain private clubs.

The dramatic action came in the house Thursday as a 10-member conference committee completed final work on the budget bill, with expectations of making their report on the $65,000,000 appropriation for the biennium, which they estimated at 3 P. M. Friday.

An agreement on the delinquent lands bill, in which the senate refused to accede to amendment written into the bulky measure by the house, also was before the legislature.

Brilliant Coup May Shorten War

Flight to South Seems Only Refuge for Nazis

The surprise crossing of the Rhine by American Army units south of Cologne is one of the most brilliant coups of the entire war—and one which may shorten the conflict greatly, especially since it synchronizes so perfectly with the new Russian offensive across the Oder against Berlin.

No wonder Gen. Eisenhower...

Reds Confirm Berlin Drive

Kuestrin Entered; Stettin Blasted

LONDON (UP)—Moscow dispatches reported today that the battle of Berlin has been resumed in full fury as the 1st White Russian army drove to within 35 miles of the capital.

Hitler Visits Front

LONDON (UP)—The German radio said today that Hitler had visited the Oder River front.

Swift Assault *Troops Gain 5 Miles*

Dashes Hopes *After River Crossing*

Of Long Fight

Rigid Blackout Covers Maneuvers; Light Nazi Counter-Attacks Halted

NEW YORK—A new U. S. army—the 15th—has gone into action on the western front as part of Lt. Gen. Omar N. Bradley's 12th army group, an NBC broadcast from the front said today.

PARIS—The American 1st army swiftly reinforced and built up its Rhine bridgehead at a point south of Cologne which the Germans said was Remagen 20 miles southeast of Berlin.

Remagen is about 30 miles...

Youthful Officer Wins Credit for Quick Breakthrough

WASHINGTON—The war in Europe has taken such a dramatic turn overnight that military observers here are prepared for almost any kind of news from Germany.

Coal Royalty Bid Attacked

Operators Report Plan Unanimously

WASHINGTON

Stock Market Breaks

NEW YORK (UP)—The American stock market...

Coal Controls Due

WASHINGTON

[photo caption]
VICE ADM. R. K. TURNER

Marines Split Iwo Japanese

Adm. Turner Predicts Fall of Island Soon

GUAM (UP)—U. S. marines virtually split in two the last Japanese holding on Iwo...

Tokyo Admits Yank Landing On Mindanao

77 Ships Reported Pouring Men Ashore In Zamboanga Area

MANILA (UP)—Americans have landed on Mindanao, second and largest of the Philippines, said an unconfirmed Tokyo radio broadcast heard in London today. An earlier report by Tokyo said U. S. warships were shelling Zamboanga, on the southwestern tip of Mindanao, and that a 77-ship invasion armada was lying off the coast.

American forces on Luzon...

Battle in Mandalay

CALCUTTA, India (UP)—Fierce hand-to-hand encounters raged today as Maj. Gen. William Slim's British 14th army fought savagely in attempts to storm entrenched Japanese defenders in the battlefront north of Mandalay.

The Crossing of the Rhine

BY CAPTAIN N. B. LAWLIS, *Ninth Armored Division*

Would you like to hear a story of the crossing of the Rhine.
    By the rough and ready soldiers of the famous Armored Nine.
They're the first to force its waters since the ancient by-gone days
    When the armies of Napoleon stormed across with Marshal Ney.

When the lads first saw the bastions of the grim and brooding Hun,
    All the armies were regrouping and war was all but won.
So they sent them to a sector in the forest of Ardennes
    To a front that wasn't active, just a place to train the men.

But the wildly raging Wehrmacht turned its Tigers on Bastogne,
    And the cleated boot fell hardest where old Nine stood all alone.
At St. Vith they struck her fiercely and at Echternach the same
    They reported her destroyed — nothing left except her name.

For the reddened snow told mutely of their presence on the line
    In so many different places that they called them "Phantom Nine"
They threw all their hoarded power at each lightly held redoubt,
    And they cut the Ninth to ribbons but they couldn't drive them out.

When "Old Blood and Guts" came northward to engage the Rundstedt flanks
    And relieve the Armored soldiers with their brave but thinning ranks,
They stood fast to their mission and the static Alsace plain
    Was the scene for their re-fitting to join the fight again.

They fought long, comrades murdered, but the death's-head storm-troop, swine
    As they readied to make history at a town upon the Rhine.
When the losses were recovered and the bright new Armor shone
    They again took battle station South and West below Cologne.

And they started driving eastward to the stream that broke the heart
    Of the legion of invaders since the time of Bonaparte.
All the Armor speeded eastward through the rubble-laden streets
    While the master race civilians stood in doorways waving sheets.

Till at last they reached the river where they saw the Teuton Line
    From the heights above the Remagen, keeping watch upon the Rhine.
Said the Armored doughboys' leader "What a sight is here below;
    There's a bridge of best construction that the Krauts have yet to blow."

We can put Old Nine in headlines and its place in fame make sure
   If we take that bridge and hold it, so our tanks can reach the Ruhr.
With a will that raced upon it, and that quickening reddening tide
   Made the river ever-hallowed to the Army's Armored pride.

For the hail of hostile firing halted in the thinning rank
   Till their standard would hit Erpel on the Rhineland's eastern bank.
While behind them rising nobly was a prize they'd fought to win,
   They had forged the final bridgehead on the highway to Berlin.

And it stood in steely glory for the troops to cross the flood,
   Bought by crimson coin of soldiers, for a soldier pays with blood.
Mars must give his glory blessings to the Armored Cavaliers
   'Cross the stream that baffled Caesar, and Augustus moved to tears.

There can be no higher honor that the Orders may define
   Than the laurels resting lightly on the troop that cracked the Rhine.
You can tell these Armored soldiers by the look that's in their eyes,
   By the pride that is in their bearing as their ranks go marching by.

But the proudest of the Armor in the days of Auld Lang Syne
   Well, I know
It will be
   The veterans of the Crossing of the Rhine.

Preface

· · · · · ·

MARCH 7, 1945, was a gray and drizzly afternoon. I was at the headquarters of III Corps, some twenty miles west of the Rhine River. One of the corps objectives that day was a town called Remagen (pronounced Ray-mah-gun). I'll never forget the scene as a little sergeant in the Corps G-3 (Operations) section threw down the telephone and yelled:

"Hot damn! We got a bridge over the Rhine and we're crossing over!!"

At this point the corps headquarters was thrown into one of those wildly happy turmoils which have few equals except in the headquarters of a presidential candidate during a tense moment in the convention balloting.

On the day Remagen Bridge was captured, I was lucky enough to be commanding a four-man team of combat historians charged with recording the on-the-spot story of the war in Europe. To be right at the point where a sensational and unexpected story broke was a real prize. And the story had many elements rolled into it—personal heroism, mystery, fantastic rumor, strategic importance, and a dramatic wallop.

Not long after receiving the electrifying news, I went down to Remagen and talked personally with some thirty officers and men directly involved in the crossing. Again and again I was told: "Be sure and see Lieutenant Karl Timmermann; he led the first men across and he was the first officer over the Rhine." I found this tall Nebraska youngster shaving in a bombed-out house east of the Rhine. His first reaction was to wonder what all the excitement was about. But he filled me in with careful details on what he had experienced, and his men and the tankers and engineers helped put the complex jig-saw puzzle together while the events were still fresh.

Lots of things ran through my mind as I looked at that shaky bridge, already wounded mortally by the German attempts to destroy it with dynamite, artillery, bombs and other means. I kept thinking that it must have taken a lot of strange coincidences to make it possible for the Americans to cross. There is a framed inscription on the wall of a house in Remagen which reads: "If God be for us, who can be against us?" Curiously, this inscription was also on the wall of the house where five German officers were sentenced to death by a Hitler court martial for failing to blow the Remagen Bridge. In Remagen I pondered the tremendous significance of that first word "If." God was surely smiling on Karl Timmermann and his men that day.

The action at Remagen Bridge is also a moving human story as well as a brilliant stroke of military daring. In gathering the military details, I became fascinated by other angles such as what kinds of people were really involved here, what kinds of families and home towns they came from, and how they reacted on each other at Remagen. At that time I was not thinking in terms of creating a sort of "Bridge of San Luis Rey" in reverse, but I resolved that if the opportunity ever arose I'd try to keep in touch with these heroes of Remagen and visit them in their home communities.

It soon became apparent that the full story of Remagen could never be told unless we could piece together what happened on the German side. Soon after the close of the war in Europe, the War Department sent President George Shuster of Hunter College and three other experts to interrogate some of the top Nazi officials. Thanks to the recommendation of my commanding officer, Colonel S. L. A. Marshall, I was assigned to this War Department mission as the fifth member and charged with covering the broad area of "military strategy." This enabled me to talk freely and in relaxed circumstances with Göring, Jodl, Keitel, Kesselring, and a score of other top German leaders interned at a Luxembourg château—before any of them had an inkling they would be tried at Nuremberg. Naturally, I talked with many of these leaders about Remagen and began to gather the story of what went wrong on the German side.

When most men get out of the service they put aside the concerns of military life. Like others, I too developed new interests—three stimulating years of teaching politics at Princeton University, four exciting years of working for Harry Truman, riding the campaign train from coast to coast in two presidential campaigns, and getting a lot of fun out of life. During Christmas vacation of 1953, I was cleaning out some old files when I came across the wartime notes and interviews concerning Remagen Bridge, decided they had rested long enough, and set out to complete the story.

Where were the men who had captured the bridge—and what would they add to the record? It used to be possible to get from the Adjutant General, for a dollar a name, the most recent addresses of Army veterans. This was a little expensive and not always accurate, but it helped put me in correspondence with over 500 men who had served in the units at Remagen. I asked them all to write me about themselves and what they remembered about the events at the bridge. The responses produced many invitations, and whenever I could steal a few days off I travelled around to see people like Emmet Burrows in Jersey City, Joe Petrencsik and Nick Brdar in Cleveland, Alex Drabik in Toledo, Myron Plude in Chicago, Joe DeLisio in the Bronx, and many others.

These letters produced a cryptic note from West Point, Nebraska, stating that Karl Timmermann was no longer living and that the town never quite understood or appreciated what he had accomplished at Remagen. This led to several trips to Nebraska to talk with Timmermann's family and try to figure out why the town felt the way it did about his exploit. In 1995, West Point honored Timmermann and his family with a special ceremony and a monument, as well as naming the Timmermann Bridge over the Elkhorn River.

In the summer of 1954 I returned to the quaint little resort town of Remagen, Germany, and spent several weeks there talking with the residents and old soldiers in the vicinity. The bürgermeister, Dr. Hans Kemming, opened many doors for me, and I am particularly grateful to Frau Karin Loef for assisting me at every turn with documentary and personal information. H. Heitman gave help with some translations and conversations. Manfred Michler of Cologne, a deep student and excellent publicist of the events at Remagen, was most generous with his help.

While in Germany I tracked down the German commandant at the bridge, Captain Willi Bratge, who was teaching mathematics in a one-room schoolhouse many miles from Remagen. I drove him back to Remagen and we spent two days walking around the town while he explained in great detail what had happened while he was in command at the bridge. I then did the same with the German engineer commander, Captain Karl Friesenhahn, who was living in Koblenz. Two ex-sergeants, then around Remagen – Gerhard Rothe and Jakob Klebach – also helped me extensively in reconstructing the German story.

During the war, the following combat historians were very helpful to me at Remagen: Robert E. Maxwell, Harvey R. George and Thomas Lyddane.

Numerous members of the staff of the Army Office of the Chief of Military History have been most generous in their help including Martin Blumenson, Major James F. Holly, Charles V. P. von Luttichau, and Israel Wice. I want to mention particularly Joseph R. Friedman, who as Editor in Chief of the Army's official series of World War II histories has had wide experience in dealing with fractious writers. This book owes much to his creative editing. Naturally, such muddy English as crops up in this book is exclusively mine.

Ken Hechler, Huntington, W. Va.
Col., Armor, USAR (Ret.)

Ken Hechler shortly after completing Officer Candidate School and receiving his commission in the Armored Force at Fort Knox, Kentucky.

Foreword

. . . .

By Brig. Gen. S.L.A. Marshall

WHEN AS HISTORIAN OF THE EUROPEAN Theater in the 1945 summer I began to bring the German commanders and their staffs into our operation so that we might know their side of the World War II combat story, nothing more astonished me than their shock at the Remagen Bridge.

Their reverses at Avranches, Utah Beach and in the Ardennes they could understand and even accept with no feeling that the results were other than the mathematically inevitable. But toward Remagen they had the demoralized view of men who feel lost because fate has mocked them and black magic fights on the other side. When the first Rhine bridge was lost, the Hitler Army reeled and its combat leaders became gutted of hope. This was the real significance of the Remagen episode, which was not a battle in any real sense but rather a military accident.

Until Remagen occurred there was always another barrier behind which this fraying army could dream of collecting itself and holding until some terms could be made. Thereafter the dream died.

"Remagen killed us," the German generals said over and over. "How could it have happened? We are a military people. We are not the careless." Their tone reflected that what had shattered hope was also the death stroke to pride. The German soldier is a precise individual. He glories in his ability to engineer all things well in war, to build and plan beyond possible intervention by chance, and to look good even in defeat. Remagen dispelled the legend even for those who are readiest to proclaim it.

In that hour we could not tell them in detail by what weird circumstance their line at the Rhine had become unhinged. The story of human failure and daring, of technical miscalculation and of tactical hazard, which composed the mystery, was of small-bore concern compared to the vast battle operations of the Theater. It was bound to be a wonderful tale replete with the values ever present when in war people stake their lives on their personal decisions. But it had to wait.

We knew that on our side many men, at varying levels, claimed part of the credit for the seizure and exploitation of the Remagen bridgehead. Not all who deserve it will ever be acknowledged their full due. That is true of all operations in war. At first only a few men may see the opportunity, as young Timmermann and the commander, General Hoge, saw theirs, when gazing from the height above Remagen they thrilled to the sight of the Ludendorff Bridge still intact. But unless upward through the chain of command there is an immediate, acute appreciation of the full military significance of what men forward know by sight, there is no pay-off. In war it is infinitely difficult to change plans already in motion and give new direction to forces already under momentum.

Still, at Remagen this was done. After the bridge was taken the penny press heaped much cheap scorn on the High Command, trying to make the point that the energy and imagination of a few determined fighters had embarrassed the well-laid plans of its master strategists to their undying chagrin. Nothing of the kind happened. General Bull's words of consternation, quoted in this book, were a first momentary reaction; he thought better of them within a few minutes. General Eisenhower, hearing by telephone of the Remagen wonder almost immediately, responded: "Get all the troops across that can be moved." Field Marshal Montgomery, with his army group already set for a full-scale go at the Rhine, got the news and replied: "That is just bully." But the legend dies hard that military brains love to do all things the hard way.

As I have said somewhere in my military writings, no decision in combat is more difficult to make, and to time correctly, than the blowing of a bridge. There is an awful finality about it even when troops are moving offensively and view the bridge both as an avenue to high enterprise and a fire-slot inviting counterattack.

When commanders on the spot stay in doubt about their main decisions, inevitably there can be no unity of resistance by their troops and fire quickly flags to the vanishing point. The clear marks of weapons and tactical near-paralysis among the Germans on both sides of the Rhine at Remagen may be read between the lines of this narrative.

Among United States troops in the attack there were the ever-present few hardy spirits who love to skate on thin ice. When the opening looms and well-organized fire is not directly grouped and going from behind it, the mere smell of a possibly overwhelming danger will not stop them. The risk has to be palpable and thickly present to keep them from boring in. There are adventurous men like Timmermann in every American unit; one mistake made by the German command in World War II was that it too lightly esteemed their energizing influence over all American operations.

I have known Ken Hechler since 1944, when Normandy was invaded. While the fighting lasted he was a combat historian, working always in the fire zone. It was after V-E Day that he drew the heaviest assignment of his life. When I decided that we had to fold the German commanders into our show to complete the history of the Theater my own time was taken up with bulldozing a right of way for this unique program through our own General Staff. Someone else had to do the pioneer work in the field, dealing with the Germans in person to determine the potential for the work while they remained in the POW camps. Out of this research we expected to develop our rules of procedure and the physical setup which the operation would require.

That assignment fell to Ken Hechler as a one-man team and monopolized his time during the 1945 summer and autumn. In its course he got to know well such men as Göring, Keitel, Jodl, Dönitz and the other culprits of Nuremberg and they unburdened themselves to him in an amazingly frank set of interviews. He set the foundation for an entirely new kind of field work in war. My debt to him is considerable.

In a niche of my study are two filled wine bottles, the only souvenirs I have ever brought back from war. What makes them different is only that, though carefully corked, they are filled with muddy river water. With Ken Hechler at Remagen were two of our staff artists, Bernard Arnest and Harrison Standley. They painted the Ludendorff Bridge while it still stood. They were still at their easels when it fell. So they painted again, showing the crumpled structure lying in the Rhine. But, like Ken, they had strayed several times to the east shore. On one trip they filled the bottles, painted special labels for them and shipped them back to me. I have lived since with this grand jest. The labels read: "Here's the best German wine of all—water from the east bank bottled by Arnest and Standley, Importers."

Ken's story revives memories of why fighting men spoke of Remagen as if it spelled magic. It explains why two bottles of unpotable water are held dear after many years.

S. L. A. Marshall
Chief Historian, ETO
Birmingham, Michigan

S. L. A. Marshall

One
. . .

The News Comes to West Point, Nebraska

MARCH 7, 1945, WAS A BUSY EVENING at the Goldenrod Café in the wealthy little farm town of West Point, 75 miles northwest of Omaha, Nebraska. The school kids were just starting to pile into the booths along the edge of the walls for their evening round of milk shakes, and to take a couple of turns to the rhythm of the giant, rainbow-lighted juke box. Above the chirp and chatter came the insistent ring of the telephone.

To Bill Schäfer, the pudgy, bald-headed proprietor of the Goldenrod Café, the telephone was a nuisance. It always rang when he was busiest. His cooks and waitresses were constantly interrupting their work to take calls. The biggest annoyance was the long-distance call, which took so much time to get through from Omaha during wartime, and usually resulted in elaborate efforts to shush the gayer customers at the Goldenrod. So when Schäfer shuffled to the phone on the evening of March 7, 1945, he was in bad humor when the operator said with authority: "Long distance for Mrs. Mary Timmermann, Omaha calling."

Schäfer grunted uncomfortably: "Timmy, get this phone again. Make it short. You got lots of customers."

An ample, middle-aged lady wearily placed a wet rag on the edge of a table and plodded across to the phone. She was a little afraid of telephones, because her broken English was hard to understand and she had some difficulty figuring out what the other person was saying. She was also afraid because her two oldest sons were fighting in Germany, her pretty daughter was in the WAC, and her youngest son was threatening to run away from home to join the Army before he was old enough. A long-distance call could mean trouble.

Mrs. Timmermann, a German war bride from the first World War, had several brothers fighting in the German army in the second war. She was sick of war, sick of her back-breaking 11 A.M.-to-midnight job at the Goldenrod, and jumpy and nervous about the safety of her sons and brothers who might be firing at each other at this very moment. She jabbered incoherently when a stern voice on the other end of the phone demanded: "Are you Mrs. Mary Timmermann, the mother of Second Lieutenant Karl H. Timmermann?"

The voice kept boring in, disregarding Mrs. Timmermann's frantic mixture of German and English.

1

Mrs. Timmermann feared the worst. She left the receiver dangling and jounced over to get Bill Schäfer. "Bill, help me, it's something about Karl, I don't know what."

Schäfer was not very sympathetic. He took the phone. The determined voice said: "This is the Omaha *World-Herald* calling. Would you tell Mrs. Timmermann that her son, 2nd Lieutenant Karl H. Timmermann has just crossed the Remagen Bridge, and he was the first officer over the bridge?"

Schäfer, who had grown up along the Rhine, knew where the Remagen Bridge was. He could guess that this was something pretty important, or else Omaha wouldn't be calling. But he wished that the voice wouldn't keep booming away as though Karl Timmermann had captured Adolf Hitler single-handed.

"Here, you take the phone, Timmy," said Schäfer impatiently. "Karl is all right. He just crossed the Remagen Bridge, that's all. Now talk to the man."

Mrs. Timmermann was still scared, and trembling. The voice kept saying: "Your son Karl has just crossed the Remagen Bridge. You know what it means?"

"I know what it means to me: Is he hurt?"

"No, he's not hurt. But listen to this: Karl Timmermann was the first officer of an invading army to cross the Rhine River since Napoleon."

"Napoleon I don't care about. How is my Karl?" The conversation was inconclusive. The *World-Herald* collected a few basic facts from Bill Schäfer and Mrs. Schäfer and then settled down to write a story about the heroism of Karl Timmermann.

Many telephones rang all over the country on the evening of March 7, 1945, as the word spread to families that there were many heroes at Remagen Bridge.

For to the bridge at Remagen had come Americans from many parts of the land—a devil-may-care little sergeant named DeLisio from the Bronx; a shy, gangling butcher named Drabik from Toledo; a hard-driving general named Hoge from Lexington, Mo.; a methodical engineer named Mott from Nashville; a sleepy-eyed tanker named Goodson from Pendleton, Indiana. . . . These along with Timmermann and many others equally courageous had brought off one of the war's most electrifying feats.

The big events of a war are confused things in the making. And after they are made, the passage of time tends to blur the original hazy outline of events into something unrecognizable. The story of the Remagen Bridge has many versions. An infantryman may tell it one way, an engineer another, a tanker still another. The general commanding a huge army has a different view of it from the enlisted man in the ranks. The real story has honors enough for all—including many who never lived to see the light of day on March 7, 1945. And it begins long before that date, long before a few combat soldiers on their way to a town called Remagen unexpectedly caught sight of a lone bridge still spanning the waters of the Rhine.

Two
. . .

How We Planned to Cross the Rhine

THE TOWN OF REMAGEN IS ON the Rhine River midway between Cologne and Koblenz. It is an old Roman town, with a population of about 5,000. Tourists come to Remagen to stroll the river bank, climb the grape-covered hillsides, and join in throaty songfests at the local cafés. But as a place from which to launch an attack across the Rhine, Remagen offers enormous difficulties.

One glance at a map would explain to any military man why Remagen is a terrible place to try a river crossing. The roads from the west are narrow. Even if troops succeed in crossing, mountains, forests, streams and ditches confront them—all conspiring against an attack—and poor secondary roads and rugged terrain unsuitable for tanks stretch eastward for a dozen miles, as far as the Bonn-Limburg autobahn.

The current at Remagen is swift and turbulent. The Ahr River, which swells to an angry torrent in the springtime, flows into the Rhine about one mile above the town. Between this junction and the town, the Rhine takes a sharp bend through a gorge and picks up speed through Remagen, where it is about seven hundred feet wide.

Directly opposite Remagen on the east bank looms a six-hundred-foot cliff of basalt whose sheer face is black against the sky, called the "Erpeler Ley." From the top of the cliff, or from the rude trails that lead to the summit, the observer has a commanding view of the countryside on both sides of the river and for ten miles in either direction.

North of the Erpeler Ley rise the famous Siebengebirge ("Seven Mountains"), including the Drachenfels—where Siegfried slew the dragon. To the east and south are other heights. The rugged Westerwald area to the east, back from the Rhine, is peppered by thick, wooded areas and forbidding slopes and gullies which make natural tank traps. Several defunct volcanoes are prominent across the Rhine. This terrain not only is difficult for an attacker, but also provides excellent observation and protection for a defender.

At Remagen was a double-track railroad bridge, a little over 1,000 feet long, built at the end of World War I and named Ludendorff Bridge after Germany's wartime commander. The railroad, after crossing from the west, passed through a twelve-hundred-foot tunnel in the Erpeler Ley, and continued along the east bank toward

Erpeler Ley, the 600-foot basaltic cliff, which loomed over the Remagen Bridge.

the Ruhr. The bridge was important because it linked the Ruhr and the Ahr valley with the Eifel and Moselle regions. The townspeople resented it because it destroyed the beautiful view up the Rhine, but they were proud of its contribution to the war.

At the time of the Normandy landings, neither the American nor the German planners dreamed of a Rhine crossing at Remagen. The inch-by-inch fighting in the hedgerows during June and July was bloody and frustrating. But August of 1944 was a glorious month for the American Army in France, a month of sweeping movement through open country, with tanks in the lead, and the American military planners began to think seriously about how to cross the Rhine.

In August the unit that would be first to cross the Rhine – the 9th Armored Division – boarded the *Queen Mary* at New York and set out on a stormy voyage to Europe. Specifically, the hour was 7:45 A.M., the date was August 20, 1944, and it was the ship's seventeenth eastbound crossing. Second Lieutenant Karl Timmermann and his buddies had spent twelve days at Camp Kilmer, New Jersey, boning up on ship-boarding techniques, taking physical examinations and making out last wills and testaments. They all had received passes for a last fling in New York. Timmermann stayed sober. He wrote to his wife at West Point, Nebraska, that he was planning to see a good movie, "Woodrow Wilson." It did not inspire him to make the world safe for democracy, but it gave some strength to his spirit and to his mental outlook toward the future.

Timmermann, an infantry platoon leader in Company A of the 27th Armored Infantry Battalion, hated the ocean. He liked little streams like the Elkhorn River back at West Point, which were ideal for swimming and fishing. He dreaded the ocean crossing.

The trip was longer and rougher than usual. While the ship zigzagged toward Scotland, big plans were being made and exciting developments occurred in France that were to influence the combat role of the voyagers. One day after the 9th Armored steamed out of New York harbor, a company of General Patton's foot soldiers in the 79th Division made a quiet and dramatic crossing of the Seine River. The night was rainy and all who were present testify it was the darkest night they had ever experienced. They found a wobbly footbridge alongside a dam across the Seine. Not a shot was fired. One nervous soldier lost his helmet, but there were no casualties.

Then came the liberation of Paris, that tumultuous and continuous celebration which seemed to go on all day and night for weeks. The flowers and the champagne and the kisses flowed on without interruption. And in the Allied ranks, optimism reigned supreme. From Paris, the tankers and their truck-borne infantry comrades were streaking toward the Siegfried Line and the Rhine.

Now the chief barrier to advance seemed to lie in the rear, for a critical shortage developed in supplies—especially gasoline. To be sure, the supplies were at Cherbourg and near the beaches, but when truck transport to the front took five days it became apparent that careful rationing was necessary. General Patton's tanks stormed ruthlessly forward without too much opposition until they were choked up short without gasoline. Rigid priorities were imposed, but they alone could not solve the basic problem of an overall shortage.

East of the Seine, the problem boiled down to who was going to push with the main effort—the British in the north, or the Americans in the south. Field Marshal Montgomery stressed the advantages of an advance through Holland which would open the way for a thrust across the north German plains directly to Berlin and victory. It was an intriguing prospect. Opening the vital port of Antwerp would ease the problem of supplies, and crushing the Ruhr, on which the enemy war machine depended, might bring about a German collapse.

General Omar Bradley, commanding an army group that included the First Army and General Patton's Third Army, had other ideas. He wanted to head for the Saar and the Rhine near Frankfurt. This route led directly through central Germany and would rob Germany of a coal-rich area.

As the debate between Montgomery and Bradley raged during August, nobody mentioned a town named Remagen on the Rhine. Montgomery wanted to left-hook far north of it, and Bradley to right-hook deep to the south. On the large-scale maps they were poring over, Remagen looked small and insignificant.

Late in August, General Eisenhower decided tentatively in favor of Montgomery's plan to make the main effort along the Channel coast. At the same time, he allowed Bradley's troops to close up to the Rhine and link up with General Devers' forces coming from the south. Only when the supply situation was well in hand would they launch the final push toward Berlin. The Eisenhower plan called for the first crossing of the Rhine to be made by Montgomery north of the Ruhr.

The American armies were still on the move August 27, when the *Queen Mary*

View of Remagen Bridge from atop Erpeler Ley. U.S. ARMY SIGNAL CORPS, NATIONAL ARCHIVES

docked in Scotland. There it was cold and clammy. "I put on my wool underwear today to keep my legs warm. They look like trapeze pants," Karl Timmermann wrote home. "I ate my three regular meals today; breakfast was the only one that came up." The top American planners had no special role in mind for Timmmermann's comrades. They weren't due in France until early in October, and by then the war might be over for all practical purposes.

To follow up Montgomery's crossing of the Rhine, Bradley prepared his First Army to attack and cross the Rhine in the vicinity of Koblenz, Bonn and Cologne. This plan he unfurled in a field order dated September 10. Events quickly demonstrated that the planned crossing of the Rhine was premature. September proved to be a month of shattered dreams. Gasoline ran out. The tanks sputtered and ground to a halt. The Germans, after a long and harrowing retreat across France, suddenly found their second wind when they began fighting in defense of their homeland. The Siegfried Line and fortified cities like Metz were stubbornly held, and Field Marshal Model, a dedicated, fanatical improviser, injected a new fighting spirit into the tired German troops. On September 17, Montgomery made a brilliant gamble to cross the Rhine with daring paratroop drops at Arnhem and Nijmegen. But the German panzers closed in on them and methodically killed an appalling percentage of them. At the end of September, the Rhine seemed much farther away. President Roosevelt wrote to Winston Churchill that he had bicycled over most of the terrain "in the old days" and therefore was less optimistic than some of his field commanders about the ease of crossing the Rhine. Arnhem-Nijmegen proved to be "a bridge too far."

The 9th Armored spent most of September in England, training in tactical problems. The division was reequipped with new tanks and other vehicles and its equipment was in good shape. Then on September 28 it embarked at Weymouth on the south coast in an LST (landing ship, tank) for the English Channel crossing. Once again the infantrymen and tankers who were to figure in the first crossing of the Rhine were buffeted by seasickness.

France and Belgium were colder and rainier than England. There were bivouacs on damp ground, road marches and rain-swept trips by truck, then more chilly bivouacs, and finally, at the end of October, the green troops went into the line near Luxembourg. They didn't feel much like heroes, in the gooey mud and under the barren trees. Three days after going into the front lines for the first time, Karl Timmermann wrote back to Nebraska: "You know, military uniforms are pretty and smart, but really all they stand for are heartache, destruction and death, because a soldier is an instrument of war."

October and November were months of slow, painful and bloody progress through the treacherous Hürtgen Forest, and no spectacular gains were scored along the Allied front. In mid-October, First Army took Aachen. Then started a renewal of the debate between Montgomery and Bradley over where the next main thrust would be aimed in a November offensive. Bradley stressed the advantages of a two-pronged attack which would encircle the Ruhr, while Montgomery still felt that a single hammer blow north of the Ruhr was the most direct path to victory. Now General Eisenhower was more sympathetic toward General Bradley's plan than in August. This meant that Bradley's armies would attack both north and south of the Ardennes, drive on to the Rhine and seize crossings if they had the momentum. Montgomery was to push from Nijmegen between the Rhine and the Maas. Once again, the little town of Remagen was overlooked.

During this new offensive, the Ardennes sector remained quiet. The line was loosely held in what was clearly a "calculated risk" in order to free troops for the offensives to the north and south.

For two weeks at the end of October and early in November, Timmermann's unit was in the front line just west of the German town of Prüm, in positions near the Siegfried Line which had previously been occupied by the 2nd Infantry Division. On November 8 the division returned to Luxembourg for intensive tank-infantry and winter combat training. Then on December 13 portions of the 9th Armored moved up to Belgium to assist in the capture of the dams near the headwaters of the Roer River.

The men of the 9th Armored Division were moving back and forth through the area of the Ardennes, that thickly wooded, hilly area which was to become the site of the murderous Battle of the Bulge in December. Robert E. Merriam's masterful book, *The Battle of the Bulge*, tells how the 9th Armored Division got its baptism of fire. Out of the darkness on the bleak and foggy morning of December 16, 1944, German panzer troops and crack infantry units crashed through the thinly held American lines. The weather made it impossible for planes to help check the breakthrough. With a few heroic local exceptions, disaster followed disaster, in the first days of the bloody fighting.

The 9th Armored Division acted as an emergency fire brigade. One combat command was rushed south to help defend the city of Luxembourg. Another combat command was thrown into the center of the raging inferno to help the 101st Airborne Division defend the vital road-net at Bastogne. Combat Command B, which eventually took the Remagen Bridge, was in the thick of the heavy fighting around the important Belgian city of St. Vith.

Late in the evening of December 16, Combat Command B of the 9th Armored was ordered to the area southeast of St. Vith, near where the Germans had surrounded two full regiments of the 106th Infantry Division. Panic prevailed in that sector. Germans in American uniforms and equipment were infiltrating, and wild rumors were spread about the mission of Skorzeny to kidnap General Eisenhower while the attacking Nazis threw the Americans back to the beaches.

Karl Timmermann's company did not have an easy time in their first sharp brush with the German 67th Volksgrenadier Division. The entire kitchen crew and supply sergeant of Company A were captured, and their riddled bodies were later found in the melting snow near Malmedy – victims of the infamous Malmedy massacre. Timmermann himself was wounded and was to carry several pieces of shrapnel in his arm all his life. During the night of December 21-22 almost the entire headquarters staff of the 27th Armored Infantry Battalion were marched off as German prisoners. Glen Strange, the battalion intelligence officer, escaping his captors, led a tank-infantry force against them at four o'clock the next afternoon and miraculously managed to free the headquarters staff.

Late in the evening of December 23, units of 9th Armored Division relinquished their positions to General Ridgway's battle-hardened 82nd Airborne Division. Their casualties in men and equipment had been high. For a green outfit, they had fought skillfully, giving ground with great reluctance and absorbing a lot of punishment. The Battle of the Bulge also resulted in a new nickname for the 9th Armored Division. On two occasions, German official communiqués announced that the 9th Armored had been "destroyed," and the men of the division began to call themselves the "Phantom" Division.

The last-gasp German breakthrough delayed strategic Allied plans for crossing the Rhine for several months. But the engineering side of the planning proceeded steadily. Ever since the invasion was blueprinted in England, the crossing of the Rhine was contemplated, and everybody felt that only a supreme, coordinated effort could hurdle this proud defensive barrier.

At every link in the chain of command, engineers and supply officers wrestled with questions like how many assault boats and pontoon bridges were needed, how fast the current was and how wide and deep the river at various points, what air and artillery support was necessary and what other problems of supply and communications were presented. Even the Navy was involved. Over the roads of Belgium huge LCVP's, LCM's, and other monster-sized naval landing craft moved toward the front, astonishing the citizens.

The main idea was to send across a first wave of crack troops in storm boats, followed up by men in double-end assault boats powered by 22-horsepower outboard motors. The Navy would then bring up enough LCVP's and LCM's to ferry over additional troops, vehicles and supplies. When the bridgehead had been built up sufficiently, an aerial cable would be strung across the Rhine, along which Dukws, landing craft, and amphibious tanks could be guided. Heavy pontoon and steel treadway bridges would be constructed to take care of the rest.

After the "Bulge" in the Ardennes was flattened in January of 1945, the Allied armies faced the immediate task of breaching the Siegfried Line and the Rhineland. In view of Hitler's decision to hold the Siegfried Line at all costs, the Allies decided to concentrate on destroying the German forces west of the Rhine. This would clear the springboard for a leap across the Rhine into the heart of Germany.

Once again the question arose as to how this might best be accomplished. Bradley now wanted to send his First Army on the north toward Bonn and his Third Army through the Moselle River valley to the area of Koblenz—and thus reach the Rhine without fighting for troublesome Roer River dams which already had cost much fruitless combat. This time, it was Montgomery's turn to get the nod. General Eisenhower in February, 1945, billed Montgomery's forces for the "main effort"—a southward drive from Nijmegen, between the Maas and the Rhine and behind the fortifications of the Siegfried Line. At the same time, the northern wing of the American forces would help fashion a gigantic trap by attacking northeastward to join Montgomery opposite the vital Ruhr.

As Montgomery's forces progressed, General Bradley's army group was directed to support Montgomery's attack by capturing the dams on the Roer River and then contriving a vast bear-hug to trap German forces west of the Rhine. After this operation was completed, Montgomery would storm across the Rhine north of the Ruhr. The Americans in the area of Remagen weren't supposed to cross the Rhine at all under this master plan.

The February offensive got under way slowly, hampered by heavy rains. The Germans blew up the Roer dams and flooded the valley, so that high water made an attack across the Roer River perilous in spite of the capture of the dams. Melting snows swelled the streams and rivers all along the front. And the roads were churned up into sticky, soupy messes which slowed the attack.

In the north, Montgomery ground forward slowly. The day after Washington's Birthday, the American First Army crossed the swollen Roer River and started toward

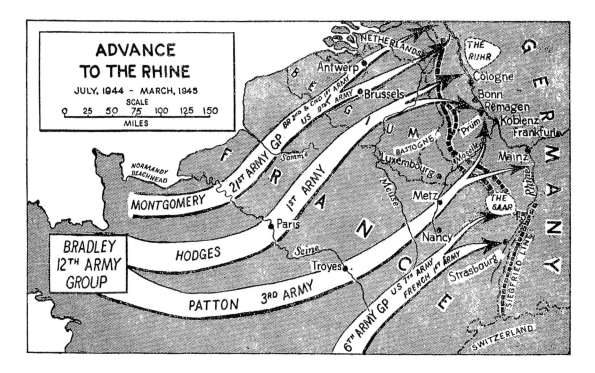

the Rhine, while General Patton's Third Army surged east and northeast toward Koblenz.

While all of these big plans were being formulated and carried out, the men of the 9th Armored Division were still back of the front, training in tank-infantry tactics and preparing for the relatively minor role assigned to them. According to plan, the 9th Armored was to cross the Roer River in the zone of the 78th Infantry Division, and then help in the drive to the Rhine. It was to follow up in the rear of several infantry divisions which were protecting the right flank of the big effort to the north.

In short, the 9th Armored Division had a walk-on part in the Rhine drama. Nobody expected that this virtual newcomer to the European Theater would steal the show.

Three
. . . .

Clearing the Springboard

THE RHINELAND STRETCHES SOME forty miles west of the Rhine River. The rolling countryside, dotted with hills and lined with rushing streams, was the springboard that had to be cleared for the leap across the Rhine.

General Omar Bradley had high hopes for this campaign. Even though he was only protecting the right flank of the British in the north, he felt he could destroy a huge German force west of the Rhine. "If I were asked what campaign in the war brought me the greatest professional pride," Bradley later wrote, "I would point unhesitatingly to this one."

To trap the Germans west of the Rhine, General Bradley told General Hodges' First Army to form the northern pincer of the trap, and General Patton's Third Army to drive in from the south to help spring the jaws closed.

There was a vast difference between General Hodges and General Patton. Patton never walked; he swaggered. Hodges strode purposefully, but did not strut. Patton insisted on boldness in attack, and administrative details were to him a "goddamned nuisance." Hodges, quiet and methodical, insisted on a tidier approach with the strings more firmly in the hands of his staff. To most of his subordinate commanders and to his men, Hodges was a superb administrator rather than an inspiring leader. Even General Bradley, who did not have much color as an individual, was hailed by the doughboys as the "G.I.'s general"; General Hodges could never inspire such accolades.

There is no question but that Hodges was a smashing success as a commander. Leading First Army, he reached the pinnacle of his success through sound decisions, an imaginative grasp of details, and a rare ability to pick and depend on staff and subordinate commanders. The most powerful arrow in General Hodges' bow was the dashing young J. Lawton Collins, who commanded the VII Corps in the First Army.

It was perhaps more than coincidence that General Collins, dubbed "Lightning Joe" early in his combat career, nearly always turned up with the toughest and swiftest divisions in the First Army—outfits like the 2nd and 3rd Armored Divisions, and the 1st, 4th, 9th and 30th Infantry Divisions. From the day General Hodges assumed command of the First Army, "Lightning Joe" always seemed to have the main assignment in the Army's role. This led some observers to comment acidly that General Collins as a corps commander had General Hodges "wound around his finger." Actually,

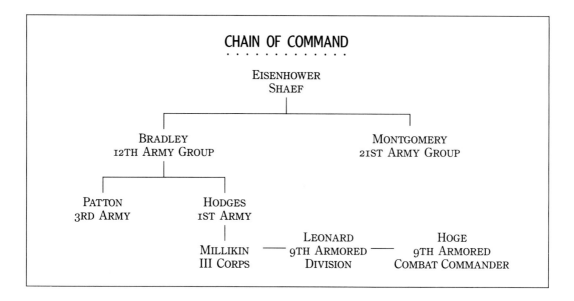

CHAIN OF COMMAND

· · · · · · · · · · · ·

EISENHOWER
SHAEF

BRADLEY
12TH ARMY GROUP

MONTGOMERY
21ST ARMY GROUP

PATTON
3RD ARMY

HODGES
1ST ARMY

MILLIKIN
III CORPS

LEONARD
9TH ARMORED
DIVISION

HOGE
9TH ARMORED
COMBAT COMMANDER

the arrangement worked out beautifully, for General Collins and his spirited troops never failed to deliver the goods. General Hodges calmly pressed the button, and General Collins shot forward to conquer. The system seemed infallible.

When plans were drawn for First Army's advance to the Rhine in February, 1945, it came as no surprise to anyone that General Hodges assigned the most desirable task to General Collins – to capture Cologne and reach the Rhine first.

South of Collins's VII Corps, Hodges assigned less important roles to the III and V Corps. They were to go east and then southeast and eventually close the trap by linking up with Patton's 4th Armored Division coming up from the south. Everybody more or less assumed that III and V Corps would not reach the Rhine until after General Collins had planted his banners on the river bank. Nobody mentioned a town named Remagen and its bridge. It just happened that Remagen and the bridge fell in the zone of advance of the III Corps.

The commanding general of III Corps was Major General John Millikin, a tall officer filled with nervous energy. Millikin, a cavalry officer, liked to go places, and fast. His chief of staff, Colonel James H. Phillips, and his G-3 (Operations) officer, Colonel Harry Mewshaw, were also cavalry officers. The whole corps, imbued with the traditionally bold cavalry spirit, liked working in General Patton's Third Army, to which it had initially been assigned during the Battle of the Bulge.

Having become accustomed to General Patton's mode of operation, General Millikin had to make adjustments in February, 1945, when his corps was reassigned to General Hodges. There seemed to be a personality conflict from the start. Perhaps General Hodges felt that General Millikin was too quick and impulsive. Perhaps General Millikin felt that General Hodges was slow and unimaginative. The staffs of First Army and III Corps, taking their cue from their commanders, revealed some of the same friction.

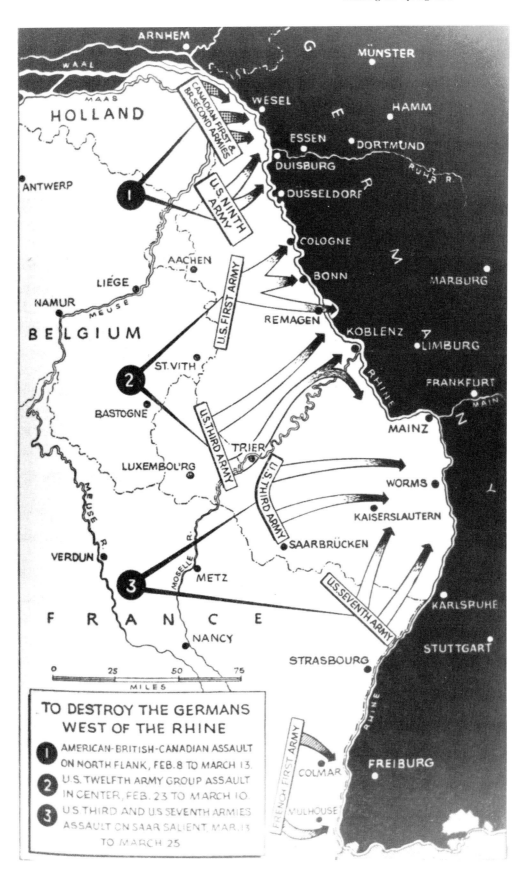

TO DESTROY THE GERMANS
WEST OF THE RHINE

1 AMERICAN-BRITISH-CANADIAN ASSAULT
ON NORTH FLANK, FEB. 8 TO MARCH 13.

2 U.S. TWELFTH ARMY GROUP ASSAULT
IN CENTER, FEB. 23 TO MARCH 10.

3 U.S. THIRD AND U.S. SEVENTH ARMIES
ASSAULT ON SAAR SALIENT, MAR. 13
TO MARCH 25

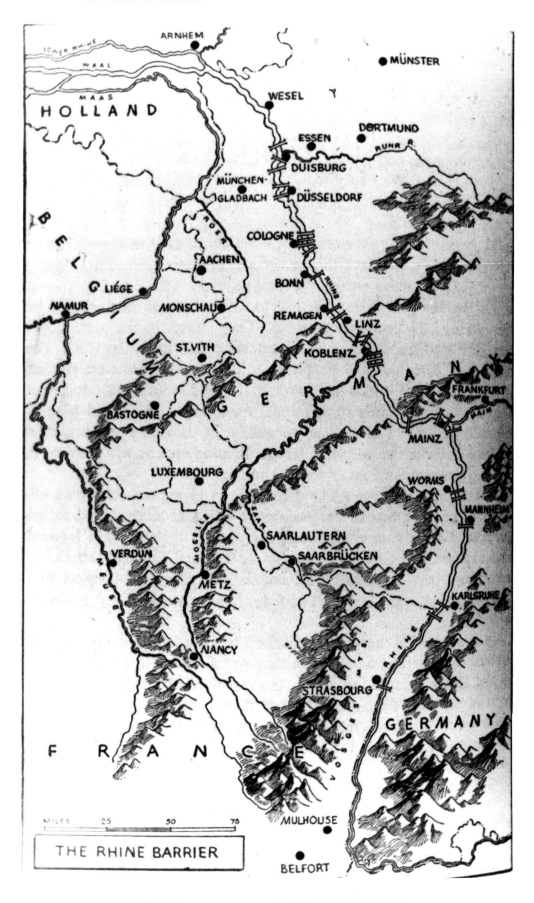

THE RHINE BARRIER

General Millikin moved his III Corps in to replace General Matthew Ridgway's XVIII Airborne Corps in February and First Army staff gave the new general and his top staff a briefing on what lay to the east between the rivers. At this briefing, General Millikin asked the very natural question: "And what about bridges over the Rhine?" First Army staff confidently and crisply told him not to worry, that there would be no bridges over the Rhine by the time he got there; they would all have been blown up by the Germans.

This was a sound and sensible answer—it was inconceivable that an army as thorough as Germany's would neglect such an obvious precaution as blowing up a bridge over a river as defensible as the Rhine. And Millikin subscribed 99 percent to First Army's certainty. But there was just a slight reservation in his mind, a tiny prod of skepticism that was to keep him on the alert for the long chance.

As the units of First Army moved from the Roer up to the Rhine, they developed a series of maneuvers which in football parlance would be termed "mousetrap plays." The technique consisted of first sucking in enemy troops, then clipping them off or encircling them, after which tanks and infantry would plunge ahead through the gaps in the enemy line. This was not too costly because of the disorganized state of the German front-line troops. Nearly everybody talked, planned, and acted in terms of a push to the river followed by a pause and consolidation. Neither the planners nor the troops carrying out the operation dreamed of scoring a quick success.

To the north of First Army, Ninth Army was making a concerted advance with a larger body of troops because of its more important role in the master plan. Montgomery, making the main effort, used Ninth Army as the southern pincer of the vast trap which the British and Canadians on the north were springing on the German divisions that protected the doorway to the vital Ruhr area.

As the Ninth Army plunged toward the Rhine in the early days of March, two interesting actions occurred whose meaning was not lost on the men of First Army. On the night of March 2, the 83rd Division quietly assembled a task force which consisted of all the German-speaking American troops that could be scraped together. These men donned German uniforms and discarded their olive-drab helmets for the black, low-cut German helmets. Tanks, tank destroyers, and other vehicles were disguised and camouflaged to look like German vehicles. Tricks like this had been pulled by the Germans during the Battle of the Bulge, and they had usually created a great deal of temporary confusion without much strategic success.

This trick worked better than anyone had hoped. The task force set out after dark on March 2, its goal the bridge over the Rhine at Obercassel, a suburb of Düsseldorf. The picked men slipped through the German lines, outwitting enemy sentries by fast talking when challenged. When dawn broke, the column was cautiously picking its way through the outskirts of Obercassel. A German motorcycle messenger challenged the column, refused to accept the hasty explanation, and raced his motorcycle back toward Berlin to spread the warning. Members of the American column vainly tried to bring down the motorcyclist with shots, but the firing only helped to

alert the Germans that much quicker. Before long a big fire fight had started in Ober-cassel. The American task force was strong enough to bull its way through this opposition. But the noise of battle warned the town's chief *Luftschutzwart* (air-raid warden). He set off the alarm that spurred the Germans to demolish their precious Rhine bridge just as American tanks were rolling up to it.

Later on the same day the 2nd Armored Division made a manful attempt to capture the Rhine bridge just south of Ürdingen. The division used no disguises or camouflage, but just charged forward and tried to steam-roller the opposition. Some tanks actually got onto the west end of the bridge, but, as at Düsseldorf, the Germans blew it up in time.

Both of these near-misses happened on a Saturday. On Sunday March 4 General Eisenhower drove to Ninth Army headquarters. Staff officers told him about these daring, albeit unsuccessful attempts. The Supreme Commander nodded his approval, but took no steps to encourage First Army to make similar attempts at seizing any Rhine bridges in its area.

Nobody at First Army or III Corps was excited by the news of these unsuccessful attempts. That both tries had failed only confirmed the general opinion that it was fruitless to hope for seizure of an intact Rhine bridge.

In the early days of March, First Army requested the Air Force to continue bombing the Rhine River bridges in the Army zone of advance, in order to disrupt German communications and also to pin down German troops west of the Rhine and destroy their escape route. But the first few days of March were rainy and foggy, and bombing missions had to be canceled.

Within the III Corps zone, the most important Rhine bridge was considered to be the one at Bonn, in the path of the 1st Division on the north flank of the Corps. Its route of advance was directly eastward, while the other Corps units were advancing southeastward. Because of the shorter distance which the 1st Division had to advance, it was expected to reach Bonn before any other Corps unit reached the river. Also, Bonn was the most important objective in the III Corps zone, because of its historic significance and its setting in a more level section of the Cologne plain. So it was anticipated that the Corps would drive to reach Bonn first.

As the 1st Division advanced, its commander, Major General Clift Andrus, asked his corps commander, General Millikin, whether he should try to take the Bonn bridge if the opportunity arose. Millikin, without thinking much about it, told Andrus to go ahead. When General Hodges, the First Army commander, drove down from Düren to the III Corps command post at Zülpich on March 4, Millikin mentioned this brief conversation. But since III Corps troops were still thirty miles from the Rhine on March 4, and since the idea itself seemed so fantastic, the discussion was not pursued far.

AT LEFT:
Ken Hechler with Maj. Gen. Norman B. "Curly" Edwards, who was rapidly promoted after Remagen.

The next day an interesting conversation took place within the G-3 (Operations) staff at III Corps headquarters. III Corps had a very able group of officers in its G-3 section, two of whom stood head and shoulders above the others: Colonel Harry Mewshaw, Assistant Chief of Staff, G-3; and Lieutenant Colonel Norman B. Edwards, his brilliant young deputy. Colonel Mewshaw's age and courtly manner made him seem to belong in the Victorian era, but his slightly bowed legs stamped him as modern cavalryman with years of service. "Curly" Edwards was a deputy who complemented him perfectly. "Curly" tackled everything with zest, whether he was bounding across camp to chow at the crack of dawn, or putting the finishing touches on a field order long after midnight. He bounced up a steady stream of new ideas, which the older and more cautious man usually accepted and improved. More important, Mewshaw could sell ideas to higher authorities with the necessary finesse and maturity.

On March 5 Mewshaw and Edwards were drafting a field order which called for the closing of III Corps units to the Rhine River. Edwards ran his fingers through his wavy, taffy-colored hair and suddenly said: "Look at those two bridges at Bonn and Remagen. Why don't we get some paratroopers and take 'em right out from under the Krauts' noses?"

"We could try," answered Mewshaw, "but if the Air Force can't even get off the ground for our bombing missions, it would be a pretty big risk to send paratroopers. I wonder if you couldn't do the same kind of a job with a picked band of rangers who'd sneak through the German lines and then fight their way to the bridges?"

"What an idea!" exulted Edwards, throwing his grease pencil down on the writing table. "We'll be over the Rhine before anybody else gets near there."

The pair discussed the idea back and forth with enthusiasm, and then started picking the bugs in it. It soon became apparent to them that Army and Corps planning had progressed to such a point that the idea would cause more trouble than it was worth. It would take some sudden and radical decisions. Troops far from the battle-front would have to change direction and be shifted hundreds of miles. The two officers knew that First Army would shudder at the thought of such disruptive moves at this stage of the game. Reluctantly, Mewshaw and Edwards scrapped their idea and did not mention it outside the G-3 section.

The field order on which Mewshaw and Edwards were working, and which was issued on March 6, was the subject of another very significant discussion over the bridges at Bonn and Remagen. There was a strenuous argument between the G-3 and Artillery sections of III Corps as to whether artillery fire should be directed at the bridges. Although bombers had been attacking them, the time had arrived when some thought was being given to protecting them for friendly use. Few people had any illusions that the structures would be captured unharmed; but to play the game according to the book you had to make every effort to capture a bridge intact. There-fore, the G-3 officers insisted that no artillery fire be placed on the bridges, lest shells destroy them. Colonel Phillips, the Corps Chief of Staff, upheld this view, even though the Artillery commander pounded on his desk and yelled: "You are letting the Krauts get away!" A compromise was offered by Colonel Thomas M. Watlington, III Corps Artillery Executive Officer. He suggested that the way to avoid destroying the bridges and at the same time to attack enemy personnel trying to escape across the bridges was to limit artillery fire to time and pozit fuse (in effect, air bursts instead of shells which struck the bridge directly). The Watlington compromise was accepted, and written into the order.

The field order which III Corps issued on March 6 directed the 9th Armored Division to continue its attack southeastward to the Rhine River, to seize crossings over the Ahr, and to "clear enemy from west bank Rhine River and north bank Ahr River in zone." The overlay for this order pointed by arrow to the Remagen Bridge, and stated: "Cut by fire." Remagen and Sinzig (to the south, on the Ahr River) were specifically named as 9th Armored Division objectives, in a large goose-egg along the Ahr River, with Remagen at the northeastern tip of the division objective. Significantly, the objective outlined in the overlay included the town of Remagen, but specifically excluded the bridge at that point.

Even though III Corps forbade direct artillery fire on the Rhine bridges, Colonel Edwards telephoned the 9th Armored Division at ten o'clock in the morning of March 6 that the Ludendorff Bridge should be destroyed by fire "if necessary, to prevent enemy from using it." Later in the day on March 6, the First Army Operations Officer, Brigadier General T. C. Thorsen, came down to the III Corps command post. Among scores of other questions, Millikin reopened the issue of the Rhine bridges. Millikin smilingly remarked that in the cavalry it was the custom to seize opportunities when they presented themselves. Thorsen, who regarded the remark as gratuitous, simply grunted his general approval. Neither officer harbored any serious hope that such a windfall would materialize.

On the evening of March 6, General Millikin thoroughly reviewed the division and corps strategy and objectives in a telephone conversation with the 9th Armored Division commander, Major General John W. Leonard. In this conversation, as in the talks General Leonard held with his own commanders, the emphasis was placed on trapping the Germans west of the Rhine. The mousetrap technique was still in vogue. Neither Millikin nor Leonard really planned seriously on seizing a Rhine bridge.

About ten o'clock on the morning of March 7, Hodges telephoned to Millikin, evincing an unusual degree of enthusiasm for the prospects of a big bag of enemy troops west of the Rhine. Millikin mentioned that his forces, racing along without rest or hot food, were desperately tired and needed a pause for showers, sleep and a few good meals which didn't come out of cans. General Hodges answered: "Well, soon you will join up with Patton, and then we can all take a rest for a while." Hodges further directed that when III Corps reached the Rhine the river should be outposted and guarded by no more than one combat team from each division, and that the other two combat teams should be pulled back for rest.

The conversation between the two generals was amiable enough. Everything seemed to be tidy, just the way General Hodges liked it. Soon he would have completed his part in cutting off the German escape route. General Millikin would be able to relax his pace. The countless thousands of man-hours that went into the planning of how the Allies were to close up to and cross the Rhine seemed to be paying off.

The men in the lower echelons of the 9th Armored Division would have been appalled at the magnitude of the decisions and efforts that had been made in their behalf. But Karl Timmermann and the other one-time travelers on the *Queen Mary* had other things to occupy their minds at the moment. They remained ignorant of higher-level plans, and fittingly so, for the job that they were about to do was one that no one had planned for them.

Four
····

Able Company of the Twenty-seventh

"MAIL CALL!"

A twangy hillbilly cry, soft and wavering, tentatively came from the orderly room.

It was echoed and reechoed as parodists by the dozen spread the joyful news. Scores of G.I.'s poured out of their billets into the company headquarters area.

Try as they might, nobody was ever able to duplicate the mournful tones of Paul Poszich of Jenkinjones, West Virginia, the mail clerk of Company A, 27th Armored Infantry Battalion, 9th Armored Division. Nor could anybody in the company jump quite as high when unsuspectingly prodded from the rear.

Poszich secretly enjoyed his role as the clown of the company, and he consciously cultivated the impression that he was naïve. Only his closest friends knew that he had great mechanical aptitude, and that he was very imaginative when it came to "living off the land." One of his favorite tricks was to go into a dark building where there was no electricity, and somehow rig up a motley collection of tin cans and wire so that everybody had heat and light for the night.

But when it came to mail call, Poszich reverted to his pose as buffoon. He rarely pronounced a name correctly. But any officer suggesting that Able Company get a different mail clerk would have had a mass mutiny on his hands. Poszich was an institution, a symbol of permanence in an uncertain world.

"Del-zo," he would start out, head bent low in an effort to decipher the handwriting.

"DeLisio," came a derisive and corrective chorus from the front row.

Poszich never deigned to accept corrections. "Del-zo," he started again, in a quavering and questioning voice. A small, agile man with a perpetual grin and a mustache bounded up to claim the first piece of mail.

The ritual continued, and Poszich went on down the pile of letters. He made several false starts and cleared his throat at great length before tackling such names as Mercadante, Chiccarelli, Gutierrez, Azukas, Fleischauer, Czyzewski and Papushak. He breathed a sigh of relief when he came to such names as Bates, Ayres, Miner, Davis, White and Lyons, and then stalled again on Petrencsik and Santomauro. But the men let up on Poszich after the first few names, and concentrated their gibes on the lucky ones who got some mail.

"Hey, plough jockey," one of the Brooklynites called out to Sergeant Alex Drabik, "don't they ever plough in a straight line in Ohio?" Drabik, a former butcher, hailed from Holland, a little suburb of Toledo, and was the homeliest soldier in the company. Also he was the shyest. He simply grinned from ear to ear and ambled off to his quarters with his precious letter. Drabik seemed to have a standing rule never to answer a taunt unless someone had the temerity to compare the state of Ohio unfavorably to Missouri.

Poszich stumbled over the last names on the list, and mail call came to an end. But the gibes always continued, with the big-city boys from the East lining up against the farm contingent from Kansas, Missouri and Ohio. The midwesterners were the original core of the 9th Armored Division, and they had been together ever since the division had been activated at Fort Riley, Kansas, in mid-July, 1942. To the epithet "plough jockey," applied by the city faction, their standard counterattack was: "How's it feel to be eatin' without your neighbor's wash in your face?"

The repartee may not have been scintillating, but it served the men of Able Company well. Being members of a combat unit, always eager to divert themselves from too many grim realities, they reacted uproariously to the most ordinary attempt at humor. And they cherished such characters as Roy Amick, who was forever singing "Long Ago and Far Away"; Helmer Larson, who made political speeches whenever he got drunk; Harry Bennett, who was called "Harry the Horse" because of his raucous laugh; rough and ready Charles Penrod, who would laugh and whoop at German shell fire with cries of "*Hot* damn, that was close"; and Noble Foster, who tried to ride every German horse he could catch.

Another of Able Company's institutions was "Kentucky" Drake, the mess sergeant, who was backed up by an able crew including LeRoy Gorrell, Glennus Davis, William Ash and Charles Schmidt. There may have been better mess sergeants in the army than Drake, but few were more colorful and ingenious. He once issued an edict, published as an official order, that all men in the company should turn in their excess Christmas hard candy to be melted down for pancake syrup. The result was a whopping success and turned Drake overnight from "character" to hero of the company. Then there was the time when the chaplain was holding church services over the kitchen, and Drake let loose at his kitchen help with a series of his most voluble curses. The chaplain's attempt to suppress his own laughter brought a roar from the men, and Drake added fuel to the flames by yelling upstairs: "What the goddammed hell's the trouble up thar?"

One of the most important influences in making Able Company a tightly knit organization was its First Sergeant, Nick Brdar, a giant of a man from Cleveland. Brdar combined just enough of the classic, hard-boiled manner of a top-kick with a warmly sympathetic concern for his men. He called them all by their first names. He wrote letters to their wives and parents on how they were getting along. He went out of his way to soothe hurt feelings when the C.O. chewed somebody out. He never overlooked his two letters a day to his wife in Cleveland, keeping her extremely well informed on the personal trials and tribulations of men in a front-line armored infantry unit.

Able Company, like other combat units that lived dangerously, had more than its share of company commanders and platoon leaders. These officers and noncoms constituted a varied assortment of personalities, each one requiring different adjustments from the men.

One of the first company commanders was a little captain who had the job when Able Company went through maneuvers in the California desert and in Louisiana. His favorite expression during training was, "Now we're going to separate the men from the boys." Some skeptics promptly dubbed him "the Kid," which occasionally was changed to "Captain Kidd" when the men desired to make a formal reference. He imposed a strict discipline on the company, insisted on visible signs of respect, and habitually called attention to minor shortcomings.

These tactics won him few friends among the enlisted men, and may have led to the startling exhibit in Able Company's orderly room at Fort Riley. One day the men went out onto the firing range to fire their rifles for record scores. A minute after the order, "Cease fire!" the company commander sauntered out to inspect targets. A couple of shots rang out, and he scurried for cover. The next day every man who came into the orderly room was greeted by the sight of the company commander's field jacket hanging on the wall, with several bullet holes distinctly burned through the back of the garment. No one was willing to clear up the mystery of how the holes got there, and the captain feigned unconcern. He had taken the occasion, however, to issue a grisly warning. Hanging below his bullet-riddled field jacket, a sign in the captain's bold handwriting read: "Don't let this happen to you." The jacket and the reminder were on display in the orderly room as long as Able Company remained at Fort Riley.

Once the company got overseas, it had a new series of commanders. "Captain Kidd" was afflicted by a stomach disorder at the height of the Battle of the Bulge, and was replaced by big, easy-going Carl L. Edwards, a Second Lieutenant who had been Special Services officer in the States. Lieutenant Edwards filled in until Christmas Day, 1944, when Second Lieutenant Jay C. Swisher, a young South Dakotan, took over the company. Swisher, a popular commander, lasted until March 1, when he was wounded while reconnoitering in his jeep. Then came a bewildering series of new commanders for Able Company in the early days of March, and the number of casualties among C.O.'s was very high. On the night of March 6, Second Lieutenant Karl H. Timmermann took over the command of the company.

Timmermann was a seasoned veteran of Able Company. He had commanded the company's first platoon since its Fort Riley days. Almost all his men liked and respected him. "He was a good leader, tough and hard-boiled," one soldier recalls. "Being a disciplinarian, he got called chicken sometimes, but I always felt secure in combat under his leadership." "Maybe he didn't have the finesse for garrison duty," says a noncom from Timmermann's old first platoon, "but he sure was a good combat officer. He was always out in front. The men admired him and knew that he'd never ask anyone to do a job he wouldn't do himself."

Karl Timmermann of West Point, Nebraska. He was the first officer to cross the Remagen Bridge.
U.S. ARMY SIGNAL CORPS, NATIONAL ARCHIVES

One of the men who served under Timmermann over three years and got to know him well relates that he was sort of a "Mister Roberts" to his men. Once when the higher brass were living comfortably in houses a few miles back from the stabilized front, it became necessary to rotate some men in damp foxholes. Tenting was the only protection against the elements. The first group of privates from Able Company were still volubly griping at their plight when they looked up to see a tall figure trudging toward them with his bedroll slung over his shoulder. "I'm going to stay with you fellows awhile," he said simply. One of the privates in the group said: "That's the kind of guy he always was. Whenever he thought one of his men was getting a rough break, he wanted to be up there too."

Lieutenant Swisher, one of Timmermann's predecessors, termed him "an enlisted man's officer." With some of his fellow officers, and with higher ranking officers, Timmermann's relationships were not so successful. He had some sharp rows because he always spoke his mind and never hesitated to tell a superior officer when he thought he was wrong. An enlisted man in battalion headquarters has reported: "Timmermann used to read the riot act to the battalion staff, and it made sense, but the battallion staff didn't have much love for him. I do believe Timmermann got the short end of the stick when it came to honor and glory or medals for that reason." Timmermann's bluntness did not endear him to field-grade officers, but it won the admiration of the men who served under him because they instinctively felt he was fighting their battles.

Karl Timmermann had had a stormy childhood. He was born in Frankfurt am Main, less than a hundred miles from Remagen. His father, a native Nebraskan, served in the American occupation forces in 1919 and was stationed in Koblenz. The elder Timmermann wandered off one day from Koblenz to take unto himself a German war bride in Frankfurt. The Army of course took a dim view of the elder Timmermann's escapade, and his record of desertion plagued him all his life. Destitute, unemployed, starving, and hounded by the authorities, Mr. and Mrs. Timmermann decided in 1923 to take their eighteen-months-old son Karl to America. The difficulties seemed insurmountable. At last the American Friends Service Committee and a group of British Quakers extended a helping hand, untangling the maze of complications through a series of cables to the State Department and paying for the ocean voyage. Early in 1924 the Timmermann family arrived in the United States, and later they settled at West Point, Nebraska.

Karl grew up on the wrong side of the tracks in West Point. Lieutenant Swisher said: "He always told me with a laugh that the reason he joined the Army was 'the garbage can lids all froze down' and he had to find a place to eat." The actual reason was more complex. As a youngster, Karl was exposed not only to poverty but to taunts about his father's Army desertion, magnified and distorted all over town. The father made things worse by kidding a little himself about how he had "outsmarted" the Army. He moved lightheartedly from job to job, never earning enough to support his family. Mrs. Timmermann struggled long and hard as a cook and waitress, and took in laundry after hours in an effort to feed the hungry mouths. As Karl watched his father being destroyed by his reputation, and as he watched his mother in her long, uphill fight against poverty, he unconsciously was drawn to thinking about the Army. This was not so much because the Army offered regular pay, security, and an opportunity to break the bonds which held him in Nebraska; rather it was an urge to live down his father's Army record and bring honor to the Timmermann name.

People in West Point thought it peculiar that Karl Timmermann should talk so much about the Army. In the 1930's, isolationist Nebraska provided a climate far more favorable to public addresses on the crime of America's entrance into the First

World War. Yet the chauvinistic spirit was strong enough to condemn the elder Timmermann as a "yellow-bellied coward who deserted under fire on the front lines"—an exaggeration which was accepted as gospel, and which hurt Karl. He studied up on military strategy, learned the nomenclature of guns, and startled his classmates with an endless patter of figures on how far the newest weapons could fire and the sizes and shapes of modern airplanes. People still thought it was strange that Karl hitch-hiked to Omaha one summer at the end of his junior year in high school, and signed up for the Citizens' Military Training Corps. That was in 1939, three months before Hitler struck at Poland, at a time when West Point was still profoundly isolationist.

Karl Timmermann had followed through on this urge which impelled him toward the Army. He left home on his eighteenth birthday—June 24, 1940—enlisted for three years, and became a private in the infantry. He worked his way up through the ranks, and earned his bars at the Infantry Officer Candidate School at Fort Benning. He was sent to Fort Riley to join Able Company in 1943.

When Timmermann was tapped to become company commander of A Company on March 6, 1945, the first platoon was left with no officers. Into the breach moved the platoon sergeant, little Mike Chinchar, an ex-milkman from Pennsylvania and New Jersey. Chinchar also had served a long apprenticeship with the company, enabling him to pick up the reins with an experienced hand.

The second platoon in Able Company was commanded by Second Lieutenant Emmet J. ("Jim") Burrows, a tall and toothy Jersey City clerk, slow-moving, unexcitable, and generally liked as a regular guy. Lieutenant Burrows was the first man to join up from Jersey City in World War II. He was sent to Able Company as a replacement in December, 1944, and his first experience with it was one he didn't forget. As he reported for duty, his new battalion commander adjusted his neat silk scarf and said briskly: "Glad to have you with us." Before Burrows could muster up an appropriate reply, the battalion commander waved his swagger stick in the general direction of the front and continued: "Your first job will be to take a jeep and go out there to reconnoiter for a forward assembly area for your new outfit."

Burrows was green. Fresh from commanding a quartermaster trucking outfit on the "Red Ball" express, he had no idea of what to do in this new situation. So he just stumbled forward with a map. When he thought he had a suitable spot, he came upon several 82nd Airborne Division men who were zeroing in on a cow. Preoccupied with the serious business of obtaining fresh steak for dinner, they paid little attention to the second lieutenant. "Where are the Germans from here?" Burrows inquired. "Oh, they're all around," the paratroopers replied airily, and proceeded with their more important task of bringing home the steak. Burrows was astounded at this seemingly casual attitude toward the enemy. It didn't sound like the "Kill or be killed" stuff drilled into him at Benning. But all this happened before he became seasoned under fire. Burrows soon learned that being casual in the face of the enemy was only a front which combat soldiers sometimes used to hide their feelings.

In early March, after several successive days and nights of hard fighting, he succumbed to what was literally an aggravated case of combat fatigue. He sat down on a chair in the kitchen of a bombed-out house one night and fell asleep. Somebody charitably lifted him, chair and all, and carried him down into the cellar to escape the shelling. When the company was ready to resume the attack, nobody could rouse Burrows. He dimly saw the figures of medics bending over him. The next thing he remembered was the sight of more medics over him in the aid station, the sharp stab of one of the Army's perpetually dull needles giving him a morphine shot, then deep sleep. Morning dawned, and he bounced up, refreshed, demanding to return to Able Company. He got back to his platoon on March 5, in the midst of the dash toward the Rhine.

The third platoon, initially commanded by Dartmouth-trained Lieutenant Charles McDowell, was left leaderless early in March when McDowell was wounded. By almost unanimous consent its redoubtable sergeant, Joe DeLisio, a product of the Bronx, took over the platoon. DeLisio was one of the scrappiest and most impetuous soldiers in Able Company. Argumentative, adventurous, and at times irresponsible, DeLisio never had to be told twice the direction to Berlin. One day, angered at reports of Nazi executions of innocent people without trials, he stormed into a German town and set up a fake execution of the mayor. Through an open window he took pains that the mayor's wife and family should hear him order: "Ready, aim, fire!" He carried the realism up to the point of having the firing squad discharge its weapons into the air. Then he restored the badly shaken man to his hysterical family with a reminder of how the families of Nazi victims felt.

Lieutenant McDowell, whom DeLisio succeeded, has said of him: "DeLisio was a completely fearless individual and was always the first to volunteer for a tough patrol. Sometimes I used to suspect that he wanted to be on these patrols so that he would get first crack at any loot, but I could never prove it." DeLisio was one of an inseparable trio that included a pair of mortarmen named Kenny and Rusakevich. "What a combination," the irrepressible DeLisio used to say, "an Irishman, a Russian and a Wop!"

Able Company's anti-tank platoon was led by a tall, young Ohioan, Dave Gardner. Gardner joined the company as a second lieutenant in December, 1944, on the same day that Burrows arrived. His joviality, high spirits and utter fearlessness under fire quickly won him a high rating among his men. They also cherished a story about his first meeting with one of the early commanders of the 27th Armored Infantry Battalion. Gardner found himself in the middle of a tactical map drill during which the battalion commander was testing what each officer would do under simulated combat conditions. The colonel pointed a long finger at Gardner and asked for a quick answer. Gardner had two alternatives he wanted to present; he started the first with the words: "Well, if—" No sooner had the word "if" escaped from Gardner's mouth than the commander slammed his fist down on the table roaring: "Gardner, in this battalion we never use the word 'if.'"

The lieutenants and the sergeants who backed them up in Able Company did a remarkable job in pulling together an outfit which included many independent characters. Most of the company—officers and men alike—were citizen soldiers, and Karl Timmermann in moments of exasperation might refer to them as "you bunch of quirks and jerks." But when Timmermann took command of Able Company late on March 6, 1945, he took over a battle-trained and seasoned outfit that functioned smoothly and knew its combat business.

The Ludendorff Bridge and the Rhine River always sparkled at sunset.

Five

. . . .

The Ninth Armored's Advance to the Rhine

"WHERE THE HELL ARE the doughs?" rasped a grimy tank commander from a roaring General Sherman tank. This was a favorite complaint, even when the infantrymen were riding on the back of the tanks.

"Goddam those tankers, they always expect us to spearhead for them," swore the foot soldiers struggling through a wooded ravine.

These were familiar cries in the 9th Armored Division, where the tank-infantry team took its objectives although plenty of argument followed as to who deserved the credit.

On the road toward the Rhine on the morning of February 28, 1945, it was pretty clear that the tankers were out in front in the attack, and leading the procession was a First Lieutenant named C. Windsor Miller.

Miller was a platoon leader in another Able Company—Company A of the 14th Tank Battalion. His mates recognized him as a budding young financier. He had left a responsible job with the British Purchasing Mission in Washington when Uncle Sam sent for him in 1942, and had done brilliantly in Officer Candidate School. Upon receiving his commission in 1943, he had been assigned to the 14th Tank Battalion; and he had served with the unit ever since.

Just before the attack started on February 28, Captain George Soumas, Company C.O., took Miller aside and said: "Oh, Charlie, your platoon will lead the company this morning." The lieutenant's back arched a little. It wasn't so much at being out in front again as at being called "Charlie." He preferred to be called "Windsor," but, even though nobody got around to calling him that, he liked the pull-together spirit of the company.

Able Company of the 14th Tank Battalion, Miller had discovered early, pretty much ran by itself. Most of the enlisted men were together in the company even before the officers came out of O.C.S. Captain Pete Zillick of Cincinnati, an old National Guard officer, had welded the company together in the rough maneuvers in Georgia, Louisiana and the California desert. A heart murmur prevented him from going overseas with the company, and George "The Greek" Soumas, a sharp-eyed Iowa attorney, took over in France. Soumas had an excellent group of platoon leaders, including John Grimball, a towering young lawyer from Columbia, South Carolina, and Sidney Moskovitz, a fearless youngster from a Kansas City department store family.

As Able Company of the tankers spearheaded across the Roer River and pointed toward the Rhine on the morning of the 28th, Miller began to feel that he and his tank were all alone out in front. He looked around and could see no friendly forces either to the right or to the left. He stuck his head up from the turret and turned around to see if his platoon was really following.

The second tank, manned by Sergeant William J. Goodson, came around a bend in the road, and Goodson opened the turret to wave to his platoon leader. "Good old Speedy," mumbled Miller to nobody in particular. Goodson had won the nickname "Speedy" because that was the farthest thing from what he was. A first glance left everyone doubting that this sleepy, slow-moving, perpetually tired Indiana boy would ever make a good combat soldier. A little combat acquaintance changed the men's minds in a hurry. Despite his mask of indolence, Goodson proved to be tough, durable and as cool-headed as any tanker in the unit when under enemy fire.

On the first day of the big attack toward the Rhine, Company A pushed forward about two miles in rough fighting. The Germans had dug in their deadly 88-millimeter guns in well concealed positions from which their fire could sweep along the level ground. When their tanks had run out of fuel, they had dismantled the hulls and buried them at ground level to step up their fire power.

Miller's platoon stayed out front in a night attack on the evening of the 28th, and it was out front all through the morning of March 1. The men were getting sleepy, grouchy, tired of a constant diet of K-rations, and almost rebellious at being in the lead position all the time. Miller too felt this resentment, although he had started the attack in good spirits. His irritation mounted as he led the company through twenty-four hours of constant attack.

He kept seeing a situation map in front of his eyes. There was Ike's headquarters with a prim flag on it, there was a smaller flag for Bradley and one for First Army; then here was the front line, and far, far out in front of all the Allied forces was a little black lozenge which represented Windsor Miller's tank.

After thirty hours of being a spearhead, Miller was almost tempted to ask Captain Soumas to give him a break and rotate the platoon leaders. Finally, at 2 P.M. on March 1, Captain Soumas, as if in reply to Miller's unspoken plea, halted the company and ordered Lieutenant Moskovitz to take over the lead with his platoon.

There was a brief pause as the platoon leaders prepared for the big switch.

"What about radios?" somebody asked.

"Open nets from now on," Soumas replied. "We had radio silence when we crossed the Roer River, because we didn't want the Krauts to know we were jumping off. But I guess they know by now that the 9th Armored has really hit 'em!"

A little after two o'clock in the afternoon of March 1, Company A of the 14th Tank Battalion jumped off again, with Lieutenant Moskovitz and his platoon as the spearhead. Shortly after they got under way, Miller saw the tanks ahead of him stop. There was a pause, and a few 88's whooshed through the air. Over his radio, Miller heard Captain Soumas talking to Lieutenant Moskovitz:

"What's going on up there, Sid?"

"Somebody's firing on us."

"Well, let's go, now."

Part of a sentence came over the radio from Moskovitz: "I gotta find out—"

There was silence over the radio, but not from the German 88's. Bursts of fire and explosions ahead told Miller right away that the Germans had found their mark. Lieutenant Moskovitz was killed. Three of his tanks were destroyed. One of the tanks from company headquarters was knocked out. The stretcher-bearers dashed back and forth. But the attack couldn't wait, and Miller was put back in to spearhead the advance.

For five more days, Miller's platoon led the way toward the Rhine. Sometimes there were brief pauses, but there was little rest. It was always Clean those guns, Get more jerricans of gasoline, Load up with ammunition, and Grease, grease, grease. Luckily, the division had been outfitted with new tanks in England in the fall, so that maintenance was not too serious a problem.

"You know, Charlie," said Soumas after the attack had been going for three days, "I wish I could put Grimball out front. But with the new Pershing tanks that his platoon has, they just can't get over these little bridges."

"Sure, I understand, George," Miller answered, almost resigned to fighting the rest of the war as that little black lozenge in the van of the Allied forces.

The 9th Armored Division had to cross a lot of little streams, swollen by spring rains. The special bridging equipment built for the narrow General Sherman tanks could not hold the wide-tread, low-silhouette General Pershings which had been added to one platoon in every company. The new General Pershings had 90-millimeter guns, and they packed plenty of additional firepower for the division, but in the early stages of the attack toward the Rhine they did not seem to be contributing very much.

The 9th Armored in its attack from the Roer to the Rhine was operating in good tank country, especially after reaching the rail junction of Euskirchen. It was a fairly level and open valley floor, with good opportunities to make long dashes if anti-tank guns could be by-passed. Nearly every town along the route provided good defensive capabilities for the Germans, but the faster the American forces moved, the fewer prepared defenses the Germans were able to throw up. The German policy of refusing to allow planning for defense in depth in rear areas clearly benefited the American attackers. After breaking the initial crust in the first few days of the attack, the 9th Armored found no anti-tank ditches, barbed wire, trenches or extensive anti-tank mines.

But the first few days of March were no romp for the tankers. A small group of fanatic Nazis and Hitler Jugend fighters, supported by a few tanks and 88's, could slow down the advance and usually cause some casualties. On the 4th of March, Windsor Miller took a tentative glance outside of his turret and was amazed to see the commanding general of Combat Command B, Brigadier General William M. Hoge, nonchalantly walking alongside his tank with the accompanying infantry. General Hoge, the man who had built the Alcan Highway and had commanded an engineer

Brigadier General William M. Hoge, Combat Command B, 9th Armored Division. U.S. ARMY SIGNAL CORPS, NATIONAL ARCHIVES

combat brigade on the beaches at Normandy, was driving his command as never before.

Hoge was utterly fearless and expected his men to follow his example. If they faltered, his normally quiet voice took on sharpness and lacerated the offenders. Quick to make decisions, he had the reputation of being a bulldog in carrying them out and a cat in jumping to meet new circumstances.

As Miller watched from his tank, Hoge boarded a jeep and the vehicle spurted forward. Miller could feel the pace of the entire tank column quicken as the general drove ahead.

Later that day, just after the combat command had taken Bodenheim, north of Euskirchen, General Hoge and his aide were slowly driving into town to make sure that all units were organized and in place. General Hoge turned around to the rear seat of his jeep to say a word, and found his aide slumped down with a sniper's bullet through his heart. Whatever Hoge's feelings, he gave no outward sign. He couldn't afford to. There were jobs to be done for the living, and he pressed on.

At noon of the next day, March 5, General Hoge assembled his unit commanders at Bodenheim and issued these instructions: "Mission of combat command to advance in its zone . . . and seize Stadt Mechenheim, then Rheinbach and on down to Ahrweiler. CCA advance abreast of us with similar mission on our right flank. Boundaries set up between the two. They are somewhat advisory. If something in the other man's zone is in your way, you have to get it out. . . . Go around resistance, don't get in a fight. . . . Infantry battalions will leapfrog. Will by-pass towns if possible. . . . Get help from tanks as you can. If no AT guns, shove tanks out in front. Will give additional objectives as thing develops. Will rest battalions as it is possible to do so. . . . If tanks can work fast, infantry will mount up in half-tracks. Those not involved in today's attack will remain in place until we get room."

This was the kind of order by which General Hoge transmitted his own driving energy into his troops. He knew that they had the massive force and shock power to roll ahead over the German opposition if they kept grinding forward. He recognized that the route toward the Rhine furnished an ideal opportunity for use of armored capabilities. By emphasizing that the tanks should keep pressing forward to find an opening, and by relentlessly following up his orders to make sure the maximum speed was achieved, General Hoge was able to move his combat command fast enough to achieve a wholesale disruption of German communications and troop disposition back of the front lines. The German difficulties of scanty supplies and dwindling manpower were aggravated by the punishing blows which General Hoge's forces meted out.

The 9th Armored Division had to pay in casualties for the ground they were gaining. On March 5, General Hoge began to be particularly concerned about officer casualties among the tankers, and he applied for a fresh batch of replacements to fill the gaps in the ranks. During early March, G-1 of the 9th Armored Division received a number of passes allotted to the division for leaves in Paris and London. All such allotments were ruthlessly rejected. The fast-tiring officers and men stayed on the job, and there were no reinforcements during the drive to the Rhine. By using refined forms of the needle and whip, all echelons of command drove their subordinates. The momentum continued, but the spirit of the men was none too good in the last stages of the drive.

Even "Speedy" Goodson was no exception. Lieutenant Miller's platoon sergeant was groggy with loss of sleep. One day Miller's platoon slipped up an alleyway and began to look cautiously around the cover of a few buildings to see whether there was any German armor out on the main highway. Goodson dismounted and wandered

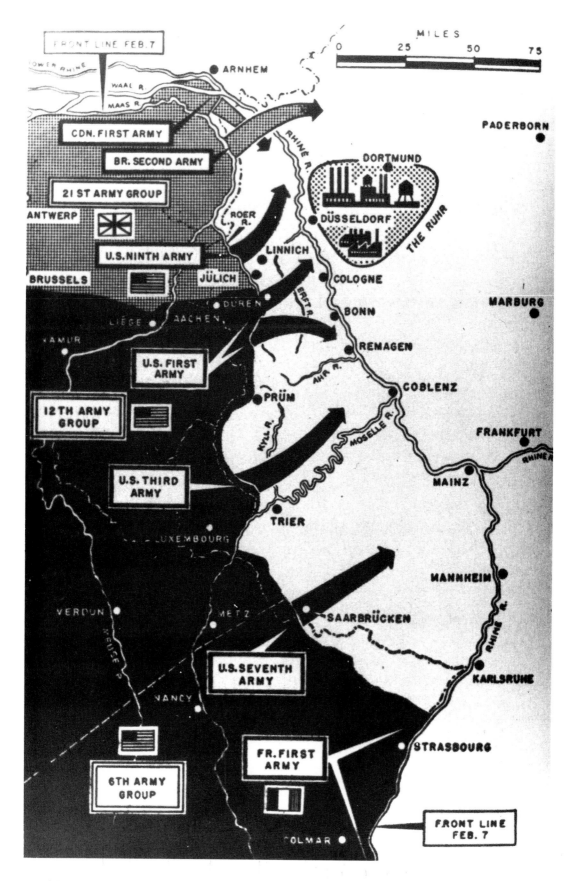

Advance to the Rhine.

aimlessly out into the open just as a few artillery shells started pumping in.

"Speedy, for crying out loud get back under cover," Miller shouted.

Goodson turned around slowly, with a dazed expression on his face.

"Aw, it won't make any difference, Lieutenant. They'll get us sooner or later as long as they keep sticking us out here in front."

That was the mood of most of the men as they slogged forward in the early days of March. It was cold, clammy and rainy. Sweat mixed with grime, and underwear stuck and stank. Nobody looked forward to chow out of cans. On the road, German 88's exacted frequent tolls. The minute the column stopped, the men faced the same necessities: gas up, grease up, check tank treads and ammo. The gains they were making gave them no sense of achievement. Too many mangled bodies of their comrades had to be pulled out of their tanks in payment.

Nobody's heart was really in the fight. They kept on only because their training had made their actions mechanical, and they were so tired out that, like Speedy Goodson, they just didn't give a damn. Then along came the needle and the whip, and they moved out again, driving toward the Rhine and a succession of objectives that seemed to stretch to infinity.

Close cooperation between the tankers and the armored infantry was vital to the success of an armored division. U.S. ARMY SIGNAL CORPS, NATIONAL ARCHIVES

Captain Karl Friesenhahn, engineer commander at bridge, and his wife.

Six
· · ·

The German Troops at Remagen

THE INVASION OF POLAND on September 1, 1939, had been the signal for putting all German military installations and strategic points on a total war footing. Among the many towns caught up in the fever of war preparations was the little tourist town of Remagen, where the Ludendorff Bridge, designed for rail traffic, crossed the Rhine. To protect the bridge, two rifle platoons and one engineer platoon descended on the town and took up positions.

As the years of offensive war proceeded and the demands for riflemen mounted on the fighting fronts, there were changes in the composition of the troops defending the bridge. The rifle platoons were taken away for combat duty, and the engineer platoon was built up into a full company.

Neither the infantry nor engineer troops at Remagen were kept very active during the early years of the war. They checked the passes of persons allowed to travel back and forth across the bridge on the narrow footpaths on each side of the railroad tracks. They planted mines on the bridge approaches, put up wire entanglements, dug gun emplacements, and took other defense measures designed to protect against a surprise enemy attack by air. They also placed nets and other obstacles to block floating mines. Finally, they practiced in "dry runs" the placing and firing of the demolitions which might some day be necessary to destroy the bridge as a defensive measure.

During the summer of 1943, when the Germans began to feel that it might pay to bolster up a few of their defenses, the engineer company at Remagen was placed under the command of Captain Karl Friesenhahn. Friesenhahn was chosen for the task because he was a combat veteran of the First World War and was thoroughly reliable. He had been a Nazi party member since 1933.

Gray-haired, physically slight, Captain Friesenhahn was pushing the fifty-year mark when he was assigned to Remagen. He had enlisted in August, 1914, and had made a distinguished record in the First World War. Gassed at Verdun and wounded three times in France, he had also fought on the eastern front in Kurland. As a member of an engineer combat battalion he had risen to the rank of sergeant, and felt that he would have become an officer had it not been for his battalion commander, a Roman Catholic who, he thought, favored only those of his own religious faith.

After discharge at the close of that war, Friesenhahn returned to his native Koblenz and worked in his brother-in-law's prosperous brewery distribution plant. When Poland was invaded in 1939, he was drafted. Because of his age, he was assigned to non-combat duty as a mine detection specialist in the engineers. He served with engineer companies at various bridges up and down the Rhine and, after attending officer candidate school, secured his lieutenancy in 1940. In 1942, he was promoted to captain.

Friesenhahn was both liked and respected by the men in his company, aside from a handful who felt he was too enthusiastic in his adherence to the Nazi Party line. His combat record commanded the respect of his men. He did not have to insist on the disciplinary measures that many younger officers felt were necessary in order to win a reputation for toughness. Instead, he went out of his way to make things more comfortable for his men at the Ludendorff Bridge. In the shadow of the bridge he constructed some rude tables where they could sit while off duty and drink or play cards in the open when the weather was fine. At a time when the local authorities demanded a court martial if so much as a branch was missing from a Remagen tree, this was regarded as a big feather in Friesenhahn's cap.

Not long after the tables were put into use, an engineer colonel came down to inspect the bridge and its defenses. When he saw the recreation facilities that Friesenhahn had set up, he exploded in anger.

"You're treating your men too damned well!"

"That's the highest praise you can give me, Colonel," rejoined Friesenhahn. Only a battle-hardened veteran with guts would have risked crossing a superior officer with a remark like that. The captain later commented: "The colonel would have exploded even more if he had known that we had filched some of the wood for the tables from one of the mine barriers in the river." Eventually, Friesenhahn was forced to take the tables down, but his standing with the men in his company was none the worse for the episode.

Two days after the invasion of Normandy, Friesenhahn's little company of engineers at the Ludendorff Bridge was reinforced by a company of 300 convalescent soldiers from the 80th Grenadier Replacement and Training Battalion. These combat soldiers – mainly infantrymen – had been wounded and were on the mend. Many of them still had their wounds dressed daily at the army hospital in Linz, across the river. The addition of this company did little to strengthen the defenses, as the convalescents, when they became strong enough, were sent to rejoin their combat units. Very few replacements were available. So the number of riflemen assigned to defend the bridge slipped from 300 to about one-third that number by the fall of 1944.

On November 1, 1944, Captain Willi Bratge was assigned to Remagen as commander of the bridge security company. In the middle of December, Bratge was also designated combat commander of the whole Remagen area, while Captain Friesenhahn retained his position as bridge commander in charge of engineer operations at the bridge itself.

Captain Bratge was quite a different type of person from Captain Friesenhahn. Both men were short, only a few inches over five feet tall, but there the resemblance

Capt. Willi Bratge, German commander at Remagen.

ceased. Bratge was about ten years younger, far more serious, and somewhat sharper of intellect. He was a schoolteacher by training. Some of his men felt that, as an officer, he remained too much of a schoolteacher, though others eventually realized that he was trying to teach them sound military procedure.

Bratge had completed his schooling in 1924 and had looked for a teaching job. Inflation was near its height, and there was none to be found. He turned to the best thing available—the 100,000-man Reichswehr. Unlike Friesenhahn, whose family had tried to discourage him from joining the Army because they preferred that he learn a trade first, Bratge received sympathetic support from his family for his military career. Born in that section of Germany which later became Poland, he was one of a fanatically loyal group who hoped some day to wrest their homeland from the Poles. In the border area where he grew up, the Army and a military career were quite natural—and the pay and prestige were far superior to a schoolteacher's.

Because of his proficiency in mathematics, physics, and the natural sciences, as well as his teaching ability, Bratge was assigned as an instructor of army personnel in evening classes. In 1927, he left the Army and returned to teaching; but he continued to take part in military maneuvers, and in 1937 he received a reserve commission as infantry second lieutenant. Pressed into active service at the outbreak of the Polish campaign in August, 1939, Bratge took particular delight in accompanying German blitz troops through the country which he believed had wrongfully taken over his birthplace. He became a first lieutenant in July, 1940, with an infantry unit that invaded France, and received two Iron Crosses for a reconnaissance mission and for bravery under fire. With the completion of the French campaign, he was assigned to an Army noncommissioned officers' school to teach "future noncoms." Then followed a period with the occupation forces in Bordeaux, and at the end of 1942 he requested transfer to a unit in training for the Russian campaigns. In the spring of 1943, Bratge got his wish and participated in the counteroffensive against Kharkov. The next year he fought in many battles in Russia, Italy and Romania. Wounded on the Russian front in August, 1944, after he had become a captain, he was then transferred to Remagen.

Bratge neither welcomed nor complained about his Remagen assignment. He was so thorough a soldier that he did not question the justification of placing him so far behind the lines, and he set about to make the most of it.

Captain Bratge soon discovered that the defenses at Remagen were pitifully inadequate for protecting the Ludendorff Bridge. The handful of walking wounded whom he commanded were armed only with a few rifles and two English and two German machine guns. It was a great event in December when Captain Bratge obtained three heavy Polish machine guns, three Russian mortars, and an Italian anti-tank gun to bolster the defenses.

Training his men in the maintenance and use of these foreign weapons was not simple, and the task was complicated by the fact that as soon as one of Bratge's convalescents became well enough for combat he was transferred out of the unit. Then the intricacies of the foreign weapons had to be taught to newly wounded personnel. Always more men seemed to be getting well and leaving for combat than were replaced by newly wounded. He suspected that he wasn't getting his fair share of the newly wounded. During January and February of 1945, there was a threefold turnover among his company's enlisted men. Fortunately, the same officers remained, but without cadre and noncommissioned officers the job of training became even more difficult. First, the new noncoms had to be taught to operate the foreign guns, and then they in turn taught the new recruits. These recruits were "raw" in more ways than one. Some of them were unable even to bend their trigger fingers; others were plagued with joints and muscles so stiff and sore that they were virtually useless in a combat situation. Worst of all, by the end of February, Captain Bratge counted his company and found it had slipped to 41 men, as against 300 at the time of the Normandy invasion.

Like many German commanders who stubbornly fought on as if they had the same troops as in 1940, Captain Bratge organized the defenses of the Remagen area along grandiose lines. He set some foreign laborers to digging foxholes and constructing bunkers. He designated "main lines of resistance," created posts for sentries, set up an alarm system and planned both a series of outposts and a close-in defense. There was a frenzy of activity as these elaborate plans were mapped out, and the digging and construction started.

The odds were against Bratge. The unsmiling combat commander exhorted and whiplashed his men in vain at the back-breaking preparation of foxholes and emplacements. Remagen, still considered as an area far behind the combat lines, operated under very stringent regulations on the use of lumber for reinforcing bunkers. Bratge was blocked at every turn from getting sufficient wood. The task was discouraging, but he did his best to build defense positions on both sides of the Rhine from which a reinforced regiment could effectively block an attacking force. Most people poked fun at his desire to have enough defense positions for a reinforced regiment, because most people realized that that many men just weren't available. But Bratge played the game according to the book as he knew it.

A bewildering series of command channels complicated the problem of setting up the Remagen defenses. In and around the town, Captain Bratge dealt with many people in his efforts to mobilize the defense of the area. The Volkssturm—that last-gasp army of the people which was hastily formed from among nearly all male civilians left in the town—received its orders from the Nazi party officials in Remagen. The job of the Volkssturm was to construct anti-tank obstacles and road blocks. Captain Bratge as combat commander could make suggestions and offer criticisms, but the Volkssturm were not answerable to him. It is questionable whether a sufficient number of strong road blocks and obstacles could have been constructed with the time, material, and men available, no matter who had commanded the Volkssturm. Many of their obstacles were much too weak to block tanks, many so-called road blocks allowed ample room for tanks or vehicles to pass around them, and some obstacles were actually placed in open territory where they constituted no obstacle at all.

All over Germany, Volkssturm troops were recruited and committed close to their homes in the hope that they would fight to defend their homes and localities. The ersatz troops soon discovered that every time they showed some resistance, the Americans took no chances but methodically demolished every structure that might house defenders.

It did not take the Volkssturm troops long to discover that a quick surrender spared not only their lives but their homes and property. This process was infectious, and usually made it easier for the regular army troops to surrender also. In the Remagen area, the Volkssturm troops naturally had less effective arms and equipment even than Captain Bratge's little handful of troops, and they were hastily and inadequately trained. In any case, Bratge had little control over them and could scarcely depend on them in any organized defense scheme.

In the early stages of his command at Remagen, Bratge's troops were responsible to the Replacement Army. The German ground forces were split between the Field Army and the Replacement Army, the latter being jealously commanded by Heinrich

Himmler. The two headquarters vied for authority in a competing and conflicting way. This caused Bratge no difficulty in the early days when the zone of combat was many miles to the west; but it resulted in serious command complications when the battle lines began to approach Remagen.

When Bratge first arrived he discovered that Remagen was technically part of the rear area of the German Seventh Army. Although he was receiving some replacement troops from the 105th Convalescent Battalion under the Replacement Army, the commander of the rear area of the Seventh Army also took a general interest in the defense of Remagen. In the first days of March, 1945, the Seventh Army headquarters was moved and Bratge did not hear from them again.

Prior to March, the defense of bridges and river crossings was the responsibility of the "Wehrkreis"—the administrative areas into which Germany was divided for combat purposes. When the battle lines came close to a particular area, the Wehrkreis yielded control to the Field Army—the combat troops. Himmler and the SS controlled the Wehrkreis administration, furnishing another source of rivalry and jealousy with the combat troops.

Although the defense of bridges and river crossings was not supposed to be under control of the Field Army, a few farsighted commanders realized that some day in the future they might have such a responsibility thrust on them if the fortunes of battle turned a rear area into a combat area. Hence, the engineer officer at Army Group B, General Janowski, had busied himself since September, 1944, with plans for protecting bridges and ferries along the Rhine. His job was not easy, because there was rivalry between the Wehrkreis and the combat troops, and because he could never be sure what channels he should deal through. After a period of several months in which he had built up a good relationship with the officials of Wehrkreis VI, which initially had control over Remagen, the Wehrkreis lines were altered in February, and he had to start all over again to build up relationships with Wehrkreis XII, thenceforth in control of the Ludendorff Bridge.

Although relations between Captain Bratge and Captain Friesenhahn were excellent, and the older and more experienced engineer officer deferred to the younger combat commander, Bratge had trouble with the other military and semimilitary units, which were so proud of their membership in the Luftwaffe that they would not take orders or suggestions from a mere infantry commander. There was little exchange of information, lack of mutual respect, and not very much cooperation between the anti-aircraft units and the infantry and engineer units. Even in an emergency, Captain Bratge could not give a direct order to the anti-aircraft units regarding their commitment, because they were under the Luftwaffe.

The peculiar thing about the other units around Remagen was that *only* in an emergency did Bratge have the authority to commit them. This meant that, although he could use them if a fire started, it was difficult to know how much he could depend on them without advance, coordinated training. Knowing they were callable only in an emergency, these units naturally cultivated a spirit of independence. They were ordered to cooperate "as much as possible" with the combat commander of Remagen, but this order was a weak reed for Captain Bratge to lean on. Among the units in the area were SS troops, the Volkssturm, the National Labor Service organization, Organisation Todt, Organisation Speer, local police forces, the Hitler Jugend organization, elements of an air signal company, a supply company (consisting of twenty German cadre and one hundred and twenty uncertain Russian soldiers who had "volunteered" for duty with the German Army), a propaganda company at nearby Kripp, and some miscellaneous rear echelon units who went about their business of baking bread, controlling traffic, or burying the dead somewhere in the environs of Remagen.

Not only were the channels of command confused, but the means of communication and transportation available to the troops at Remagen were very meager. Until the beginning of March, neither Bratge nor Friesenhahn had a vehicle. Occasionally Frau Friesenhahn would visit her husband at the bridge on week-ends, and the bicycle on which she rode was one of the few means of transportation that the officers saw—except, of course, the railroad trains that chugged across the bridge, or the limousines used by visiting staff officers. The National Labor Service (Reichsarbeitsdienst, or R.A.D.) maintained a woman's leader school at Remagen, and although its "students" were scarcely worth winking at they all had bicycles. There was great rejoicing when the school departed suddenly in early March because of the threat of advancing American troops, leaving behind a number of women's bicycles which were immediately pressed into messenger service.

The radio and telephone apparatus available to the Remagen commanders, although serviceable enough for normal times, was totally inadequate for an emergency. One telephone line hooked up from the bridge to the regular German Army line running between Bonn and Koblenz, and another line was connected by a civilian hookup to Wehrkreis headquarters in Wiesbaden. Frequent bombings disrupted the lines for long periods, and even when they were undamaged they were so busy that it usually took a full day to complete a telephone call. The combat commander of a seemingly insignificant installation like the Ludendorff Bridge was rather low in the system of telephone priorities under which much more urgent business was conducted in the latter stages of the war. For contact with the attached units in Remagen Captain Bratge had to depend on the civilian dial telephone, fairly reliable in normal times but questionable in time of emergency. Electric current was needed to operate the line, and this could not always be obtained during combat; furthermore, the line had a disturbing tendency to go dead suddenly when jarred by shelling, and it was always dead for a few weeks after a sizable bombing attack.

In the final weeks while the German forces were in control of Remagen, several changes occurred in the anti-aircraft units in the area which materially weakened the Remagen defenses. Anti-aircraft guns may frequently be depressed for effective ground artillery and anti-tank use; but whenever Bratge and Friesenhahn tried to get the anti-aircraft commanders to work up a plan of cooperation these showed no interest. Finally, after protests to higher headquarters, the Luftwaffe assigned a local flak officer to work with Captain Bratge and interpret his orders to the anti-aircraft units in the Remagen bridgehead. The local flak officer, who arrived in mid-December, 1944, had the authority to set up emplacements for anti-aircraft ground artillery fire, to organize anti-tank defenses, and to arrange for the emergency commitment of flak units for ground combat as needed by Captain Bratge. He and Captain Bratge concluded an amicable arrangement which considerably strengthened Bratge's artillery power, and also made available groups of anti-aircraft soldiers for emergency use as infantry.

In mid-February, 1945, the following anti-aircraft units were in or near Remagen: two platoons with 20-millimeter four-in-one guns on the bridge, atop the Erpeler Ley, the six-hundred-foot height across the river, and in the town of Remagen; one battery of a heavy and two batteries of a light railroad flak battalion with 20-, 37- and 105-millimeter guns; one battery of a light flak battalion. The troops had rifles, bazookas, and light machine guns for ground use. There was also a chemical company attached to the anti-aircraft, which had the mission of releasing smoke generators to set up a smoke screen. This company was of dubious value in combat, since it consisted largely of Russian prisoners of war, guarded by about twenty German soldiers. There was also one battery armed with rocket launchers which could not be used in ground combat, and which were so secret that the troops carrying them were under orders to withdraw to the east bank of the Rhine or destroy the equipment in the face of enemy attack. This battery was commanded by Lieutenant Karl Heinz Peters.

By the end of February, the bridgehead was seriously weakened by the withdrawal of all the railroad flak batteries. The command complex was further confused and weakened by the withdrawal of the local flak officer, and the transfer of his function to an unsympathetic anti-aircraft major who moved in with his battalion across the river from Remagen. Major Halbach, whose battalion was operating mainly outside the bridgehead area, suggested that he assign a lieutenant as a deputy local flak officer, but Captain Bratge rejected the idea as unfeasible. He also turned down the suggestion that the duties of local flak officer could be exercised from the major's command post, thinking it totally unrealistic, because it would leave the two officers six miles apart without adequate means of communication. Less than a week before the capture of the Remagen Bridge, these vital arrangements were still not concluded because Major Halbach had terminated his conversation with Captain Bratge with the observation that the issue was not urgent.

By early March, Captain Bratge had available in his own bridge security company a total of 36 men. Captain Friesenhahn's engineer company consisted of 120 men. About 180 Hitler Jugend members of varying qualities were scattered around. There were 120 Eastern "volunteers" of uncertain loyalty. The anti-aircraft units could muster about 200 men, and there were 20 men from the Luftwaffe rocket battery. The total paper strength of the Volkssturm in the villages on both sides of the river near the bridge amounted to some 500; but its commanders admitted that only a tenth of this number could be counted on to appear, and fewer still would fight.

All in all, the number of men available for the defense of the whole Remagen area was well under 1,000. It varied considerably from day to day, and an accurate count of the combat effectives was never possible. The picture was a sorry one for Captain Bratge, accustomed to discipline and veteran of the crack units that had blitzed through Poland.

During early March, the officers and men in Remagen had an inescapable sense of impending doom. They did not talk about it, but they did not have to be told that they were in a tight spot. On Sunday March 4, Frau Friesenhahn cycled up to the bridge for her customary week-end visit with her husband. He had persuaded her to give up their home in Koblenz because of the rising fury of the bombings. So she moved to the little village of Hümmerich, on the east bank. Every week-end she visited her husband, who had private quarters in one of the bridge towers. They didn't see much of each other on March 4, because Captain Friesenhahn was working all day trying to plank the bridge for vehicles and supervise the reconstruction of the earth-work defenses damaged by the spring rains and thaw.

On the morning of March 5, Frau Friesenhahn kissed her husband goodbye. She knew something was troubling him deeply. He said: "Whatever happens, don't move out of Hümmerich. Stay where you are, no matter what happens." She cycled away, and looked back to wave cheerily. He seemed to be thinking of something else as he lifted a tired arm to return the farewell. Just before she turned a corner to disappear in the distance, she looked back again and he was still standing there, just gazing into space. Frau Friesenhahn knew at that moment that it would be a long time before they saw each other again.

The Remagen Bridge against background of town.

Seven

· · · · ·

The Town of Remagen

THE TOWN THAT WILLI BRATGE, Karl Friesenhabn and their troops were trying to defend was an unhurried and relaxed community. Karl Timmermann of West Point, Nebraska, would have noted a number of differences between his home town and Remagen.

Both towns were on rivers which sometimes overflowed to leave muddy reminders in people's basements; but the similarity ended right there. In West Point, Timmermann's parents had found that those who lived down by the grimy Elkhorn were known as "river rats." In Remagen, it was fashionable to live close to the Rhine. Nobody ever made the Elkhorn River of West Point the subject of song and legend. But Remagen's river inspired ballads and poetry. The townspeople claimed that one verse was written especially for Remagen:

> Beware of the Rhine, beware of the Rhine.
> My son, mark well my advice,
> For there you'll be getting too much wine
> And you'll get too big for your size.

Remagen boasted many fine hotels and superior restaurants. It was a resort town, whose major industry was tourists and whose major attraction was the rich scenery of the Rhine and the mountains and valleys beyond. It was less industrious, earnest and ambitious than West Point. People came to Remagen to buy souvenirs and trinkets, to dine at its elegant restaurants, and to slap their friends on the back and break out into song. Visitors clambered up and down the hills around town or simply strolled along its narrow and crooked streets. West Point was a town of swirling dust, cattle feeders, blue overalls and frontier spirit. People came to West Point from the surrounding farms to buy food, clothing and farm machinery, to go to ball games and wrestling matches and to drink beer in the cafés. Theodore Roosevelt and Wendell Willkie had posed in West Point with prize Hereford cattle; in Remagen, when Goethe paid a visit the townspeople presented him with a barrel of red wine.

In Remagen, there were none of the wary, measuring glances with which Timmermann's home town appraised visitors; everyone was greeted with the open-hearted spirit of the Rhineland.

Secure in the knowledge that Nature had endowed it with far more treasure than human effort could create, Remagen showed no zeal for economic progress. Industry, smoke, and noise were virtually unknown. There was only one large factory, the Becher Veneer and Plywood Works, on the river close to the bridge. There were about eighty retail shops, most of them small ones. Under Hitler, almost all of the proprietors of Jewish faith had been driven from Remagen.

Perhaps the biggest excitement in Remagen before the war stemmed from the argument over whether the main road between Koblenz and Bonn should pass through the middle of town or skirt it. Like shopkeepers the world over, the local merchants fought to have through traffic directed through the center of the business district, hoping to get more customers. Their fight was a vain one. A higher authority outside of Remagen ruled against contaminating the town with gasoline fumes and the hazards of traffic, and the main road, Route 9, was built at the edge of town. To please the merchants, the buses from Bonn and west to the Ahr River were still routed through the center of town, but some local people still felt that the municipal authorities should have agitated harder to keep the Bonn-Koblenz road in town.

Dr. Hans Kemming, the chief town official, had been Bürgermeister since 1932, and he ruled Remagen with a benevolent hand. Though some of the businessmen blamed him for the loss of their cherished highway, they forgave him because of his achievements in building up and transforming the Rheinwerft, a winding promenade along the river bank, into a major tourist attraction. This drew visitors in great numbers for its view of the shimmering stretch of greenish blue water and the mountains beyond.

South of Remagen, a fairly good road from the Ahr valley joined the Bonn-Koblenz highway. This was the most logical and most traveled route into Remagen from the west. But the first American troops were to enter Remagen instead by the thin, tar-covered secondary road from Birresdorf that wound out of the hills in an S curve past St. Apollinaris Church to the Bonn-Koblenz highway. Thence several different routes could be used through the town to the bridge. One route knifed directly to the Rhine and to Dr. Kemming's beautiful Rheinwerft hugging the river bank. Another followed the Bonn-Koblenz highway, crossed the railroad tracks near the railroad station, followed one of the main streets – the "Alte Strasse" – past the cemetery, and then forked off to the bridge. Either way, it was over a mile from the heights of St. Apollinaris Church to the Remagen Bridge on the southeastern edge of town.

From a strictly military standpoint, the town of Remagen had advantages for both attacker and defender. The attacker could direct operations from perfect points of observation above the town. The narrow and crooked streets were ideally laid out for tanks to sneak around corners and blast out opposition. On the other hand, Remagen's streets, village squares, and embankments afforded excellent defensive strongpoints for a tenacious force if it had the weapons and the will power.

The most imposing building in town was the four-towered Gothic Church of St. Apollinaris, with traditions that went back to the Middle Ages. The church was

The famous Apollinaris Church at Remagen. U.S. ARMY SIGNAL CORPS, NATIONAL ARCHIVES

Remagen's proudest shrine. It was on the approximate site of an old Roman castle, and its chapel also had its origin in Roman times. The bishop for whom the church was named had had rather independent and forthright ideas, later became a martyr to these ideas, and was beheaded in Italy in A.D. 79. The remains of St. Apollinaris were buried in Ravenna, thence moved to Milan. When Emperor Frederick Barbarossa conquered and destroyed Milan in 1164 he authorized the Archbishop of Cologne to transport the remains of St. Apollinaris and other valuable relics to Cologne.

Out of the trip down the Rhine to Cologne was born one of Remagen's oldest legends. It is said that when the ship bearing the remains of St. Apollinaris reached the point on the Rhine opposite Remagen, it mysteriously stopped despite the rapid downstream current. After refusing to budge, the ship gradually turned toward the Remagen shore. Not until the body of St. Apollinaris was placed ashore at Remagen would the ship move again to complete its journey to Cologne with the other relics sent from Italy.

The magnificent St. Apollinaris Church housing the remains of the martyred bishop was rebuilt several times, once in the thirteenth century and again after its towers were destroyed during the Thirty Years' War. Toward the end of the seventeenth century it was reconstructed, and about a century before the arrival of American troops it was enlarged and rebuilt. The redesigning was done under the supervision of Zwirmer, who did the final work on the Cologne Cathedral.

Remagen was called Ricomagus in Roman times, and among its many Roman landmarks was a well preserved Roman gateway. In the early eighteenth century a Roman milestone bearing the date 162 A.D. was found in the town. This milestone recorded that the Roman road through Remagen had been started under the emperor Marcus Aurelius. Even earlier Drusus, the commander of the Roman Army of the Rhine, had built a string of forts along the river, one of them at Ricomagus, which became an outpost of civilization against the marauding Teutons that populated the wooded areas east of the Rhine.

During the fifth century, when the Romans withdrew from the Rhine, as they did in what is now England, the towns, villages and castles fell to the Teutons; and through the centuries that followed, waves of war and occupation rolled over Remagen. Although the Thirty Years' War did not touch it at first, from 1631 onward it was alternately occupied, robbed, and burned by Hessian and Swedish troops. By 1633 only two score of the two hundred or so buildings before the war remained. In 1635, Spaniards under their lieutenant colonel Don Pedro forced the citizens to supply a daily ration for each man of a quart of wine, a pound of meat, and two pounds of bread.

Throughout the rest of that century, Remagen suffered a number of severe pillagings. After each war many soldiers were left in the town, frequently without pay, and they took their food, clothes, and lodging where they could find them.

Soon after 1700 Remagen was in the middle of another war—the War of the Spanish Succession. To the usual depredations were added the raiding of granaries, the requisitioning of leather and cloth, high taxes, and debts. The same horrors prevailed in the early nineteenth century, and Remagen in Napoleonic times was whipsawed between French and Russian troops.

World War I scarcely touched the town, although it chafed under the French occupation that followed—a "correct" occupation with little of the requisitioning and pillaging of previous years. Not until American bombs started to drop in 1944 did Remagen feel the full impact of World War II.

Down through the years Remagen had developed a psychosis. It shuddered at war and dreaded even more the aftermath of occupation. The inhabitants could never forget the centuries of spoliation, but paradoxically they also indulged in the glorification of war common to old soldiers everywhere. War was hell, but it was great to sentimentalize about the battles of the past. Out of this feeling had grown a tradition.

One manifestation of this tradition was Remagen's "St. Sebastian Shooting Society," founded in 1478, which met and trained frequently. Its members were strongly bound together. Dr. Kemming wrote lyrically on one anniversary of the society: "The old rifleman's heart keeps on beating bravely throughout the years, loyal to his flag. And so it is with us in Remagen. May these festive days fill the hearts of our riflemen with pride and joy and the knowledge of their old tradition. May also our home town be filled with the same pride, and in unanimous devotion participate in this festive event. Their testimonial to the genuine rifleman's spirit, their joy in that which is noble and beautiful shall become a grand confession of creed for the perpetuation of the customs of home and the Fatherland."

It might have interested Karl Timmermann, expert rifleman, to know that here was a locality where the "genuine rifleman" received his due.

Dr. Hans Kemming, Bürgermeister of Remagen in 1945.

German highway signs: "Brücke" means "Bridge."

Hans Peter Kürten, Bürgermeister of Remagen, was a pioneer in the establishment of the "Friedensmuseum" (Peace Museum) in the Remagen Bridge towers.

Eight

. . . . .

The Ludendorff Bridge

KARL TIMMERMANN HAD BEEN no great shakes as a student in Nebraska, where he attended Guardian Angels High School, a mile's walk uphill from the little house by the Elkhom. The sisters and the priests constantly had him on the carpet for "unexcused absences," which always increased after the ice in the river started to melt; but two subjects, Latin and History, held his interest. A classmate was taken aback one day, when they had played hookey to go fishing, by hearing him launch into a vehement exposition of the relative merits of Julius Caesar and Alexander the Great. Karl loved to read Caesar's Commentaries, and he soaked up the military strategy of Caesar with a thoroughness that delighted his Latin teacher and confounded his playmates.

Precisely two thousand years before the Remagen Bridge gained world-wide fame, Julius Caesar had constructed the first bridge across the Rhine and made one of the first assault crossings. Karl had been only sixteen years old when he read in Book IV of Caesar's Commentaries:

"Having finished the war against the Germans, Caesar believed he should cross the Rhine for several reasons. The most important was that, since the Germans crossed into Gaul so often without excuse, he wanted them in turn to fear for the security of their own country, showing them that the army of the Roman people dared to and could cross the Rhine. . . . Caesar did not deem it worthy of either himself or the Roman people to make the crossing by boat. Therefore, although the width, fast current and depth of the river made the construction of a bridge extremely difficult, he believed that a bridge would have to be attempted or the crossing would not be undertaken at all. Here is the plan of construction which Caesar adopted. Timbers about a foot and a half in diameter, somewhat pointed on the ends and of a length proportionate to the depth of the stream, were linked together two and a half feet apart. When these had been lowered into the river and set in place by mechanical devices, they were driven in by pile-drivers, not perpendicularly, as piles, but on a slant to resist the flow of the current."

Caesar's first bridge over the Rhine was located near Neuwied, about a dozen miles south of Remagen. The Roman troops crossed it and spent eighteen days on the far side. Upon returning to the west bank they destroyed the bridge. Caesar evidently had a demolition plan that worked even without explosives. Two years later he built another bridge near Andernach, somewhat closer to Remagen. This he also destroyed once it had served his purpose.

The Roman emperor Drusus crossed the Rhine in 10 B.C. on a permanent stone bridge north of Cologne, probably at Neuss. This remained standing until the Middle Ages. Gradually, other "permanent" bridges were thrown across the river, although the swift current and the difficult river bed made the construction of a bridge a great engineering feat.

Just before the Rhine reaches Remagen it takes one of the many right-angled turns which add to its charm. There the angry Ahr River races down to throw its waters into the other. At the town the Rhine narrows to about 700 feet confined by the precipitous Erpeler Ley on the east side. These factors contribute to a brisk current of seven and one-half feet per second, which scours the rocky bottom and sweeps it clean.

Directly across from the Erpeler Ley, in the early days of World War I, a young housewife named Frau Maria Bayer had a perfect view of the river from the front of her house at No. 8 on the Rheinwerft. She could see for miles up and down the river, and the train conductor's announcement of the station of Erpel on the other bank, echoing against the rock of the Erpeler Ley, was a pleasantly familiar sound that reached her clearly on her porch. She used to sit and watch when the absurd little ferryboats started from Remagen for Erpel, pointing their snub noses directly upstream and reaching the opposite bank only after battling crablike against the current.

One morning Frau Bayer was surprised to see official-looking cars drive up, and men start taking measurements and soundings. More men came, bringing heavy equipment and it was soon apparent that her view would be destroyed by a bridge. Why did they have to build a bridge at Remagen?

Before the First World War, Field Marshal Count von Schlieffen was chief of the German general staff, and he formulated the famous "Schlieffen Plan," one of whose essentials was that if war should come to Germany on both the Russian and western fronts Germany should reach a decision on the western front before attacking east. As early as the turn of the century he started agitating for the construction of three new Rhine River bridges, to speed the transportation of German troops and supplies from east to west in the event of war. One of his staff officers, General Erich Ludendorff, continued the fight for more Rhine bridges and stressed the need for better transportation facilities between the Ruhr and the regions west of the Rhine—the Saar and Eifel. For a bridge to link these crucial areas, Remagen was picked as one of the crossing points.

The firm of Grün & Bilfinger of Cologne received the contract to construct the bridge at Remagen, and in 1916 hundreds of workmen were employed on a round-the-clock schedule. Other workmen started building viaducts over the highways, and began drilling a tunnel into the solid rock of the Erpeler Ley. Frau Bayer got precious

Air view of Rhine, showing right-hand turn above Remagen.

few peaceful periods for meditation during the next two years. But she was lucky that the job could be done in two years. There were no shortages of men and of steel and other materials, and there were no air attacks.

The Remagen Bridge was one of the most stately of the Rhine bridges. Although many of the Remagen people felt, like Frau Bayer, that it destroyed the natural beauty of the Rhine landscape, it had a man-made beauty of its own. The majestic sweep of the bridge arching to the Erpeler Ley had an unforgettable grandeur, especially at sunset. Even those most bitterly opposed to the structure grudgingly admitted that the end result was not altogether displeasing.

The bridge had three symmetrical arches, resting on four stone piers, with spans

Ludendorff Bridge, showing stone towers. U.S. ARMY SIGNAL CORPS, NATIONAL ARCHIVES

respectively 278, 513 and 278 feet long and an over-all length of 1,069 feet.

Four heavy towers, two at each end of the bridge, sternly commanded the surrounding landscape. They were of dark brown stone and resembled small castles in design and ruggedness, and each tower had small apertures for gun emplacements. Winding circular stairways led from floor to floor. There was ample provision in its three stories for the quartering of troops, storage of supplies, and all-round defense and observation. From the flat roof of each tower a lookout had an unobstructed view of the surrounding countryside, with the protection of a thick stone wall around the edge. Passageways connected each pair of towers, making it possible to go from one to the other under cover. The four towers contained enough space to house a full battalion of men.

The bridge enabled railroad trains to pass in both directions, with a yard-wide planked footpath on each side. It was also possible to plank over the railroad tracks to provide for vehicular traffic.

A great celebration attended the dedication and opening of the new bridge. The highway bridge at Cologne was finished about the same time, and the two structures were named after Germany's greatest World War I field commanders – Hindenburg

1st Battalion Headquarters, 15th F.A., Second Division, A.E.F. crossing Rhine at Remagen bridge on December 13, 1918. Major E. H. Brainerd, U.S. Marine Corps, commanding, in foreground. Behind and to the right of Major Brainerd, is Captain Elmer Hess (wearing overseas cap) who was battalion medical officer and who was president of the American Medical Association in 1955.

and Ludendorff. The one at Remagen received Ludendorff's name because of his particular interest in seeing a bridge built at this location.

Not long after the Armistice ended the First World War and within a month after the Armistice, the American occupation troops began to arrive at the Rhine. In December, 1918, the III Corps had the honor of being the first American troops across the Remagen Bridge and the first across the Rhine. Deane J. McAlister, a Greenville, Illinois, private in the 2nd Infantry Division, recalls: "We shoved off from the German-Luxembourg border on December 1, 1918, and crossed the bridge at Remagen on the 13th. The two large towers at each end reminded me of some of the big silos in the Midwest, only they were fatter. We carried full marching packs weighing 80 pounds, including rifle and ammunition, and I don't need to say my powers of observation were somewhat dimmed after twelve days of continuous hiking. I did not even see the bridge as we approached and the first thing I knew someone said, 'We're on the Rhine!' and the platoon commander ordered us to break step. Then there was a mixup at the head of the column and we halted in the middle of the bridge. They had the railroad tracks planked over so we could march over more easily."

As 1919 wore on, more and more American occupation troops marched across the Ludendorff Bridge and in July the Nebraska private John H. Timmermann, of Company M, 8th Infantry Regiment, Karl's father, crossed the bridge, three years before Karl was born.

Remagen was at the north of the American occupation zone, just south of the British zone. When the American occupation forces went home, the French moved in. Unwittingly, the French, performed a great service for the American troops in World War II. While in charge of the Remagen Bridge, they discovered that each stone pier supporting the bridge contained two large demolition chambers which could be packed with TNT for easy destruction in the event of enemy attack. They methodically filled the chambers with cement. During World War II, when the Germans were formulating plans to demolish the bridge in case of attack, they discovered that the only way to remove the cement from the wells in the piers was to remove the main supports of the bridge. This could not be done without dumping the entire structure into the Rhine.

In the years after World War I, the bridge was used primarily as a foot passage. In those years of hardship and inflation, only a few freight trains chugged over at infrequent intervals. There were no passenger trains.

Residents still tell in hushed and horrified tones of the time when a French Moroccan soldier murdered an elderly German woman on the Ludendorff Bridge one moonless night, and hid her body in one of the towers on the east end. This seemed to be about the only event out of the ordinary near the structure between the wars. In the winter of 1938–39, coals from a passing locomotive set fire to the temporary planking on the roadway and caused some damage. After considerable delay pedestrians were allowed again to journey along the catwalks. Such incidents were soon forgotten, and the Ludendorff Bridge became known only as one of many ways to cross the Rhine.

In some respects, the people of Remagen felt self-conscious about their bridge. It brought back too many unhappy memories of World War I and it embarrassed them in other ways. The noise and smoke of the freight trains lumbering over the bridge marred the fresh and peaceful atmosphere of the quiet town. Furthermore, because its approaches lay fully a mile south of the town's center, in a somewhat desolate and underprivileged section, few people other than those who had to cross took the trouble to visit the bridge.

With the rearming of Germany in the 1930's, and especially with the outbreak of the Second World War, the citizens felt a little more pride in their bridge. It played an increasingly important role in delivering the sinews of war. More traffic used the bridge, and the visible evidence of Germany's growing power stirred the residents of Remagen as they watched and listened to the rolling stock clicking across the Rhine.

By the eve of World War II, the Ludendorff Bridge had become strategically important in German military planning. Few people in Germany dreamed that the day might come when such a bridge as this might have to be blown up as a defensive

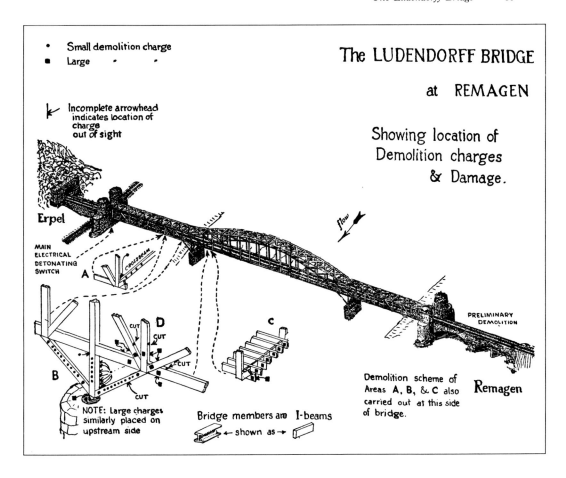

The LUDENDORFF BRIDGE

at REMAGEN

Showing location of
Demolition charges
& Damage.

- • Small demolition charge
- ■ Large • •

⤹ Incomplete arrowhead
indicates location of
charge
out of sight

Erpel

MAIN
ELECTRICAL
DETONATING
SWITCH

A

CROSSBEAM

flow

D

CUT

CUT

CUT

C

B

CUT

NOTE: Large charges
similarly placed on
upstream side

Bridge members are I-beams
← shown as →

PRELIMINARY
DEMOLITION

Demolition scheme of
Areas A, B, & C also
carried out at this side
of bridge.

Remagen

measure. But Germans are thorough. It was for them only standard operating procedure to prepare a specific plan to demolish any strategic bridge in order to keep it from falling into enemy hands. In 1938 – a year before the outbreak of World War II – they devised and put into effect a careful demolition plan for the Ludendorff Bridge.

Sixty zinc-lined boxes, each capable of holding eight pounds of explosives, were placed underneath the railroad tracks on the bridge and at points where an explosion would do the maximum amount of damage. Engineers removed the explosives and stored them close by in order to protect them against the weather. The explosives could be replaced in the boxes quickly if needed. The firm of Siemens & Schuckert carefully worked out the installation of an electric fuse, the cable for which was encased in a thick steel pipe laid underneath the tracks in the lower part of the bridge. The ignition switch for the fuse was at the entrance to the railroad tunnel on the opposite side of the bridge from Remagen. The apparatus was designed to set off each of the sixty charges in the circuit, and unhinge the bridge at its most vulnerable points, causing it to collapse into the Rhine. A circuit-tester enabled engineers to check the electric ignition system to make sure it was in good working order. As insurance, the Germans had an emergency device: a primer cord to be lit by hand could be used to set off the charges if the electrical ignition failed to work.

At the end of 1944, because of the rapid American armored advances, it became necessary to add a new feature to the elaborate demolition plan. In order to prevent enemy tanks from making a surprise crossing, it was decided that if tanks neared the bridge the engineers would blow a ditch about thirty feet wide and twelve feet deep at the Remagen side of the bridge. This would give the bridge defenders sufficient time to set off the main demolition with the electric fuse.

The plan looked like a masterpiece. It seemed to take care of all foreseeable contingencies. But a talkative little sergeant named Jakob Klebach, who had worked as a carpenter on constructing the bridge and who was also a member of the team that carried out demolition maneuvers at the bridge in 1939, discovered something that may have been only a straw in the wind. "We tried to test the circuit during a trial run, and found it didn't work. We groped around all night on the bridge trying to find where the break was, but we couldn't find the damn thing." The demolition maneuvers were held many times after 1939, and the circuit always seemed to work. It was inconceivable to the Germans that something could go wrong again.

Another view of the Apollinaris Church, the town of Remagen, the Rhine River and the Ludendorff Bridge at Remagen.

Nine
· · · ·

Bombs Over Remagen

THE AREA AROUND REMAGEN and the bridge invited air attacks. Besides the Luden-
dorff Bridge itself, a prime target because it carried war freight and troops over the
Rhine, there were many other points where bombs could do a lot of damage to the
German transportation system. Just south of Remagen was Sinzig, an important rail
junction which linked the railroads coming from the north with the Ahr valley line.
Here an important bridge crossed the Ahr River. Three highways passed through
Remagen, and the Bonn-Koblenz highway was an important conduit. Ferries plied
across the Rhine at and near Remagen.

Although Remagen itself had no targets of strategic military importance, it was
known to quarter a large number of German troops; and other military installations
in and around the town made legitimate targets.

During 1940 and 1941, there were a few sporadic air attacks, ostensibly aimed
at the Ludendorff Bridge. The bombs did not come close to the bridge nor did they
do much damage to other installations or to the town. Not until 1944 did bombing
start in earnest. During the early months of 1944, twelve direct hits were scored on
the bridge at Sinzig.

By the time American forces swept to the German border in September, 1944,
the Ludendorff Bridge and other Rhine bridges had become vital targets. Every hit
on a bridge had a direct effect on the speed with which troops and supplies could
be transported to the front lines. Also, the rail junctions near the Rhine became more
important as American troops approached.

In mid-September, the Ninth Air Force started a campaign to disrupt German
movements of troops and supplies by interdicting rail lines running westward from
Düsseldorf, Remagen, Cologne and Koblenz. There were cheers in air force headquarters on October 19 when thirty-three planes of the 36th Group reported that they
had "destroyed" the Ludendorff Bridge at Remagen in a mass attack that day. Although
the report was inaccurate, the damage did create a vast amount of consternation and
subsequent hard work for the General of Transportation West in the German command. Thanks to the construction of some pillars in the early days of October, which
prevented the superstructure from falling into the Rhine, the repair was not an impossible undertaking. Furthermore, special equipment and manpower had been ear-

marked to speed bridge reconstruction. In the fall of 1944 8,000 tons of steel girders and 6,000 meters of steel piles—very precious items at this late stage of the war— were allocated to the German railway directorates of Karlsruhe, Mainz, Cologne, Essen and Wuppertal. They enabled the hard-working German transportation laborers to get the Remagen Bridge back into operating order by November 3, just fifteen days after it had been "destroyed."

During the remainder of November and the early part of December, 1944, the Ludendorff Bridge escaped further damage, for most of the Allied air attacks in the vicinity were directed at the rail junction south of Remagen. With the onset of the Battle of the Bulge, the Ludendorff Bridge was marked once again as an important target. The fog was too thick for effective attacks on the bridge until Christmas-time, but on December 29 a full-scale attack scored heavily. About one o'clock in the afternoon three waves of American bombers swept in from the Eifel and carpeted the town and the bridge with bombs. They made four direct hits on the bridge, inflicting the most serious damage near the end of the bridge across from Remagen. The bombs ripped up the steel girders under the railroad track so badly that the bridge hung only from its upper girders. The German transportation records reveal that this attack was expected to put the bridge out of commission "for several weeks." Both Remagen and Erpel were badly damaged. Remagen's city hall was so thoroughly damaged that it could not be used, and the city government had to move. In the last days of December and on New Year's Day, the bombing of bridge and town continued as the American Air Force attempted to stifle the last gasp of the Ardennes offensive.

During these trying days, the whole populace was torn among many tasks: to get in line early enough for food, to get the children into the woods before noon, and to carry on the necessary official wartime functions in the town. The people grew to hate the bridge, which seemed to act as a magnet for the American bombers.

On the morning of January 2, Mrs. Schmitz arose early to do her family chores and to get her three small children into the woods above Remagen before the usual noontime air raid. She set forth with her ration cards, and called first at the bakery shop. The line was a block long, and moved slowly. She fretted about the children, whom she had asked a neighbor to look after while she secured the rations for both families. After a long wait she had advanced close to the head of the line when the air-raid warning siren started to moan. The people in line scattered for the nearest cellar, but Mrs. Schmitz, half mad with fear, ran down the street. Near the Convent of St. Anne an air-raid warden caught her by the shoulders, shook her, and yelled: "Away from the street!"

"I must get to my children," she cried, trying to pull away, but the warden gripped her firmly and dragged her into the cellar of the convent. The priests and the nuns assembled the shivering people who had found refuge from the streets, and prayed. When the iron gates of the nunnery were blown open, again and again, and the crash of the bombs was felt all over the town, the terror-stricken people knew that this was the worst that Remagen had experienced.

A short while before the bombing that day, Captain Bratge prepared to stroll from his command post near the bridge to his living quarters with the Koch family, five hundred yards distant. He was a stubborn man, determined to stick to a schedule come weal or woe, and rarely missed his afternoon nap, despite the fact that most of the bombing attacks occurred during the lunch hour or early afternoon. Because his first sergeant had brought in some papers for him to sign just as he was about to leave the command post, he was in a bad humor when he arose to go to the door. Just then the air-raid alert sounded. He started as though to defy the siren, but thought better of it and settled down to wait. The *thwump* of the bombs seemed to be getting closer and shook the buildings. He heard screams up and down the streets. He still wanted to get home for his nap. Finally, there was a lull, and he went out. He was aghast at what he saw. Mangled bodies, shattered lumber, uprooted trees and inert cattle on their backs. The Koch house had been leveled. Frau Koch and her two children were dead. The Remagen Chief of Police and twenty others had been killed by a direct hit on an "air-raid shelter" across from the Koch home. Mrs. Schmitz was more fortunate. She managed to stumble tearfully down the road to her home. Up from the neighbor's cellar ran her sobbing children, transforming her anguish into heartfelt gratitude.

After that, she took them to the woods early every morning to get away from the hated, horror-stricken bridge. Each morning, along with all the other families not required for urgent wartime tasks, they loaded a few knapsacks and trudged into the hills above Remagen and picked a peaceful spot. Everybody seemed to know where to go, and each family went to the same spot, returning home in the late afternoon to attempt makeshift repairs on the bombing damage of the day. In the woods, quarrels and jealousies were forgotten in the face of common danger. The housewives bragged about their latest recipes to make the food rations stretch out, and the men concentrated on trading the latest information heard via shortwave.

The January 2 attack collapsed a wooden platform which had been built on the approach side of the bridge. One railroad track was ripped up, but the second track was still able to carry traffic. Heavy bombers of the Eighth Air Force continued to plaster the Remagen and other Rhine bridges on an increased scale. American reconnaissance planes recorded in mid-January that the Ludendorff Bridge had received direct hits on two of its spans and another on the east end of the bridge near the tunnel. One of the damaged sections of the bridge was reported to be twenty feet wide and eighty feet long, with rail traffic impossible.

The next large air attack took place on January 28, causing new and more severe damage to the platform at the bridge approach. Beams were used to bolster up the platform, and a new railroad track was quickly laid. Periodic investigations by American air reconnaissance in the last days of January and early February reported heavy damage, but on February 10 the flight noted that repairs were under way although eight bomb craters were still clearly visible on the bridge. On February 13 the report was that the bridge was "still undergoing repairs and is still unserviceable," but two days later it was reported as "completely repaired."

From both sides of the Rhine, the Remagen bridge dominated the landscape. PHOTO BY WILLIAM MUSTANICH

At the beginning of February, fighter bombers attacked the heavy railroad flak unit on one of the high hills above Remagen. As the American planes swept in for the attack and the German anti-aircraft was preparing to fire, a hospital train waited to cross the Remagen Bridge. The railroad flak unit hurriedly placed its guns in firing position—and in so doing blocked the track. Observing the frenzy of activity around the anti-aircraft battery, and the big guns swinging around, the American planes aimed their bombs at the railroad battery. Panic broke out in the hospital train, and a large number of wounded German soldiers, many of them dressed only in flimsy nightshirts, jumped out into the snow. The bombs which rained down on the anti-aircraft guns killed many of the wounded as they searched in vain for cover.

In mid-February, air attacks sank the ferries which operated between Remagen, Kripp and the east side of the Rhine. Loss of the ferries placed a greater burden of foot passenger traffic on the bridge, for there were many who lived on one side of the Rhine and worked on the other side. The constant stream of civilians taxed the troops who had to check passes and unsnarl the traffic and kept them from working on plans for the defense or possible demolition of the bridge.

The net effect of the air attacks was twofold: the bridge was seriously hurt by the bombs, and civilian morale was so shattered that the Remageners wanted nothing more than a quick end to the war. They had thought the war lost even before the large-scale attacks started. The bombs only underlined for them the hopelessness of continuing resistance. Some were resentful that the Luftwaffe never showed up, or that Hitler's long-promised secret weapons never effectively materialized. Others sullenly blamed the bridge for all of Remagen's troubles. Many felt like the Remagen girl who wrote to her friend in the Army: "If they would only end it soon. We can't stand these bombings any longer." A Remagen man wrote to his sister: "It is about time we put an end to this war. It only costs the lives of more of our people and keeps destroying the homes and possessions of many more. It is a sad but true fact that humanity has to be bled to death because of a few men who have fixed ideas in their heads."

The plain citizens of Remagen did not feel bitter against the Americans for the bombings. Of 250 letters which mentioned the air attacks in early 1945, only 3 referred to "damn Americans" or used the epithet "gangsters" describing the attackers. Bitterness in the town was directed chiefly against those who wanted to continue the war, and as word of American invincibility spread the citizens began to talk more and more openly of their desire to be "liberated." The cowed submission and fearful silence of the early days of the war gave way to widespread and open talk of a bloodless surrender. Soldiers quartered in homes not only heard and participated in the talk, but had reason to share the sentiments. As the American bombs killed more people and destroyed more homes, the citizens of Remagen were not stirred by anger to resist, or steeled like the British to a determination never to give in; they added to and reinforced the feeling of the soldiers that arrival of the Americans would spare their lives and their town. Without the deep-seated fear of the Russians which caused bitter opposition to advances on the eastern front, both civilians and soldiers looked forward to the day when they would be relieved from suffering, starvation and bombs. It cannot be claimed that the air attacks had already crushed the fighting spirit of the professional soldiers detailed to protect the Ludendorff Bridge. It can be said justly, however, that their fighting edge was dulled, and that the civilians' will to resist was virtually buried in the débris of the bomb-shattered town.

Ten
. . .

The German Predicament in the Rhineland

DEFEATS ON THE BATTLEFIELD always threw Hitler into a blind rage. He looked for scapegoats, and usually invented them when none could be found. Hitler was enraged to hear that an American bomb had blown up the Mülheim Bridge at Cologne with a lucky hit on the demolition chamber. He ordered that henceforth igniters should be attached to demolition charges only at the last moment, and that the order to prepare a bridge for demolition as well as the order for the demolition itself must be given in writing by the responsible tactical officer. Further, in areas more than five miles behind the front lines, only initial preparations should be made—that is, the demolition charges were to be stored in the vicinity. To leave no doubt in anyone's mind, this strict order was underlined by the stern announcement that court-martial proceedings had been initiated against those "responsible" for the loss of the Cologne-Mülheim Bridge. The order had a great psychological effect on the defenders of Remagen, the burden of which was: Don't arm these explosives too soon, or it will be somebody's neck.

Another Hitler order—to hold out in place to the last man—also had its effect on developments at Remagen. This policy had been in effect since the fighting in Normandy, but it was reinforced in far more stringent terms late in 1944 and made to apply specifically to troops in the West Wall fortifications. Morbidly suspicious of his field commanders after the attempt of July 20, 1944, to assassinate and overthrow him, Hitler viewed any withdrawal from the West Wall as either timidity, cowardice, or treason. He therefore required a written report whenever such a position was given up, and many court-martials followed planned withdrawals from the West Wall. Conspicuously posted notices named the officers and men who had been executed for "treason" and specified the other retaliatory measures taken against the families of the unfortunate victims of this drumhead justice.

On the surface, it might seem that such an order would strengthen the sagging backbone of the German Army by terrorizing the commanders and troops into a will to fight. To some extent, it produced this effect. But it had other effects which were dangerous from both a strategic and a tactical standpoint. A unit that knew there had been a break-through on either side of its position, leaving it vulnerable to attack from a flank or the rear, or to encirclement, still had to remain in position. It had the choice of being captured or cut to pieces. There was no provision for withdrawing in order to maintain contact with a flank unit, or making a reconnaissance to determine a good defensive position in the event the troops had to pull back. Any commander who gave thought or effort to finding a good position back of the front lines was regarded as "defeatist" and was a likely candidate for the next court-martial.

To hold the main line of resistance "to the last man," the last handful of scanty reserves had to be committed. This meant that when a break-through occurred there were no reserves left to seal off the gaps. One corps commander, General Hitzfeld, commented later: "Letting oneself be shot and killed in the main line of resistance might be reasonable, but one can only let oneself be killed once."

The knowledge that withdrawal would lead to a court-martial tempted many commanders to falsify their reports and to shift blame to others for their misfortunes. Strength figures of units were doctored to cover up losses. Commanders who engaged in this form of trickery subsequently became suspicious that their fellow officers were practicing the same deception. Any report was subject to second-guessing as to whether the information it contained was based on a frank appraisal of the true situation. Everybody got into the act of writing and issuing impossible orders to subordinate units, because evidence of a written order usually afforded a commander some protection at a court-martial. He could then claim a defeat was not his fault: hadn't he issued an order which would have saved the whole situation if it had only been carried out? Naturally, such bad manners quickly undermined comity of feeling in the German Army, and suspicions and jealousy were rife. Hitler's suspicions and his warped efforts to shore up the German front-line defenses only hastened the final American break-through.

The morale of the German troops in the Rhineland in March of 1945 was generally poor. Yet it would be a mistake to classify them all as defeatists who quickly laid down their arms at the first sign or sound of American soldiers. The German fighting forces were liberally sprinkled with men who still idolized National Socialism and were willing to die for the cause. Resistance to the American advances was sparked by fanatics who still felt that Hitler had brought glory to Germany and would bring more. For example, the diary of a twenty-four-year-old German parachute sergeant who was captured on the 9th Armored Division front at Zülpich contained the following entry in early March: "Men, at present, are not good enough; they must develop themselves into supermen. The only living example of this is Adolf Hitler. He alone has the faith, the belief and the ability . . . The enemy is menacing our vital industrial regions. Our new weapons must be committed, regardless of any humanitarian feelings." Fanatics like this sergeant were not in the majority, but it was difficult to tell the difference when Americans spotted the gray-green German uniform at the business end of a menacing burp gun or panzerfaust. Most German soldiers, no matter how low their morale, responded well to discipline and did their best to put up a firm defense. Only when outflanked or surrounded did they submit by mass surrender.

Lack of supplies, shortages of ammunition, and inadequacy of equipment were serious drawbacks to the German troops in the Rhineland in early 1945. Fuel and vehicles had always been short, and the situation steadily worsened. Frequently, general staff officers in desperation took to motorcycles and went out to search for fuel trains stalled on bombed rail lines. With communication wire in short supply, wires constantly being cut by bombings, and radio equipment scanty, the problem of maintaining contact with friendly units and keeping abreast of the enemy situation became almost impossible. The German confusion was compounded in the event of an American break-through, when lack of communication often left both higher headquarters and front-line troops in the dark as to what was happening.

The German situation maps in early March of 1945 reveal a frenetic resort to small detachments in an effort to plug the gaps. According to one German army commander he had available no more than "thinly scattered occupation troops, weak formations with deep echeloning, weak artillery, no mobile antitank defense and only small local reserves." Usable army reserves were non-existent, and it was almost impossible to scrape together sufficient reserves in the corps zones in time for them to be effective.

With so few troops available, the German commanders had to look for ways to economize. Despite General Patton's slashing attacks across France, the Germans convinced themselves that most American attacks were limited-objective affairs, with full time allowed for consolidation once objectives were reached. The Germans felt that, whereas the Russians showed a reckless disregard in throwing troops into battle, the Americans put a high price on human life and refused to take unnecessary chances with their troops. Early in March, for example, the American Ninth Army drew up to the Rhine and, to the relief of German observers, proceeded to consolidate its forces instead of making a concerted attempt to cross the river. The Germans concluded that between Cologne and Koblenz, the same practice of easy consolidation would be followed. From this line of reasoning, it was an easy step for the German command to gamble everything on holding the front lines, and to leave the defense of the Rhine and its crossings to the time when it was more directly imperiled. All attention was focused on holding the West Wall, on preserving the Rhineland instead of protecting the bridges and crossings of the Rhine.

The German troops in the Rhineland were commanded by General Gustav von Zangen of the Fifteenth Army. Von Zangen had gained fame as the German commander during the bitter defense of the Scheldt estuary in the fall of 1944, which has been chronicled in *The Eighty-five Days*. The Fifteenth Army command and staff had moved to the Rhineland to replace the command and staff of the Fifth Panzer Army at the end of February. In the early days of March, there were other frantic jugglings of the line-up in order to check the American advance. Divisions and regiments were reassigned and commanders were replaced, but none of the reshuffling seemed to have any effect. Frequently, units were ordered to counterattack from jump-off points that were already overrun.

The Mission of General Botsch
· · · · · · · · · · · · · · · · · · · ·

At the end of February, 1945, the First Army opened its attack over the Roer River, across the Cologne plain and down the Ahr River valley toward the Rhine. Up to this time, the Remagen area under the combat command of Captain Willi Bratge had been in the jurisdiction of Wehrkreis XII. Captain Bratge had a sealed, top-secret envelope which he was instructed to open only when Wehrkreis headquarters gave him the code word "Lorelei." He had a pretty good idea that this top-secret envelope contained orders detaching Remagen from the Wehrkreis and attaching it to a combat headquarters, but he was too disciplined a soldier to second-guess the order and make any advance contacts.

On February 26, the eve of the American attack across the Roer, the magic code word "Lorelei" came to Captain Bratge over the telephone from the Wehrkreis staff. It quickened his blood circulation. He was going to see some action again. What was more, higher headquarters would pay a little more attention to his needs from now on. He ripped open the sealed envelope, and pulled out the top secret document. It looked a trifle faded. As he suspected, the order attached the Remagen units to a combat army headquarters. But he was amazed to read that his units were to be attached to Fifth Panzer Army headquarters. It was impossible because, as Bratge knew, the Fifth Panzer Army had been replaced by the Fifteenth Army; but nobody had bothered to bring this important order up to date.

Bratge took the initiative and telephoned to the Chief of Staff of the Fifteenth Army. The call was a very confusing one for both parties, because nobody at Fifteenth Army had heard anything about a plan to subordinate Remagen to Army command. The Chief of Staff had troubles enough at the front lines without being pestered by a precise captain who kept talking about a railroad bridge forty miles back of the front. So the Chief of Staff said he had heard nothing about it, and refused to talk further until he had instructions from Army Group headquarters. That was always a quick and easy way to end a troublesome conversation, and at the same time be sure that your skirts were clean if there was a court-martial.

Somewhat nonplussed, Captain Bratge telephoned his old Wehrkreis headquarters to inform them of his plight. There followed two days of efforts to untangle the mix-up. The Wehrkreis staff finally appealed to Field Marshal Model, commanding Army Group B, to straighten out the mess. Model became convinced that it would take an officer of considerable rank and ability to bring order out of the chaos of command along the Rhine. He selected Lieutenant General Walter Botsch to set up an Operations Staff Bonn-Remagen for the defense of the area, and tapped him for the assignment on March 1—a scant six days before the American troops arrived at Remagen.

Botsch was a natural for a job of this character. He was a born trouble-shooter, had the knack of inducing people to work together, and loved to analyze complex and seemingly hopeless situations.

In the three days prior to getting his new assignment, General Botsch had gone through a fast training course in changes of command, as well as being given a number of full opportunities to participate in the fighting in the Rhineland. This kaleidoscopic series of experiences was not arranged in advance in order to groom him for the Bonn-Remagen defense mission, but it certainly helped him. During most of February, Botsch had commanded the 18th Volksgrenadier Division. On February 27, he was ordered to form Kampfgruppe Botsch out of the remnants of the 18th and 26th Volksgrenadier divisions. Then, during the time when Generals von Zangen and Manteuffel were switching the commands of the Fifth Panzer Army and the Fifteenth Army, Botsch was assigned to command a corps while the corps commander was temporarily taking over the Fifteenth Army. This mission having been performed, Botsch had barely resumed command of his Kampfgruppe when Model summoned him to head up the defense of Bonn-Remagen.

For his new job, Botsch was given most of the old staff who had been with the 26th Volksgrenadier Division, and with whom he had become acquainted while running Kampfgruppe Botsch. Field Marshal Model gave Botsch two major assignments: first, to build up a defense position west of Bonn, with a front facing north to prevent an American break-through from the direction of Cologne; second, to improve the defenses of the bridgeheads at both Bonn and Remagen.

Although Field Marshal Model initially assigned General Botsch, he placed him for command purposes under Fifteenth Army. One of Botsch's first steps was to drive to Remagen and size up the defenses. Meanwhile, Army headquarters had summoned Captain Bratge on the same day that Botsch made his trip. So the two officers missed a valuable opportunity to arrive at an early agreement on what was needed at Remagen.

General Botsch saw enough at Remagen to realize that it was woefully undermanned and weakly defended. On March 2, he proposed to Army Group that a full division be assigned to protect Bonn and a reinforced regiment be made available to defend Remagen. Model was impressed by the case which Botsch made, but he did not have the troops to carry out the recommendations. He promised instead that he would try to transfer a heavy anti-aircraft battalion to Remagen, and that the anti-aircraft forces already at Remagen would be ordered to form alert units for infantry use. The heavy battalion never arrived, but on March 5 the order went through concerning the use of existing anti-aircraft units as infantry.

In order to supervise both the Bonn and Remagen areas easily, General Botsch wanted to locate his command post halfway between Bonn and Remagen. Field Marshal Model did not like the idea, being convinced that the main American thrust would be along the Cologne plain toward Cologne and Bonn. Therefore Model felt that Botsch's command post should be in Bonn. The CP was finally located at Dottendorf, on the southern outskirts of Bonn—about fifteen miles north of Remagen.

General Botsch ran into other difficulties in untangling the chaotic chains of command along the Rhine. When he set up his command post at Dottendorf, the defense commander of Bonn, General von Bothmer, immediately started a series of critical arguments over who was responsible for the defense of Bonn. Traveling to the Fifteenth Army, which was nominally above him in the chain of command, General Botsch initially discovered that its commanders had no knowledge whatsoever of the situations at Bonn and Remagen – and did not appear to care. Their indifference was officially sanctioned: they had been ordered not to take a defeatist attitude by worrying about what went on in the rear areas. However, Fifteenth Army did order General Botsch to make another reconnaissance of Bonn and Remagen and report what ought to be done.

During the first few days of March, General Botsch spent a great deal of time driving back and forth between the command posts of Army Group B, Fifteenth Army, Bonn, Remagen, and up and down the area of his responsibility. In doing so, he probably became the one man who could figure out how the command complex operated. He studied the individuals involved, the difficulties of their operation, the status of the troops and supplies, the danger spots which might need sudden reinforcement, and the techniques to be employed when any portion of the area should be seriously threatened. He also saw the shattered German lines and disrupted communications system, and knew that the Bonn-Remagen area was in grave peril.

Meanwhile, Captain Bratge reported at army headquarters, reviewing with the engineer and signal officers the status of the Remagen defenses. When he asked that additional labor forces be sent to Remagen to construct emplacements he was sent to the G-4 who handled such matters; but the visit produced no results. Bratge asked for additional radio and signal equipment for maintaining contact with General Botsch's headquarters. Some equipment for this purpose was sent. He secured the promise of a technician and some telephone equipment. When the technician later arrived at Remagen he turned out to be a sergeant who was highly skilled technically but did not have the influence to secure the necessary telephone lines and equipment.

At army headquarters Captain Bratge overheard enough discussion to realize the dangerous strategic situation which German troops faced early in March. He now knew that the German front lines had been punctured, that in many areas troops were in full retreat, and that there were few reserves available to check the American onslaught.

On March 2 Captain Bratge received a peculiar telephone call from his old Wehrkreis command, insisting that the code word "Lorelei" had been issued prematurely, and that he was to remain under command of the Wehrkreis. He spent two precious days trying to straighten this out over the telephone. By the time General Botsch paid another visit to Remagen on March 4th, the misunderstanding had been resolved and the channel of command was a trifle less confused.

Botsch paid a final visit to Remagen on the afternoon of March 5. At that time, he secured full information on the withdrawal of certain units from the Remagen

Capt. Bratge briefs Ken Hechler on west bank of Rhine, June 1955, on German defenses at Remagen.

area. He learned that the personnel of the R.A.D. camp had been withdrawn, that elements of an air signal company had been moved, and that certain anti-aircraft instruction troops had crossed from Remagen to the east side of the river. Although these were largely non-combat troops, had they remained they might have been pressed into service to aid the badly undermanned defenses at Remagen.

At Remagen, Botsch also conferred with Friesenhahn, the bridge commander, and Möllering, the Volkssturm commander. They discussed the deployment of troops in the bridgehead, the commitment of the Volkssturm, the completion of work on a wooden platform for the bridge, the arrangements for demolition of the bridge, and relations with the local anti-aircraft commander. Once again, General Botsch saw that defense of the bridge and town was impossible with the troops under Captain Bratge's command, and he promised to see if he could obtain two infantry battalions, an artillery battalion, and a battery of 88-millimeter anti-aircraft guns.

Before leaving Remagen for the last time on the afternoon of March 5, General Botsch reviewed with Bratge and Friesenhahn the steps to be taken with respect to the demolition of the bridge. They went over again the Hitler order that extreme caution be exercised to prevent a premature demolition. They reviewed the general circumstances under which the bridge would be demolished, that is, when American troops were observed to have reached certain strategic points. Friesenhahn, on being asked under what conditions he could guarantee the demolition of the bridge, replied that demolition was certain as long as the heights commanding the bridge remained free of infantry weapons and artillery observers. He pointed out, however, that he had not yet received the military explosives which he had requisitioned.

When General Botsch left Remagen, he was reasonably sure that, despite the inadequacy of the troops and supplies available to the troops there, the defense of the bridge was in the hands of good commanders. Bratge and Friesenhahn had the feeling that General Botsch would do everything humanly possible to get them what they needed. Moreover, they felt that if anything went wrong he would quickly and sympathetically understand how to remedy it. There was a rare feeling of mutual confidence.

That evening, General Botsch reported by telephone to Model on the situation in his command. Model asked many questions about Bonn and its defenses, toward which the greatest American threat appeared to be aimed. Finally, Botsch said that he wanted to talk about Remagen also.

"Oh, yes," Model interjected in the matter-of-fact tone of a busy man who wants to be courteous, but is eager to get on to more important things, "you have Remagen in your area too. What do things look like there?"

"Conditions in Remagen are similar to Bonn," Botsch responded. "I have a bridge security company, and in addition the Volkssturm and some alarm units, but there is very little anti-aircraft." Model turned from the telephone and ordered the Army Group anti-aircraft officer to move a heavy anti-aircraft battalion to Remagen and to prepare the existing anti-aircraft units for infantry commitment in an emergency.

"Well, now that you have another alarm company available from the flak units, you have enough for Remagen, don't you?" asked Model.

"But I requested a reinforced regiment of infantry for Remagen," General Botsch protested.

"That you cannot get," said the field marshal. General Botsch then talked with General Wirtz, the engineer commander at Army Group B, and asked his advice on what additional technical measures were necessary to prepare the Remagen Bridge for demolition. General Wirtz advised him to have available triple or quadruple fuses for the charge, to prepare an emergency charge on the eastern bank of the river, to have an anti-tank gun at the east end of the bridge and to have the fuse cables checked every hour to make sure they were intact and the circuit was complete. This advice General Botsch relayed in a message to Captains Bratge and Friesenhahn at Remagen.

Events moved swiftly on March 6. General Patton's Third Army troops surprised the German commander of the LIII Corps when he was looking around for his own troops, and they painlessly took him prisoner. Good corps commanders were not easy to find at this critical stage when the German lines had been ruptured and the military situation was extremely fluid. Model liked and respected General Botsch, and felt that he had done a good job of reorganizing the confused Bonn-Remagen defense system. So late in the afternoon of March 6 Model informed Botsch that he was relieved of his responsibility for the Bonn-Remagen area and directed him to proceed immediately to take over the LIII Corps.

"Who will succeed me as commander of the Bonn-Remagen area?" Botsch asked.

"General von Bothmer, the defense commander of Bonn, will take over."

"I guess I had better brief him on the situation."

"No," Model said impatiently, "there's no time for that. The Americans have broken through the LIII Corps lines, and you have to get down there at once and take over."

This was a serious blow for the commanders and staff at Remagen. The officer whom they trusted, who had learned to weave his way through very complex command channels, and who had spent many days figuring out the best way to defend the area, was relieved just at the time when the American drive was getting dangerously close. Worse still, he was replaced by an officer who was argumentative and uncooperative, who had raised a number of jurisdictional questions of a petty nature, and who was thoroughly familiar with Bonn but knew little and cared less about the situation and defenses at Remagen. Quite apart from its military importance, Bonn was the birthplace of Beethoven, and General von Bothmer felt that it deserved his fullest concentration. He did not bother to visit Remagen. Instead, he told a liaison officer to look over the situation.

On the evening of March 6, Captain Bratge had only 36 men left in his company. Having received no word of the promised reinforcements, he decided to commit this handful of infantry to positions on the Remagen side of the river. The air was filled with rumors, and retreating German troops were already straggling into Remagen with lurid stories of the speed of the American advance down the Ahr valley. Bratge felt that he had to get in touch with General Botsch and see what steps should be taken in view of the increasingly critical situation. Of course, by this time General Botsch was already on his way to his new command. Bratge tried to telephone him but was told that the lines were out of order. He tried to send a radio message but had no success. He did not at first suspect that Botsch's headquarters had pulled out, but he began to wonder about this as the evening progressed. About nine o'clock that night, Bratge sent out two bicycle messengers with a message to be delivered in person. About an hour later the messengers returned and reported that, because of the pitch-blackness and the fact that vehicles were jammed three abreast on the road, they could not possibly get through to Bonn before morning.

General von Bothmer's liaison officer, Lieutenant Colonel von Poppelreuther, had set out from Bonn southward for Remagen after dark. Unfortunately, nobody in Bonn had an accurate situation map showing where American troops had penetrated, because nobody knew. He wandered into the American lines and was captured. Later, he and Captain Bratge met in an American prisoner-of-war camp, and Bratge told of his frantic efforts to get through to General Botsch. Poppelreuther replied: "No wonder. I was sent to tell you that General von Bothmer had replaced General Botsch. This is the first opportunity I have had to do so."

March 6 was a disastrous day for General von Zangen and his German Fifteenth Army. The day had dawned with von Zangen's troops still manning a thinly held line, forty to fifty miles west of the Rhine, with the following line-up of units from north to south:

LXXIV Corps, including 3rd Parachute Division, 272nd Infantry Division, 62nd Volksgrenadier Division.

LXVII Corps, including 277th Volksgrenadier Division, 89th Infantry Division.

LXVI Corps, including Kampfgruppe Botsch (remnants of 18th and 26th Infantry divisions), and remnants of 246th Infantry Division and 5th Parachute Division.

Counting all his service troops in the rear areas, von Zangen had perhaps 75,000 men. But in the face of the rapid American advance the units became disorganized, isolated and scarcely capable of putting up a coordinated defense. On March 6 the American 9th Armored Division ripped open the German lines with a nine-mile gain. By dusk of that day it not only had reached Stadt-Mechenheim — ten miles from the Rhine — but had broken open and driven through a wide gap in the center of the Fifteenth Army.

On the northern sector of the German front, the LXXIV Corps was completely out of touch with its neighboring corps on the left and had been bent back toward Bonn. Frantically, on the night of March 6, General von Zangen tried to close the gap and stabilize his line by organizing a counterattack. Hitler refused permission to the German troops to fall back and defend the Rhine line; instead, they were ordered to do the impossible: to recapture the ground they had lost.

General von Zangen tried to carry through the mad idea of a counterattack. By telephone, he ordered General Otto Hitzfeld, commander of LXVII Corps at his center, to attack into the southern flank of the American penetration starting from Altenahr. Hitzfeld stormed and pleaded with his army commander that such an attack was out of the question, but von Zangen insisted. Hitzfeld's signal communications had been knocked out by the American attack and he personally went to find his division commanders. En route, he was appalled by the condition of the troops. Whole sections of the front were held by weak groups no larger than a few sentries, and commanders had little or no knowledge of where their own troops were, let alone what contact they had with other units on their flanks.

At 11 p.m. on March 6, General Hitzfeld telephoned to General von Zangen and pleaded that a hopeless attack into a strong enemy flank would only hasten the American progress to the Rhine. General von Zangen held fast to his order and indicated that the fresh 11th Panzer Division would attack southwestward from Bonn to meet Hitzfeld's thrust and close the gap in the German lines. At midnight, General Hitzfeld made his third and last try to shake General von Zangen from his decision, without success. The sand was slipping through his fingers. His weak troops were unable even to hold the positions they were already occupying, let alone launch a counterattack.

In the midst of this compounded confusion, General Hitzfeld received a startling new order which hit him like a sudden shock of electricity.

The Mission of Major Scheller

At one o'clock on the morning of March 7, 1945, the commander of the German LXVII Corps, General Hitzfeld, received a telephone message from Fifteenth Army.

"Bridgehead Remagen is at once subordinated to LXVII Corps. Previous order to Corps remains in force. Strength at Remagen one battalion and anti-aircraft artillery."

At the time General Hitzfeld received this message, he was about forty miles west of Remagen. His troops were scattered at uncertain points along a broken front, trying desperately to defend their loosely held positions and at the same time assemble for a counterattack they had been ordered to make. General Hitzfeld knew that American spearheads to the northeast of him were already ten miles from Remagen. In this desperate situation, he was ordered to take over a vital point forty miles away about which he knew nothing, and had little time to learn more.

Had the front been stabilized, perhaps General Hitzfeld would have gone to Remagen personally in order to estimate the situation. As it was, the Corps Chief of Staff was out trying to find one of the divisions, and Hitzfeld himself had just returned to corps headquarters from a similar mission. He was up to his neck in the pressing and urgent issues of launching a counterattack and at the same time preventing another break-through. Therefore, he turned to his adjutant, Major Hans Scheller, an able and energetic thirty-two-year-old officer, and gave him the mission of going to Remagen to do what was necessary to organize the defenses.

It was 1:30 A.M. on March 7 when General Hitzfeld called in Major Scheller to brief him on his mission. "We have to reckon with a strong American attack on Remagen from the direction of Rheinbach," Hitzfeld said. "You take eight men and a radio set along and leave as soon as you can for Remagen. I am appointing you Commandant of Remagen, and all forces there will be subordinated to you. Report by radio to corps headquarters when you get there."

Hitzfeld gave Scheller the mission of establishing a narrow bridgehead with what forces he could find at Remagen, and ordered him "to establish a larger bridgehead with the forces you are able to get hold of during the day and those which arrive to cross the bridge." Scheller was to find out immediately about all the technical features of the Ludendorff Bridge, and to have it prepared for demolition. "If necessary, depending on the situation," Hitzfeld added, "you will give the order for demolition yourself."

Although Scheller had been under Hitzfeld's command for only a few weeks, the corps commander had come to know him as a capable and discreet officer. He had had considerable combat experience and had acquitted himself well. During the winter of 1944, he had contracted inflammation of the ribs as the result of an old combat wound, and had recuperated at his home near Cologne. Now he was fully recovered, and he had been back on duty for several weeks when Hitzfeld gave him the sudden assignment.

After talking with Hitzfeld, Scheller had a brief talk with the corps operations officer before leaving. He wanted to make sure he had all the possible information necessary for his assignment. The corps operations officer was impressed by Scheller's positive manner, and by his evident awareness of his heavy responsibility.

Out into the dripping and foggy night went Major Scheller and his little group.

The sounds of battle seemed to be all around them, and they had only a vague notion of the points to which the American troops had already penetrated. Progress was slow. Before dawn, their fuel started to run low, and Major Scheller discovered that he would not have enough gasoline in his own vehicle to reach Remagen. He instructed his men with the radio set to go on to Remagen and meet him there. He took a detour via Dedenbach, about a dozen miles southwest of Remagen, to get refueled. Movement became increasingly difficult for both groups. They were uncertain of the roads in the dark, and were constantly challenged by sentries. When dawn broke and the group of men with the radio set started to pick up speed, they observed American tanks already between them and Remagen. After first trying one or two approaches, they decided that it would be impossible to get through. Thus they stripped Major Scheller of his means of communication.

Major Scheller reached Dedenbach, which had been planned for a corps command post, and did not have too much difficulty getting the gasoline he needed. But the detour had taken him so far out of the way, and the roads were so clogged with retreating German troops, that it was after eleven o'clock on the morning of March 7 when he finally arrived at Remagen.

He was worn and haggard. He spent a few minutes futilely looking for his missing men and the radio set. Then he got in touch with Captain Bratge and Captain Friesenhahn to tell them of his mission.

Major Hans Scheller.

Eleven

· · · · ·

March 7, 1945

ON THE MORNING OF March 7, Lieutenant Karl Timmermann was awakened before dawn. A messenger had come from battalion message center to tell him that there would be a meeting of all company commanders at 0600 at Colonel Engeman's C.P. For Timmermann, this routine message had a special significance: it marked the first official recognition of his new responsibilities.

For a full week, Able Company had fought day and night as the 9th Armored Division pushed across the Roer River and through the fields and streams of the Rhineland. Although not in the lead, the 27th Armored Infantry Battalion had borne its share of the fighting, and Lieutenant Edwards, who commanded Company A, had been one of the casualties. At that point, Captain Frederick F. Kriner, a replacement officer, had been sent down from division to take command. On the night of March 6, Able Company reached Stadt Mechenheim, only ten miles short of the Rhine. But in taking that town, Captain Kriner had been hit. He had lasted just two days. Lieutenant Timmermann had organized the defense perimeter after dark, and established his company headquarters in the cellar of a bombed-out house. Now as he awoke and pulled on his combat boots in the darkness, he felt confident and strong, perhaps because he had just had a good six hours of sleep—the most he had been able to get all week—or perhaps because he was excited by the day ahead. It would be his first full day as company commander.

Timmermann had no illusions about war. He had just written to his wife in Nebraska: "La Vera, there's no glory in war. Maybe those who have never been in battle find that certain glory and glamour that doesn't exist. Perhaps they get it from the movies or the comic strips."

Five minutes after being awakened, Timmermann was climbing up out of his damp cellar headquarters. At the top of the stairs he paused a moment. Then he went out into the morning.

It was a damp, gray day, and from the overcast sky a light mist was falling. From about a block away the clatter of pans and the sound of men's voices told him that the kitchen crew had arrived. Kentucky Drake and his boys were welcome any time, but especially now. After a week on K rations, the men of Able Company were going to get their first hot breakfast. Timmermann smiled and gathered up his mess kit. Things were starting out all right.

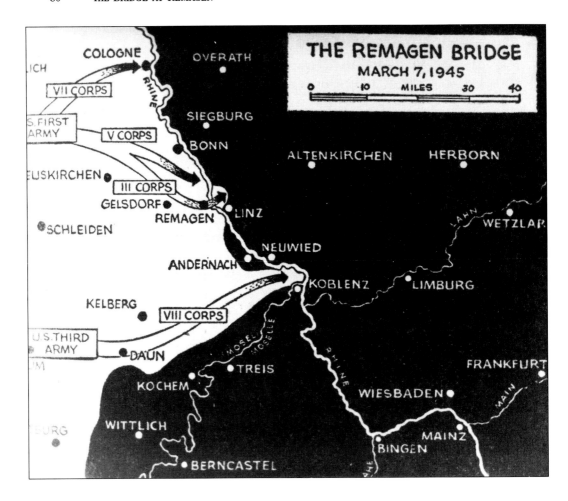

At the kitchen, Timmermann had just loaded up a stack of hotcakes and congratulated Kentucky on his food when a message center runner tapped him on the shoulder.

"Better get up to battalion, sir. Old Man's gettin' restless."

The "Old Man" whose restlessness had cut short Timmermann's breakfast was Lieutenant Colonel Leonard Engeman, commander of the task force that was spearheading the 9th Armored Division's drive toward the Rhine. Engeman, a Minnesotan, had the curious reputation of being both brusque and talkative. He had taken command of the 14th Tank Battalion just before it was shipped overseas in the summer of 1944. Ever since his days at the University of Minnesota when he took a fifty-cent chance on a $2,700 Packard and won the grand prize, Engeman had been lucky at everything he tried.

Timmermann looked at his watch as he went inside the bombed building where Colonel Engeman had his C.P. in the kitchen. It was just 6:00 A.M.–"0600," as the army called it.

"All right, break it up and let's get down to business," Colonel Engeman was saying sharply. "I just came back from General Hoge, and the Old Man wants us to push ten miles an hour today." Quickly he disposed of the business at hand in order to issue special orders to his infantrymen and tankers.

"Timmermann, you put your doughs on half-tracks, and I'll give you a platoon of tanks. You've got an important job to do today. You'll be the advance guard for our whole task force."

Timmermann nodded confidently. "When do we start?"

"Move out at 0700. The Recon will screen you on the left. Now where's Grimball?"

"Here, suh," said the tank commander in a deep South Carolina drawl that was so heavy that it seemed to be put on.

"Grimball, we haven't used your new Pershing tanks too much in the last few days, have we?"

"No, suh. They're a little wide for these country bridges."

"I know. But they sure scare the Krauts. You take your platoon of Pershings and team up with Timmermann as the advance guard. We're supposed to take a town called Remagen—that's about ten miles away, all the way down by the Rhine River. That means everybody will have to get off his rear and push hard. They tell me there's not too much enemy stuff ahead of us."

"No air support today, Colonel?"

"Don't be crazy, they couldn't get a plane off the ground in this haze and drizzle. No, there definitely won't be any air support. You'll get artillery when you need it, and they'll have their Piper Cubs up to help you spot. The Old Man hopes we'll move fast enough so we'll outrun our own artillery."

"What kind of roads do we have today? They look pretty thin on the map," observed Captain Soumas, commanding A Company of the 14th Tank Batallion.

"They'll hold your tanks pretty well. Secondary roads, sure, but they're black-topped, or tarred over, and you won't have too much trouble. But listen to this, Timmermann and Grimball: When you meet some fire, don't just stop, but try and barrel ahead and overrun it. Don't get bottled up in towns. And if there's any stopping, just remember I'll be on your neck, because the Old Man'll be on mine and he's pretty hot today."

With that, Colonel Engeman slapped together the two acetate covers on his map case, arose, and left the room. The tank and infantry company commanders saluted and left to brief their platoon leaders, as did the other unit commanders who had attended the meeting. Everything seemed routine. Most of the officers were feeling just a little better that morning, what with a few extra and unexpected hours of sleep and hot food.

Lieutenant Timmermann walked back to his C.P., and at 6:30, when the drizzly morning light was still decidedly gray, he called together his platoon leaders. Only two officers beside himself were left in the company—Burrows and Dave Gardner, the anti-tank platoon leader. All three officers were second lieutenants. Mike Chinchar and Joe DeLisio, two sergeants, had taken over the first and third platoons.

Lieutenant Colonel Leonard Engeman, commander of the 14th Tank Battalion, with his Sherman tank.
PERSONAL PHOTOGRAPH OF COL. ENGEMAN

"Jim, you put your men on half-tracks to point the advance guard," Timmermann said to Burrows. "We'll move out in half an hour, heading toward a town called Remagen. I'll show you on your maps which route we'll take. They tell us we move about ten miles an hour. I'll be running up and down the line in my jeep. Mike, you take your platoon out to protect the right flank, and, Joe, you protect the left and make contact with the recon that's screening our left. Dave, you bring up and protect our company rear with your 57's. Any questions?"

"Yeh, Lieutenant," said DeLisio, "what about radios?"

"Radio silence. That makes it important to keep in sight of the fellow ahead of you."

"I guess on a day like this the fly boys won't be up."

"Nope, you're on your own. Now before you move out, check your ammo supply and gas, and make sure everybody has their K rations. Get your drivers to check those half-tracks, treads and motors, because today we're really goin' to move. All right, let's go," Timmermann concluded—and the group separated.

Lieutenant Burrows scurried around to post his squad leaders on their mission. He made sure that his half-tracks were in good running condition and were well stocked with ammunition and supplies. Everything seemed to be in order until he investigated the road he was to use. A few yards out of town, the rubble was piled so thickly that vehicles couldn't get through. Bulldozers were manfully scooping up and removing the débris left by recent American bombing attacks, but the job looked endless. Seven o'clock came and passed. General Hoge fumed and stormed as he tried to get news of what was holding up the column. Colonel Engeman, who was just as anxious to move forward, yelled:

"What the hell's goin' on here? Why don't you get movin'?"

The cry was echoed and reechoed up and down the line, but the Air Force had done its job just a little too well, and there was a limit to the amount a bulldozer could digest in one swallow. So it was just hurry up and wait.

"Wish I had taken another stack of hot cakes," said Ralph Munch, as he coolly mounted the lead half-track. A thirty-four-year-old Iowan, he was one of the steadiest and most intelligent men in Burrows' platoon. He got set for his usual task of feeding in the ammunition belts to the .30-caliber machine gun, and keeping the empty cartridges cleaned out below. On this particular day, his teammate was Bob Crawford, a lanky Texan who as usual was wearing his pants outside his combat boots, like a cowboy.

"Let's try a burst to see how she works, Ralph," grunted Crawford as he cut loose with the machine gun on the side mount of the track. A cartridge jammed; working it loose, they tried again, and once more the gun became jammed. "Goddam headspace ain't set right," Crawford noted, but it was too late to stop for repairs.

Alex Giles, a Kansas farm boy who was driving the lead half-track, leaned on the gas, and the vehicle squeaked forward. A little later, Giles yelled back from the driver's seat: "What's that?" The men in the squad took notice when Giles saw something. His sharp eyes seemed to be able to pick out strange objects before anyone else. "Could be a tiger tank," someone mumbled as they followed Giles' long, pointed finger.

Lieutenant Burrows waved his arm to dismount, and three men gingerly crept forward to find nothing more than an abandoned and burned-out German auto. They laughed nervously.

As they remounted, Burrows turned to his men and said: "I predict a quick reaction to this, so hold onto your helmets." Sure enough, thirty seconds later Karl Timmermann, the new company commander, came steaming up in his jeep. He didn't have to say a word. Giles turned around to his buddies as he gunned his half-track, saying: "Let's give Tim a race." The men jerked backward as the vehicle shot ahead. Timmermann let out a loud laugh, waving his arm toward the east with a yell: "And keep goin'!"

Burrows climbed out onto the hood of the half-track, where he could get an unobstructed view of the countryside. He kept his binoculars glued to his forehead, searching for clues to enemy guns which even Giles' piercing eyes could not distinguish. Out there in front, Burrows and his men felt very keenly their responsibility as the "point" of the advance guard of Task Force Engeman. Munch turned around and noticed that the first support tank was a good half-mile behind. That didn't make the men feel any better about their exposed position. In this fairly open country, dotted by occasional patches of woods and with gently rolling hills, it seemed like a perfect set-up for a German ambush. Were the Germans just sucking in a large enough force before they pinched it off?

A little over a mile out of Stadt Mechenheim, near the town of Fritzdorf, Pfc. Herman Michael spotted a road block at the entrance to the village.

"I'd much ruther be shooting coyotes back in Missouri, but here goes, let's give it to them," Michael yelled. The armored infantrymen sprayed the road block with .50-caliber machine-gun fire. The two vehicles following started firing to the left and right, and Forrest Miner silenced some opposition in one of the windows overlooking the road block. As the task force advanced cautiously, small arms and an automatic weapon began firing at the Americans from an orchard south of Fritzdorf.

On the hood of his half-track, Burrows gave a long wave of his arm, the signal to dismount. The men in the lead half-tracks each grabbed the side of their vehicles and vaulted into the roadway. Two squads outflanked the German position. Charlie Penrod, who could write his name on a wall with a Thompson submachine gun, had a field day pumping out all the ammunition he could lay his hands on. The squads spread out behind the houses in the town while the half-tracks moved through on the road. On the extreme left flank, Ralph Munch heard someone call behind him and upon turning around saw a group of German soldiers coming out of foxholes with their hands above their heads. They were all youngsters. Munch sent them back under guard to the rear. Then Burrows blew his whistle for his men to remount. A quick count revealed no casualties.

At this point, Lieutenant Timmermann drove up in his jeep. After talking over the situation with Burrows, he went out in front of the column for a while. It was a good example. It not only quieted the nerves of those in the lead half-track, but also demonstrated that Timmermann was both a commander and a leader. The column plowed ahead without incident, and soon Timmermann turned his jeep and drove back to keep his column together, and also make sure there was enough dispersal between vehicles.

The men in the lead half-track started to eat their K-rations, although it was still fairly early. A mile or so down the road, near Overich, a panzerfaust opened fire and the lead half-track was almost hit. Burrows signaled back for Grimball's tanks to come up and give Overich a little plastering, and soon a timid group of prisoners emerged after cries of "Hände hoch." Once again, Burrows' men emerged unscathed.

By eleven o'clock the task force was already halfway to Remagen and moving rapidly.

"At this rate," Timmermann told the men hanging on one of the tanks, "we ought to be able to clean things up by early this afternoon and then just eat and sleep along the Rhine for a couple of days."

The column rounded a corner and went through another small town, with white flags flying. A buxom girl in a tight-fitting sweater was giving a demonstration of good posture as the vehicles rolled by. Paul Poszich turned to Charlie Ellett and said: "Don't tell me that bread and wine made all of that." The remark wasn't carried on the intercom, but somehow it passed down the column and seemed to get funnier as it was repeated.

Burrows began to worry about the overhead telephone wires. "There just isn't enough noise around here, Tim. I'll bet they're planning a trap. Don't you think we ought to do something about all those wires?"

Timmermann was cool. "Let's get to Remagen first, Jim. It's getting late."

"But shouldn't we cut those wires down somehow?"

"Never can tell. Might want to use 'em ourselves," Timmermann laughed.

Burrows was persistent. He got excited and yelled: "You want the Krauts to meet us in Remagen with a brass band? I tell you we've just got to do something about those wires before we go any further!"

Timmermann slapped Burrows playfully between the shoulders and laughed his big, friendly laugh. He reached into his jeep for his carbine and said: "I'll fix yer damn wires for you." Timmermann took a couple of pot shots at the wires. Miraculously, one of them came down. Timmermann hopped into his jeep, firing wildly as he took off in front of the column. He gave a whoop as another wire came down. After a few minutes when the fun was over, he drove back and repeated the command: "Now let's get pushing!"

The column ground on toward Niederich. On the far side of the town, a group of German soldiers was beating a hasty retreat. The Americans fired a few automatic weapons, and soon the Germans threw up their hands and started toward the American column. Burrows had one squad dismount to assemble the group of prisoners. As one German officer approached with his hands in the air, he evidently thought he would try to exact a last penalty: he drew his pistol and fired wildly at short range. It was a miracle that nobody was hit. The reaction was immediate – and deadly. The officer fell with half a dozen American bullets in him.

This was the part of war that the men hated most. They had almost grown used to killing the enemy at long range, especially when they had seen their own comrades die. But there was something terrible about shooting a man whose facial expression they could watch close up. War seemed like a dirtier business than ever that morning in Niederich. The men were mad, and it was lucky for the German soldiers that none were found in either Leimersdorf or Birresdorf. There were only white sheets flapping in the wind, and the streets were deserted.

Just outside of Remagen, hidden from the town and the river by heavy woods, the Allmang family ran a small tavern, the Waldschlösschen. It was crowded at all times, because three generations of Allmangs were always running in and out. When war came, the tavern closed down, and the Allmangs took in boarders. The younger Allmang sons left for the army, and the husbands of the younger daughters went off also. German soldiers were quartered at the tavern, but they cleared out in a hurry on the night of March 6.

About ten o'clock in the morning of March 7, several breathless German soldiers ran down the Birresdorf-Remagen road and excitedly reported to Herr and Frau Allmang that the Americans were already in Birresdorf. "Get into the cellar and stay in the cellar. We're crossing the Rhine. Good luck!" They ran down the road toward Remagen.

Infantry move toward Remagen. U.S. ARMY SIGNAL CORPS, NATIONAL ARCHIVES

The father of the household, Joseph Allmang, calmed his wife, daughters and grandchildren, with these words: "Don't get worried, now. You know, when I fought in France in 1918 it took weeks to get through the main line of resistance. If they're at Birresdorf it will take many days before they get to the Waldschlösschen. Just calm yourself." Before he finished speaking, the sound of Jim Burrows' half-track was heard around the bend, and one of the Allmang girls, blonde Frau Annie Seegmuller, swept up the little grandchildren and dashed for the cellar. Frau Allmang followed, and the rest of the family, trailed by the still skeptical head of the household, took refuge. From a window they could see the first two half-tracks rumble past. Suddenly, Frau Allmang rose and said: "This is no way to greet our liberators." Running upstairs, she took a tablecloth from the kitchen table and went out onto the lawn and waved it vigorously.

Just then Lieutenant Timmermann drove up in his jeep. He looked over at the left of the road where Frau Allmang stood half paralyzed with fear, but still shaking her token of surrender. He held up his hand gently, and then asked her in perfect German: "Any soldiers here?"

"Nein," answered Frau Allmang.

By this time, the rest of the family had emerged from the cellar. A little less peremptorily, Timmermann asked: "Any guns? Any ammunition?"

"Nein, nein, nein," they all chorused.

The flicker of a smile appeared on the face of one of the thoroughly frightened youngsters. Timmermann could see that all three of the little children were under-

Enemy artillery slowed the progress toward Remagen. U.S. ARMY SIGNAL CORPS, NATIONAL ARCHIVES

fed, and marked with the sores of a strange disease. "I'll send you some food and medicine this afternoon," he said, turning to remount his jeep.

When the food arrived, the Allmangs refused to touch it. They indicated to their benefactors that they would not dare to eat until the Americans had first tasted the food. Not long afterward, the first American soldiers were storming up to the swank Waldburg Hotel above Remagen, demanding that the proprietor bring out his best wines. But before the G.I.'s would drink, they forced the proprietor to drink a sip from each bottle used. Such are the suspicions bred by war.

Across the road from the Allmangs', Forrest Miner spotted an ammunition dump on the right side of the Birresdorf road. There were stacks of dark boxes, but nobody around guarding them. Miner took a quick look and then decided to push on. Just about that time the pangs of hunger began to grip some of the men. Miner, Drabik and a few of the others paused to try out a new form of G.I. pea soup, warmed by a wick which could be lit in the center of the small can. It tasted good. Miner swigged his pea soup in his left hand and fired a few shots, one-handed, at the edge of an abandoned German labor service camp just visible around the bend.

Carmine Sabia squeaked along the road with his reliable half-track "Aibas." Sabia tried to make a little noise with his machine gun because he did not like the deadly quiet of the pine woods through which they were passing. He glanced up at the gaps

Although this photo was taken after March 17, 1945, when the Remagen Bridge collapsed (see piers in the river), this is the point where first American troops saw that the Remagen Bridge was still intact. U.S. ARMY SIGNAL CORPS, NATIONAL ARCHIVES

in the trees which had been cut by machine gun and rifle fire. Suddenly in the distance Sabia saw the crest of a mountain looming over the top of the trees. The mountain was actually across the Rhine, but Sabia did not realize this at the time.

Up ahead, a reconnaissance car halted and the occupants told Penrod and Munch that they had been fired on. The two men moved on about fifty yards beyond the recon car. They could see that the road turned sharply toward the right. They cut through some woods on the right side of the road, working their way through the woods and back onto the road again where it turned right. Across the road was a clearing in front of the heavy woods. Near the road was a pile of brush and as they looked closer they could see an anti-tank gun hidden there, pointing almost directly at the half-track which they had left 150 yards up the road. They discovered that the gun was not manned. Suddenly, Penrod and Munch saw something which caused them to wave violently at the men in the column behind them.

Timmermann saw the excitement ahead as he left the Allmangs. He hopped into his jeep and raced forward. Rounding the bend in the road, he emerged from the woods and found himself confronted by a breath-taking view. Far below, the river wound through its narrow valley, and off to his right, clearly outlined against the sky, was the prize no man dared hope for – the Ludendorff Bridge, still intact, spanning the Rhine!

Twelve

· · · · ·

The Last Hours of the German Defenders

ON THE EVENING OF March 6, 1945, Captain Willi Bratge had sent most of his 36 infantrymen west from the Rhine to the Victoriaberg, where the old trenches which had been dug around the Waldburg Hotel offered excellent observation and good defensive fields of fire. The heights of the Victoriaberg gave a commanding view up and down the Rhine and northward across a short valley to the R.A.D. camp. There, the winding road from Birresdorf emerged from the woods to make several S-curves as it descended sharply into Remagen. This road was to assume historic importance for the Americans the next day.

To command the handful of infantrymen west of the Rhine on the night of March 6, Captain Bratge sent his first sergeant, Gerhard Rothe, a tall man with loose-jointed arms and a friendly smile.

Rothe had come to Remagen in 1928 when his father, Wilhelm Rothe, became the owner of the Central Hotel, just across the plaza from the railroad station. Gerhard prepared himself to take over his father's business, and anticipated the prospect. He had a lively sense of humor, a casual way of sizing up his guests and anticipating their wants, and an honest desire to see everybody happy.

Young Rothe was drafted into the army along with several hundred other Remagen men, many of whom never came back. After being wounded on the Russian front in 1944 he was so lucky as to be sent to his home town for recuperation. Of course he had to travel across the Ludendorff Bridge to the hospital at Linz for treatment. As one of the "walking wounded," he was assigned as first sergeant to Captain Bratge's infantry company. At first, he had difficulty firing a gun, but he could operate a typewriter and perform the necessary clerical duties.

Disturbed by the boom of American artillery and tank fire to the west and by the reddened skies over Koblenz marking a full-scale air raid, Rothe's little group on the heights spent a nervous first night with little sleep.

Back at the bridge Captain Friesenhahn's first glance at those skies over his boyhood home caused him to shuffle about nervously. He always became irritable when the fires began to burn in Koblenz, and his men sensed that this evening he was more disturbed than usual. He kept looking southward, worrying about his home and family, and before long he went to Captain Bratge and said sharply: "I don't like the idea of sending the whole bridge security company up to the Victoriaberg."

The Ludendorff Bridge was a railroad bridge, which was planked to allow vehicular traffic. U.S. ARMY SIGNAL CORPS, NATIONAL ARCHIVES

Bratge, so much younger than Friesenhahn and a trifle insecure in his authority, did not like it to be challenged. "Where do you think my men ought to be?" he demanded.

"They should be here protecting the bridge."

"But we must have outposts," Bratge responded testily. "Someone has to warn us if the Americans should try to break through here."

Friesenhahn shook his head resignedly, and took another horrified look at the deepening red glow over Koblenz. He was not convinced by the explanation, but he pressed the issue no further. Years later, he acknowledged that Bratge's decision was sound under the circumstances.

During the last days of the German troops in Remagen, Jakob Klebach was one of the busiest soldiers in the area. The little carpenter, along with scores of others, was working under high pressure to plank over the tracks of the bridge so that vehicles could cross. Many unskilled men were engaged in the task, but Klebach was such a good carpenter that he was kept on the job almost around the clock. His wife brought his meals to him. About ten o'clock on the evening of March 6, Klebach and his colleagues finished the grueling four-day task. It had been done so fast and so well that under other circumstances, probably medals would have been awarded to them for their efforts.

Because of the weak spots in the bridge underneath the tracks, the planking could not be laid in a precisely even fashion. There were gaps between the planks which made it dangerous to cross except in daylight. Although Captain Bratge wanted to start vehicles moving over the bridge at once, Captain Friesenhahn insisted that he did not want to run the danger of having it closed for hours while they extricated a truck from a hole between the planks. Therefore, the bridge was opened only for eight railroad trains that night. Most of these were hospital trains evacuating the wounded from military hospitals throughout the Ahr River valley, or empty rolling stock which there was sore need to preserve.

All through March 6, increasing numbers of troops and vehicles came to Remagen in the hope of crossing the bridge. The narrow streets were clogged and traffic control was difficult. For this reason, Captain Bratge welcomed the arrival of two military police detachments in the early afternoon. Two lieutenants, supervising the detachments, had come to clear the way for some of their staff troops to cross the river. The lieutenants and the military policemen were stationed at a number of check points on the edge of town. They were able to check vehicles and individuals for identification and combat orders, and to round up stragglers and shirkers. Suddenly, at eight o'clock in the evening, both lieutenants reported that they had received orders from Army Group B to move their detachments elsewhere. When they had gone the traffic situation became almost intolerable. The troops available could not man the check points properly, in addition to organizing the shaky defenses at the bridge.

Bratge abandoned all of the traffic check points except one about three hundred yards northwest of the railroad station, entrusted to his chief messenger, Sergeant Keilhofer. Keilhofer warmed up to his job quickly, and his commanding voice made up for what he lacked in rank. He scored his first success shortly before midnight when a depleted regiment of the 3rd Parachute Division tried to break through. After discovering that the unit had no orders to go across the Rhine, Keilhofer sent the noncommissioned officer in charge to Captain Bratge. Bratge ordered the unit to spend the night in town and move out at five o'clock in the morning to take up defensive positions near Bodendorf, about three miles to the southwest. He incorporated other stragglers into this group.

Keilhofer's luck did not hold out long. Although things seemed so peaceful that Captain Bratge decided to take a nap at two A.M., he was rudely awakened at three by motor vehicles racing through the crooked streets toward the bridge. Arising hastily, he ran toward the traffic control point and found Keilhofer in a frenzy of frustrated rage. Trucks of a retreating combat unit had broken down the crude barrier he had set up, and were rushing blindly ahead. When the next vehicle in line ignored Bratge's command to stop, Bratge fired into one of the tires; the truck lurched onward unchecked. Only when a second shot punctured another tire did the driver pay attention.

By this time, the road to the bridge was clogged with two and three vehicles abreast. Bratge realized that he would have to remain at the traffic control point to enforce his own orders, and also to make sure that when the bridge was opened for traffic the vehicles could cross in order of priority. The rest of the night he handled traffic, and when the bridge was opened at five o'clock a steady and orderly stream of vehicles passed over it. He had the traffic under control, but it took him away from other defense duties.

Having no regularly established channels of intelligence, Captain Bratge had to rely on the retreating troops for information about American movements. On the morning of March 7 he received a number of reports, which the noise of approaching guns seemed to confirm, that American armored forces were in the area west of Birresdorf. He telephoned the information to Army Group B, and after some difficulty got through to Lieutenant May, one of the assistants to the operations officer. Bratge excitedly reported that he needed help, and particularly wanted the two battalions which he thought Field Marshal Model had promised. Lieutenant May's tone indicated he had more important things to think about. Bratge insisted that the American tanks were getting closer every minute. Lieutenant May told him: "Don't soil your underwear. Those tanks are heading toward Bonn, Cologne, and Düsseldorf." Bratge answered: "They're coming toward Remagen." Finally, May broke off the conversation with the sarcastic remark that Bratge as an old combat soldier ought to know and realize that this was not the main body of American troops. Bratge banged down the telephone in a rage. In effect he was accused of cowardice, and he was livid.

On top of the Erpeler Ley two multiple, four-barreled 20-millimeter anti-aircraft guns and their crews had been stationed for several days. There was no better point in the entire Remagen area from which to observe the approach of troops from the west. Unknown to Captain Bratge or to any of the troops in the Remagen area, there had been a shift in the anti-aircraft guns and their crews on the afternoon of March 6.

The unit on the Erpeler Ley was ordered to Koblenz. Its place was to be taken by a similar unit that had been on the eastern outskirts of Remagen until then. The latter unit, unfortunately, had no prime movers to tow the guns, so that the crews had to drag their weapons by hand. That night fourteen of the gunners went A.W.O.L. Some gave themselves up to the Americans; others simply changed into civilian clothes and disappeared into anonymity.

On the morning of March 7, Captain Bratge's eyes fell on the strange sight of the crews tugging and sweating as they manhandled their anti-aircraft guns across the bridge. He immediately went onto the bridge. Only after close questioning of the crews and their commander did he discover that the guns on the Erpeler Ley had been moved. Bratge angrily ordered the gun commander to get his guns up to the Erpeler Ley as quickly as possible so that they could cover the bridge and its approaches, and to report to him the minute the guns got into position.

Perhaps the angry command by an infantry commander to a lordly Luftwaffe officer affected the speed of its execution. At any rate, the report never came; the best point of observation was unmanned when the Americans arrived.

At nine o'clock on the morning of March 7, Frau Maria Bayer, still living in her house on the Rheinwerft within the shadow of the bridge, was warned several times that this was going to be the day of decision for Remagen and the bridge. For many months, she had quartered soldiers in her house. They seemed like nice boys. They stopped in to tell her goodbye and to warn her to leave town, because the bridge would probably be blown up later in the day. Frau Bayer went uptown, and there she saw some SS soldiers who also told her that unless she got away from Remagen Bridge she surely would be hurt.

In Erpel early that morning, Frau Karin Loef, who worked across the river in the Remagen City Hall, noticed an unusual tension as people scurried around to get their rations. As she walked toward the bridge, a number of friends shook their heads and pleaded with her not to go over to Remagen. She insisted that her job of recording births, deaths, and marriages in Remagen could not be interrupted by wars, revolutions, or earthquakes. Secretly, she wanted to be on the spot if there was going to be any action. So, armed with her special pass, she crossed to Remagen.

Frau Loef was almost engulfed by the traffic that was surging across the bridge in the other direction. "I could not help comparing it to the stories of Napoleon's retreat," she said later. "The older ones could hardly march on; their eyes were cast down onto the ground, they simply seemed to stumble on without any hope. They had all sorts of animals with them, horses – poor, worn-out creatures – pulling carts or guns behind them. I even saw flak soldiers pulling their guns. In between they also had cows and oxen with them, probably taken from the abandoned farms they had passed." Later in the morning, Frau Loef crossed back to Erpel, and when she tried to return to Remagen soldiers told her they were preparing to blow the bridge, and even her special pass was of no avail.

Captain Bratge had many things to worry about on the morning of March 7. Despite lack of sleep, he was clear-headed, incisive in his orders, calm. His training in mathematics seemed to help him preserve an orderly arrangement amid all of the confusion. There was little time for what he had to do, but his good sense of priority helped him make full use of such time as there was. Beginning to wonder what had happened to the remnants of the parachute outfit that he had dispatched to set up a defense in Bodendorf, he sent Becker, the Nazi party chief in Remagen to find out why he had received no report from Bodendorf.

Becker found a horrifying explanation. In the town, white flags were already flying. The local Volkssturm had torn down the anti-tank road blocks and the people were apprehensively waiting to be liberated. Where were the parachutists? Becker finally learned that a paratroop lieutenant had encountered the motley group and ordered them to turn around and follow him eastward across the Rhine. Even the Nazi chief had to admit that the defection was inevitable. In the first place, it was an order. In the second place, the order was far more congenial to the men than the original order to bare their breasts in Bodendorf to the point of the American assault. He returned to report the disastrous development.

About the same time as Becker, Fräulein Louen had set out for Bodendorf. She did not have quite as far to travel, because her father was the official forester of the Remagen area and they lived far out in the woods above the town. She dutifully reported at the Bodendorf post office, where she had worked for several years. All through the early morning she heard the steady clump-clump of German boots on the pavement, retreating toward the Rhine. The troops were not singing or talking, but marching briskly. Then suddenly, as if by signal, white flags appeared at many windows. For a long period there was dead silence. When she stole a glance out of the post-office window she was terror-stricken to see a figure in strange khaki uniform dart past and crouch at the corner, with his machine pistol at the ready. She cranked the wall telephone to Remagen, was put through to her home, and cried: "Mother, mother, what will I do? They're here! The Americans with guns. There are lots of them . . ." Before she could finish, the telephone went dead. Bodendorf fell without a shot.

Back at the Remagen bridge, Captain Friesenhahn and his men had been putting the final touches on the preparations for demolition. They placed mines and barbed-wire entanglements near the approaches, and arranged to set off the charge which would gouge out an anti-tank ditch. This, they reasoned, would ensure enough time to demolish the bridge in case the Americans in a lightning thrust with tanks should attempt to rush the bridge.

"This will fool those damn foreign workers," Friesenhahn said bitterly as he and one of his men hung out several signs reading "Achtung, Minen" along the road where he had no intention of placing mines. He still burned with indignation whenever he recalled that the French and Russian laborers always seemed to know what was going on in his planning and disposition of troops. On that morning of March 7 Friesen-hahn had a deep crease in his brow as though he were more worried than usual and his men tried in vain to find out why. He finally asked one of them:

"Where are the 600 kilograms of explosives they promised us?"

"Haven't seen them yet, Captain," Sergeant Klebach answered.

"Well, let me know as soon as they get here, because we're going to have to place them right away for use in an emergency."

About eleven o'clock a truck drove up with the long-awaited explosives, and Captain Friesenhahn discovered to his horror that he had been short-changed. Instead of the 600 kilograms that had been requisitioned, the truck had brought only 300. Furthermore, even this was not the standard type of military explosive, but a weaker form of industrial explosive. All the engineers complained bitterly; but, knowing it would do no good to ask for more, they prepared to make the best of what they had.

It was just turning 11:15 when Captain Bratge looked up from the combat orders he was checking at the traffic control point and saw a tall, young major in a dusty and wrinkled uniform. As he came closer and spoke it could be seen that he was red-eyed.

"Major Scheller. I have orders to take over as combat commander of Remagen."

Captain Bratge was surprised, but pleased that higher headquarters was at last paying some attention to him.

He had lost all telephone contact with surrounding units; and had not dared to send a radio message in the clear lest it be intercepted. Although Major Scheller's coming was unexpected, he greeted him enthusiastically because he felt that it meant the long-expected reinforcements would shortly arrive to bolster up his weak defenses. Looking beyond Scheller, he could see no sign of reinforcements and asked:

"When can we expect the two battalions to arrive?"

Major Scheller looked blank, his tired eyes drooping. Bratge repeated his question in a rising pitch.

"What battalions are you talking about?" Scheller answered in measured tones.

Bratge's agile and imaginative mind immediately began to calculate. He recalled the story about the British officer who had impersonated a German general in France and caused untold damage by ordering units hither and yon to tangle up the whole German command system.

"Let me see your identification and your orders," he snapped.

Looking up twice from the picture on the pass that Scheller produced, he assured himself that he had the right man. He was puzzled to learn that Scheller was with the LXVII Corps, but knew that General Hitzfeld's Corps was somewhere in the Ahr valley. A few minutes' careful conversation convinced him that Major Scheller was not a spy and that his mission was legitimate. However, his spirits sank when he realized that now there was probably no hope of reinforcements for Remagen and the bridge.

Major Scheller impressed Captain Bratge as an intelligent, direct, and incisive officer. His chief difficulty was total unfamiliarity with the command channels in which the Remagen troops operated. This was a complex subject that Bratge couldn't explain in two minutes at a traffic control point, with everybody and his brother tugging at his sleeve to make decisions on other matters. Temporarily giving that up, he tried to explain to Major Scheller the plans for the defense of Remagen and the bridge. He was in the midst of this when at 11:25 A.M.—only ten minutes after Major Scheller's arrival—a messenger ran up to report that some of the troops on the hill above Remagen had been attacked by American tanks and infantry. Even as they stood there, they could see puffs of smoke and distinctly hear the staccato of rifles and machine guns at the top of the hill near the R.A.D. Camp.

Major Scheller remained calm at this startling development, and simply said: "Let's go and inspect the bridge."

Thirteen
· · · · ·

The Capture of Remagen

LATE IN THE FORENOON of March 7, a gray, drizzly day, a little group of American soldiers on the Birresdorf road near the abandoned R.A.D. camp above Remagen were talking excitedly. The Ludendorff Bridge was over a mile, away, and Karl Timmermann and his men did not dream that it would still be standing when they reached it.

Timmermann and his second platoon leader, Lieutenant Burrows, were peering through field glasses at the distant bridge.

"Jim, look at those damn Krauts going over the bridge," said Timmermann.

"Hey, look at the cows and horses, too," Burrows said. "With all those people trying to cross over, that bridge would make a good target."

Burrows glanced around quickly for his mortar squad. "Amick," he yelled, "you and Mercadante set up and prepare to fire on that bridge." There was a hasty scuffling with the heavy base plates and stovepipe tubes as the men adjusted their mortars. "Tim, I'm not so sure about this," Burrows said to his company commander. "Do you think our mortars will do the trick?"

"It sure tempts me."

"Let's plaster 'em, Lieutenant," one of the mortarmen called out.

"Well, we've got some heavy stuff back of us, and there's no sense in sticking a pin in their tail just to see 'em jump. Let's do it this way: get hold of Colonel Engeman and he can bring up his tanks and call for some artillery."

A runner took off to alert the task force commander about the big bonanza that Timmermann had found.

A few minutes later, Engeman roared up, followed by Major Murray Deevers, the commander of the 27th Armored Infantry Battalion, and Deevers' Operations Officer, Major Don Russell. They watched the procession of German troops, vehicles, and animals far below, making their ant-like way across.

"Let's lower the boom," Engeman decreed. A radio message flew out, and presently somebody shoved a reply into his hand.

"Damn. They won't fire the artillery. Claim there are friendly troops in the vicinity. How can I get it through their thick—Oh, what's the use! Murray, we've got to take that town, and it looks like the doughs ought to go down first and clean it out. I'll

"The Watch on the Rhine" is maintained by an American soldier, T/5 William Goodwin (Mayflower, Ark.) who guards one of the approaches to the Remagen Bridge from atop an armored car. U.S. ARMY SIGNAL CORPS, NATIONAL ARCHIVES

bring up my tanks to cover you. Let me know how you want to plan your attack on the town."

The minutes ticked by. The stream of traffic across the bridge slowed down. There was frustrating delay on top of the hill, as the debate proceeded on how to seize this tiger by the tail without inciting him to bite. Deevers spoke to the commanders of A and C companies, Lieutenants Timmermann and William E. McMaster: "Tim and Mac, you make a reconnaissance down into town and give me a report on how to go in there."

Timmermann and McMaster made their way a little over five hundred yards down the hill along a footpath into Remagen. They met no enemy fire, but they saw a lot of activity near the bridge and on the opposite side of the river. Timmermann paused a moment at the bottom, on the road entering Remagen, and contemplated a battered old sign: "Citizens and Friends: Preserve our parks." It had obviously been intended to restrain the out-of-town tourists from scattering trash. He laughed humorlessly and started climbing back.

On the road to Remagen lived Josef Büntgen and his wife. They were unwilling

Foundation timbers are laid at the site of the Remagen bridgehead, where a Bailey bridge is to be built across the Rhine River, March 17, 1945. U.S. ARMY SIGNAL CORPS, NATIONAL ARCHIVES

eyewitnesses, along with several German soldiers quartered in the home, of the entry of the American troops into Remagen. Herr Büntgen was a very patriotic local official, heading the construction office in the town government. The soldiers and the Büntgen family watched the American troops at the top of the hill pausing to take stock and figure out the next move. They saw Timmermann and McMaster descend the hill to reconnoiter. They saw the terrifying tanks poised for combat. They could see American soldiers start to fix their bayonets at the top of the hill. A German sergeant took a moment to say goodbye to Mrs. Büntgen. He waved his panzerfaust and shouted: "I'm going out and knock off one of those tanks."

She tearfully argued with him: "Do that, and they will level all our houses and destroy the town."

"Lady, there's no better place to stop them than at the Rhine. Heil Hitler!"

(Later, the Büntgens saw the sergeant's body in a ditch, an unnamed and forgotten German hero who had tried to create his own Thermopylae.)

Timmermann and McMaster returned from their reconnaissance, and Timmermann got the nod from Deevers for the all-important task of breaking into Remagen.

Members of the 164th Eng. Bn., 69th Div., U.S. First Army, fill box frames with large stones on a float that will anchor anti-mine nets. The anchors, weighing six tons each, will protect the pontoon bridges over the Rhine above Remagen. March 21, 1945. U.S. ARMY SIGNAL CORPS, NATIONAL ARCHIVES

Lieutenant Jack Liedike's B Company followed, its mission to clear the southeastern part of town while protecting the right flank of the advance. Lieutenant McMaster's C Company was assigned to clear the northwestern part and protect the left flank.

Timmermann held a quick conference with his platoon leaders to issue the attack order, and singled out Lieutenant Burrows to point the assault with his second platoon, It was about one o'clock in the afternoon. He told Burrows to take the main road and work his platoon through the center of Remagen, hugging the buildings because of snipers. Sergeant DeLisio was to fan out along the river road on the left flank, crouching low along the river because the Germans could observe clearly from the east bank. Sergeant Chinchar's platoon was to capture the railroad station and move through town on the right flank of A Company before heading for the bridge.

Once Timmermann's men had started for Remagen, a further series of developments put new life and speed into the attack. Major Ben Cothran, General Hoge's operations officer, had charge of moving the command post for the combat command on the morning of March 7. Because the main effort of the 9th Armored Division was to capture bridges over the Ahr, Hoge had stayed with the south column of his combat command and turned over to Cothran the job of moving his CP from Stadt Mechenheim to Birresdorf, three miles west of Remagen. Cothran, an adventurous officer, had been a newspaper editor in Nashville, and had a nose for news as it devel-

Men and equipment of the 1st U.S. Army cross the Remagen Bridge to consolidate and expand positions on the east bank of the Rhine. March 11, 1945. U.S. ARMY SIGNAL CORPS, NATIONAL ARCHIVES

oped. After seeing the combat command's bag and baggage to Birresdorf, Cothran hopped into his jeep to find out how close to the Rhine Colonel Engeman's task force had come. He got the same tingling sensation in his spine as everyone else when he emerged from the woods and saw the Rhine and the intact bridge below. He looked just long enough to see the German vehicles streaming across and several locomotives on the other side of the river getting up steam.

"Don't you think we ought to bring some artillery down on all that?" asked Colonel Engeman.

"My God, I've got to get the Old Man," yelled Cothran, scarcely aware of the question.

He radioed to General Hoge, who tore across the countryside to the scene, arriving shortly after one o'clock.

Things began to happen fast. The general encouraged his troops to take Remagen. He told everybody in sight to take the town immediately. Speed, speed, and more speed, he urged, was the key to the whole operation. Colonel Engeman, who had been trying to size up the situation and make careful plans, was spurred into action and issued a series of decisive orders to his subordinates. Directly or indirectly, every man on top of the hill felt spurred on by the combat and battalion commanders.

Satisfied that his presence and good leadership had speeded up the operation and saved many precious minutes, General Hoge began to think about the bridge that,

Reconnaissance unit in Remagen passes German sign that reads "Persons who listen to the enemy and rumor-mongers are traitors to the nation and as good as dead." U.S. ARMY SIGNAL CORPS, NATIONAL ARCHIVES

incredibly, still stood before his eyes. "You know," he said in rather subdued tones to Colonel Engeman, "It would be nice to get that bridge too while we're at it."

He quietly studied the procession of troops and vehicles crossing the river, and weighed the risks involved in trying to rush the bridge. An aide tapped his arm.

"Want me to drive back and tell General Leonard?"

Hoge continued to stare through his field glasses, and the aide waited apprehensively.

"We might lose a battalion," replied General Hoge, irrelevantly. The aide shifted his weight to the other foot and tried again: "Do you see anything special?"

"Engeman, Deevers, Russell, get those men moving into town!" General Hoge barked, taking the field glasses from his eyes.

"Already on their way," the three replied, almost in unison.

It was true—Timmermann had already led his men down the hill and into Remagen. Colonel Engeman's leadership had already seen to that.

Burrows' platoon had its biggest scuffle in the main square near the City Hall, where an automatic weapon momentarily slowed down the advance. As Burrows started to maneuver his men to flank the German gun, two of Lieutenant Grimball's tanks rumbled up and fired several 90-millimeter rounds into the square. The machine gun shut up suddenly. Grimball's tanks then intermingled with Burrows' second platoon of infantry and they pushed toward the bridge.

Infantry moves cautiously through the town of Remagen. U.S. ARMY SIGNAL CORPS, NATIONAL ARCHIVES

Timmermann's old platoon, the first, did not have too much trouble. Sergeant Chinchar proved an excellent interpreter of the frenzied remarks of Polish and Russian displaced persons and prisoners who were anxious to reward their liberators by indicating where the German soldiers were hiding.

Across the valley from the German Labor Service camp where the American troops had first appeared, Sergeant Gerhard Rothe and his small group from the German bridge security company saw Chinchar's platoon wind down into town, single file. Realizing that Chinchar's men would cut off and isolate the group atop the hill at the Hotel Waldburg, Rothe and several of his comrades started down the hill in an effort to slip past Chinchar's men. Rothe was running in short bursts across an open field when Chinchar's machine gunners spotted him and fired at him. Rothe did not fire back, because his only concern was to get to the bridge with a whole enough skin to report the situation to Captain Bratge. The machine-gun fire became more intense. He rolled into a ditch beside the main road between Bonn and Koblenz.

"Halt! Stop!!" yelled the men at the machine gun. Rothe did not hear what they were yelling. He thought they were encouraging one another to shoot him down. He waited for one more burst of machine-gun fire to rake the road, then noted a pause which he interpreted as necessary for the machine gunner to change his belt of ammunition. He sprang up quickly and started across the road. The machine gun chattered nervously, and a slug ripped into his leg. "Why doesn't the guy stop?" asked a high voice, drowned out by the boom of another voice, "This'll stop 'im!" followed by a chorus of shots. Rothe was trying to drag his injured leg across the road when another .50 caliber bullet drove into his thigh. By sheer willpower he crawled out of danger. Leaving a long trail of blood he reached the bridge and crossed it on all fours – the last German soldier to cross before the Americans barred the way.

The third platoon, headed by DeLisio, moved out rapidly under the aggressive leadership of the little sergeant.

"C'mon, you guys, just another town," DeLisio cried, waving his arm and giving a hitch to his M-1. His men fixed bayonets as they moved down the hill in single file past the stately St. Apollinaris Church. Bates, Foster, Plude, Kreps, Rusakevich, Pol, Rundbaken, Acosta, White, Kenny – these were some of the men whom DeLisio led down to the river bank. They crept carefully along, squeezing close against the walls of buildings and keeping their submachine guns and M-1's cocked for trouble. From behind lace curtains, the apprehensive citizens watched. Some shivered. Some laughed and said: "Why do the Americans hug the buildings and move so slowly? There are no German soldiers left to fight!" If Company Commander Timmermann had overheard these remarks, he would have complimented his men for conducting themselves like the combat veterans that they were – sticking to the book, taking no chances.

DeLisio came to a road block which the Remagen Volkssturm had set up and then neglected to close. He posted four men at the road block and set up a machine gun 100 yards farther inside the town. It was a perfect trap, in which they caught a number of German soldiers trying to slip through town to get across the Rhine. All were taken prisoner.

Shortly after the road block had been set up, an excited American soldier dashed up to DeLisio and yelled:

"Joe, Sergeant Foster wants you on the double! He's got a German general."

DeLisio ambled down the street behind the messenger, and soon observed a very strange sight. Foster had the muzzle of his M-1 pressed against the stomach of a gaudily attired German, with elaborately braided blouse and trousers and enough "scrambled eggs" for several admirals on his hat.

"Here's yer general, Joe," Foster announced. "Now we'll find out the straight dope about that bridge."

"Lower your gun, Foster. Lemme see him," DeLisio began. He asked the prisoner a couple of questions in halting German, and then turned to the hangers-on from his platoon who had gathered to kibitz.

"General, my ass! You know what this guy is? He's the chief station agent for the railroad! Now scatter out, you guys, and let's check these houses."

The men took off, some sheepish, some laughing, and resumed the job of locating and silencing sniper fire. At several points civilians ran out and stopped American soldiers to point out cellars where German soldiers were hiding. Thoroughly demoralized, the Germans invariably surrendered without a shot; many of them realized the futility of resistance and some had even sent civilians to bring in the American soldiers.

Still, it was not an easy job to clean out the town. Sniper fire rattled from unseen locations, some 20-millimeter German fire was landing in the town, and each quiet street carried the threat of a death trap at every corner.

Shortly after two o'clock, Timmermann's men had cleaned out enough of Remagen to turn their rifle fire directly on the bridge. Before they actually reached the bridge, the men saw a volcano of rocks and dirt erupt into the air – Captain Friesenhahn had exploded the preliminary demolition which gouged a crater thirty feet wide in the approach to the bridge.

Gradually, DeLisio, Burrows and Chinchar worked their platoons up to the bridge approach where they were joined by the tanks which had helped to clear out the town.

"Look at that hole," grumbled Grimball. "It's not enough that they want to blow the bridge, they won't even let us get near it."

Timmermann came up for a brief confab with his platoon leaders.

"Well, what're we goin' to do?" Burrows asked.

Across the river, they could see the German troops making frantic preparations to blow the bridge. Timmermann glanced along the bridge and clearly saw the wires and the telltale charges, ready to go off. Turning to his platoon leaders, he said:

"They'll probably blow it any minute now. Watch this – it ought to be good." He put his field glasses to his eyes and scanned the far bank. "They look like they want to get us out on the bridge before they blow it."

"Screw that noise," DeLisio said simply.

By three o'clock most of the infantrymen of A Company and the supporting tanks had taken up positions near the bridge. Myron ("Pluto") Plude, one of DeLisio's machine gunners, set up his gun and started throwing a few tracers across. The regular *thwump* of the tank cannon echoed against the Erpeler Ley across the river. Looking back at the top of the hill from which he had first seen the bridge, Timmermann could observe more tanks belching smoke as they threw their shells across the Rhine. Everybody was tense waiting for the Germans to deliver the inevitable *coup de grâce* to the shaky bridge.

Alex Drabik, the shy, gangling butcher boy from Holland, Ohio, ambled up to the bridge and made one of his rare utterances to his company commander. "Lieutenant Timmermann, looks like we're gonna get some sleep tonight."

"Yeh, Alex," Timmermann answered. "We'll get some hot meals, too, and shack up here for a couple of days."

The same thought had been in General Hodges' mind when he told General Millikin that after joining up with Patton everybody could take a rest for a while.

Just south of Remagen, at Sinzig on the Ahr River, an incident occurred which had a profound effect on the tankers and infantrymen in Remagen. About the time that Timmermann's men were approaching the bridge in Remagen, a task force under Lieutenant Colonel William R. Prince, making the main effort of the 9th Armored Division, was meeting considerably tougher opposition in its attempt to seize the bridge over the Ahr. Prince's task force succeeded nevertheless in rushing the bridge before the Germans could blow it up. This notable feat was accomplished almost two hours before Timmermann led his men through Remagen to the bridge.

Colonel Prince's task force captured about 400 prisoners among the rabid defenders of Sinzig. His men also rounded up some Volkssturmers and civilians who were making menacing gestures. A couple of the civilians indicated that they had information "of great importance" which they would like to transmit to the American authorities. Lieutenant Fred de Rango, intelligence officer of the 52nd Armored Infantry Battalion, interrogated the civilians. Impressed with the attention paid to them, the civilians tried to enhance their own importance by giving a good story. They could not have made a better choice in their selection of subject matter: they told de Rango that the German command planned to blow up the Remagen Bridge at four o'clock on the dot.

De Rango received this information about half past two, and he naturally considered it to be of the greatest importance. Acting swiftly, he sent a priority radio message to Combat Command B headquarters, alerting them of this new intelligence. The message had an authoritative ring, and the combat command forthwith relayed it to Task Force Engeman. De Rango, feeling there was not a minute to lose and fearing that his radio message might have to pass through too many channels, also dispatched a special messenger to carry the news to Colonel Engeman. Soon the messages started to ricochet around Remagen as everyone hurried to inform everyone else.

The German troops at the bridge later swore their plan to blow the bridge had no set time schedule but hinged on the appearance of American forces. Furthermore, it seems scarcely plausible that civilians in a neighboring town would have detailed information on a secret military plan of this nature. Authentic or not, the news spurred the American commanders and troops to quicker action in order to cross the bridge before it was blown.

It was 3:15 when General Hoge received the message that the bridge was to be blown at 4:00. He immediately stormed down to give the word to Colonel Engeman. The scrappy Minnesotan already had the news, but General Hoge repeated it. "Put some white phosphorus and smoke around the bridge so the Krauts can't see what we're doing, cover your advance with tanks and machine guns, then bring up your engineers and pull out those wires on the bridge because we're going to take that bridge," General Hoge ordered.

General Hoge waited nervously as the minutes ticked by. He directed Majors Deevers and Russell, the commander and operations officer of the 27th Armored Infantry Battalion, to get down to the bridge and order their men across. He turned again to Colonel Engeman: "I want you to get to that bridge as soon as possible."

Engeman answered: "I'm already doing every thing possible to get to the bridge."

General Hoge paused. Without waiting for another word, Engeman started down the road in his jeep to Remagen. On the way he cut open his 508-radio and called Grimball: "Get to that bridge."

Grimball's rich South Carolina accent clearly pierced the static: "Suh, I am *at* the bridge."

Engeman told him to cover the bridge with fire and keep the Germans off it. He then sent a messenger to summon Lieutenant Hugh Mott, a platoon leader in Company B, 9th Armored Engineer Battalion. The pair met, in the rear of one of the big resort hotels about two hundreds yards from the bridge.

These were Engeman's orders: "Mott, General Hoge wants you to get out onto that bridge and see if it's mined or loaded with TNT, and whether it'll hold tanks. I'll give you fire support from my tanks and you'll have infantry scouts out there too." It was a tough assignment.

Lieutenant Mott, a tall, dark and cool-headed twenty-four-year-old from Nashville, swiftly got hold of the two most reliable men in his platoon – Eugene Dorland, a big Kansas stone mason, and John Reynolds, a little North Carolina textile worker. On their way up to the bridge, they saw the crater blown at the bridge approach, and when the smoke had cleared they jumped into the crater for protection. They also saw Majors Deevers and Russell talking with Karl Timmermann, and pointing at the bridge. Mott waved his two men forward with him.

Deevers and Russell had made their way independently to the bridge, and both of them made contact with Timmermann to give the tall Nebraskan the order to take his men across.

"Do you think you can get your company across that bridge?" the battalion commander asked.

"Well, we can try it, sir," Timmermann answered steadily.

"Go ahead," Deevers snapped.

Timmermann took a split-second look at the bridge, the gaping crater at the approach, and the little knots of German soldiers making frantic preparations on the far bank.

"What if the bridge blows up in my face?" Timmermann asked quickly.

Deevers avoided Timmermann's steady gaze. He turned and walked away without a word. Timmermann knew then that this was a suicide mission. But he did not hesitate.

"All right," he barked to his platoon leaders, "we're going across."

Just as Timmermann was giving the order to cross the bridge, General Hoge back at the top of the hill was faced with a soul-searching decision. Hoge was jolted by a message from 9th Armored Division headquarters, ordering him to push south with all possible speed, objective unlimited, to link up with the 4th Armored Division of General Patton's army. The message gave him serious pause as he surveyed the bridge with his field glasses. In the light of this latest message, to concentrate on crossing the bridge instead of moving south would be a deliberate violation of orders from higher headquarters. Success might excuse such a violation; failure might mean a court martial and disgrace. Hoge could see that the Germans were preparing to blow the bridge. Suppose they blew it up while Timmermann's men were on it? Or, even worse, suppose they blew it after sucking across a large number of troops and vehicles?

General Hoge weighed his decision cold-bloodedly. He figured that he would lose no more than a battalion if the Germans blew up the bridge and cut off the first men who crossed. And if that happened there was still a chance that the men would be captured alive. Hoge also figured that he would lose no more than a platoon if the Germans chose to blow the bridge while Timmermann's men were on their way across. He made up his mind to go through with the crossing.

Back in West Point, Karl Timmermann's wife had given birth to a daughter who was now eight days old. General Hoge's command decision could not consider Timmermann's wife and baby girl, nor Drabik's eighty-year-old father in Holland, Ohio, nor Burrows' mother and father in Jersey City. Nor would Hoge, or Deevers, or anyone else in the world try to answer Timmermann's simple question: "What if the bridge blows up in my face?"

Fourteen
. . . .

German Attempts to Demolish the Bridge

AT TWENTY MINUTES BEFORE noon on March 7, a little less than half an hour after he had arrived at Remagen, Major Scheller started walking with Captain Bratge from the traffic control point near the Remagen railroad station a mile through the town to the bridge. On their way down, they had a spirited discussion of where the Remagen troops should be placed. Bratge, fearing that American forces would easily slip across the Rhine in fishing boats, suggested that the bulk of the troops west of the Rhine be withdrawn and used to set up the defense of the bridge on the east bank. Scheller, on the other hand, insisted that the troops stay where they were to prevent American attackers from taking Remagen and the bridge.

"How are you going to get enough men to do that?" Bratge asked.

Scheller answered by stopping a vehicle that contained five infantrymen and a machine gun. He ordered the men to swing around and not to cross the bridge. Turning to Bratge, Scheller started to explain that enough men could be commandeered to defend Remagen by stopping those who were trying to cross the bridge. While he was making his explanation, the vehicle with the five men and machine gun suddenly shot forward and tore down the road, headed for the bridge. It raced over the Rhine before anyone could stop it.

This incident convinced Scheller that the commandeering method was hopeless. He then directed that the small group deployed on the heights above Remagen be withdrawn to the bridge. Captain Bratge tried to telephone this order to the bridge security company. He could hear the phone ringing on the other end, but despite repeated tries nobody answered. The bridge security company had already been attacked and routed.

At ten minutes to one, Major Scheller ordered that the combat commander's C.P. be moved from the west side of the river into the railroad tunnel. Captain Bratge supervised the move, taking particular care that all his secret papers were carried along. Then both Scheller and Bratge went back to see how Captain Friesenhahn was progressing with the preparations to demolish the bridge.

At this moment the three officers were looking at their problem from three different points of view. Friesenhahn, as the officer responsible for blowing up the bridge, was concentrating on demolition and could think of little else. Although both Scheller and Bratge were concerned about the demolition, they wanted to make sure that the timing was correctly related to other tactical developments. Captain Bratge, who had been at Remagen for many months, was primarily concerned with the situation at Remagen and the proper way to fight a delaying action before blowing the bridge. Major Scheller, having recently come from LXVII Corps headquarters, was concerned about the broader fate of the retreating German army in the Ahr valley. Many of the troops had been trapped already by the rampaging American advance; others had crossed the Rhine on other bridges and ferries, or had swum across. But there were still several thousand Germans who wanted to cross at Remagen.

As Scheller and Bratge neared the bridge, an artillery captain approached to say that an artillery battalion was on its way to the bridge. He pleaded that the bridge not be blown until the battalion arrived and passed over to the east side of the Rhine. Major Scheller, aware that artillery at this stage was not easy to spare, decided to hold up the demolition. Captain Bratge, still concerned about the disappearance of his thirty-six men from the bridge security company, worried lest the already audible fire from American tanks and infantry meant that these forces would rush to the bridge unopposed and unannounced. Therefore, he asked Captain Friesenhahn to make two rifle squads available for commitment as infantry along the access roads to the bridge.

"If you take two squads of my engineers now, I can't guarantee that the demolition of the bridge will be carried out," Friesenhahn replied firmly. Bratge withdrew the request, and later said that Friesenhahn was thoroughly right in balking at it.

Shortly after Major Scheller arrived at the bridge, Captain Friesenhahn saw him talking rapidly with the artillery captain who wanted to ensure safe passage for his guns over the bridge. Friesenhahn then asked Scheller to authorize him to arm the demolition charges and make final preparations for blowing up the bridge.

"Now, don't get so excited," replied Scheller, "we're not going to blow up the bridge just yet."

"I'm not excited," insisted Friesenhahn, raising his voice, "but you know our secret orders say that no Rhine bridge shall fall into the hands of the enemy. I think it's time you give me the order to go ahead."

"The situation doesn't require it just yet," said Scheller with great calmness and deliberation. Then he went to join Bratge in the tunnel on the east bank.

At the Remagen end of the bridge, Captain Friesenhahn, two noncommissioned officers, and two volunteers waited near the time fuse that was connected to the preliminary demolition charge. The explosion of this charge was designed to rip a hole big enough in the bridge approach to prevent the passage of any vehicle onto the bridge.

Tank and infantry fire was already hitting the bridge shortly after two o'clock as Friesenhahn and his quartet of engineers watched for some kind of signal to set off the preliminary demolition. He had placed two men armed with panzerfausts to delay any surprise tank attack while he set off the preliminary charge. Suddenly Friesenhahn heard a police whistle blow, and the sound of racing motors. He caught a glimpse of American helmets several hundred yards away from the bridge, and saw American infantrymen in the Becher Furniture Works.

"Fire the charge!" he shouted.

One of the noncommissioned officers pulled the cord and the men took cover, counting off the eternity of six seconds needed for the time fuse to take effect. A cloud of dust and smoke shot up. Friesenhahn looked briefly to make sure the preliminary demolition was successful. He was elated with the results. The charge had blown a thirty-foot crater across the bridge approach, and he knew that no tank or any other type of vehicle could negotiate that ditch.

With a wave of his arm, Friesenhahn started back across the bridge, for the tunnel. One of his noncommissioned officers overtook him and streaked back to the tunnel. He looked around but saw no sign of the other three. The fifty-year-old captain started to puff as he ran across the bridge. A tank shell landed on the bridge, and its concussion knocked him down. He tried to get up, noticing vaguely that his clothing was badly ripped and he was bleeding. Gradually, the boom and rattle of the firing seemed to fade away and he lost consciousness.

For nearly fifteen minutes, Friesenhahn lay there oblivious to the shells and bullets that flew over him. Finally, he began to stir. Dazed and shaken, he picked himself up and began stumbling and staggering on toward the tunnel. Small-arms fire rattled around him as he made his way across the bridge. He had no idea how long he had been unconscious, but he was satisfied that he had done an effective job in blowing the big anti-tank crater in the approach to the structure. Now all that was left was to set off the main demolition that would crumple the bridge into the river.

It was about ten minutes to three when Friesenhahn reached the Erpel tunnel. His mind was clear when he came up to Captain Bratge and started conferring with him about blowing the bridge. A short while later, Sergeant Rothe crawled into the tunnel, bleeding profusely from three wounds in his legs and upper thighs. Rothe reported that American armor had broken through his company's positions, and that nothing was left between the Americans and the bridge. Captain Friesenhahn shouted, amid the shots and shells that were already crashing around the Erpeler Ley, that American tanks and infantry were already at the bridge approach and were getting ready to cross.

About this time, the white phosphorus shells from the American tanks across the river started to take effect. A heavy smoke screen was forming on the Erpel side of the bridge. Men rubbed their smarting eyes and screamed as the phosphorus burned. Bratge, assuming that the Russian workers were sabotaging smoke pots which had been kept ready to screen the bridge in case of an American air attack, strode out to take the culprits to task. He discovered that the smoke was coming not only from American phosphorus shells but also from German smoke pots that had been shattered by high explosive shells. Taking a quick look across the river, Bratge saw a row of American tanks lined up, firing relentlessly at the east bank of the river.

Shells began bursting all around the German positions. The screams, the noise, and the confusion heightened; Friesenhahn yelled at Bratge to return to the tunnel.

"Get me the order from Major Scheller to blow the bridge," cried Friesenhahn. The little engineer captain added that unless he received the order forthwith he would assume no responsibility for failure to blow the bridge.

Bratge rushed up to Major Scheller and blurted out: "Major, unless you issue the order to demolish the bridge, I shall have the bridge demolished myself!" Bratge took pains to see that his executive officer, Lieutenant Siegel, overheard the request. He was afraid that the major might still want to wait for the lost German artillery battalion to appear. But Scheller could see the American tanks lined up across the river, and he knew that the splattering of shots around the tunnel could only mean that American infantry was close at hand. Quickly and firmly he told Bratge: "Go ahead and have the bridge demolished!"

In spite of the tense atmosphere and the urgency of the moment, both Bratge and Friesenhahn felt that, the command situation being as confused as it was, it was important to clarify responsibility for the destruction of the bridge. So Bratge carefully directed Lieutenant Siegel to write down the exact time and wording of the demolition order. It therefore became a matter of record that the demolition order was given by Major Scheller at twenty minutes past three. Bratge then rushed back toward the tunnel. As soon as he came within shouting distance of Friesenhahn, he cupped his hands and gave the order: "Blow the bridge!"

Now it was Friesenhahn's turn to become slightly bureaucratic. Knowing that Hitler had ordered all bridge demolitions to be approved beforehand by higher headquarters or in writing, Friesenhahn said to Bratge: "I must have that order in writing." Even to a correct old veteran like Friesenhahn, the words just about stuck in his mouth. They sounded to Friesenhahn just as absurd as they were; so he didn't wait for a reply from Bratge but immediately turned around and prepared to set off the main charges to blow the bridge.

By this time, the tunnel was crowded with terrified mothers and wailing children, Volkssturmers who did not choose to fight, German soldiers who thought the tunnel a good place either to set up a defense strongpoint or to surrender, refugees, foreign workers, a few prisoners, and even some animals. It was a motley and uncontrollable group that Friesenhahn addressed with these words:

"Attention, everybody! Everybody take cover. The bridge is being blown up. Everybody lie down. Open your mouths to protect your eardrums. We are now going to blow the bridge."

There was a mad scuffle as everybody complied with the order. Most people clasped their hands over their eyes and gulped the dank air of the tunnel while they waited for the demolition.

Friesenhahn had mixed feelings when he ran up to turn the key that was to destroy the bridge. He knew that the circuit had just been tested, and he had been told a few minutes before that the circuit test was positive. He did not worry about the possibility that an American shell would break the circuit, because the wiring was enclosed in a thick pipe on the bridge. But he was concerned lest the rumbling vibrations from American tank fire upset some sensitive feature of the firing mechanism. Nevertheless, he was pleased that he would have ample time to set off the charge before American infantry ventured onto the bridge.

Taking his place just inside the tunnel, Friesenhahn gave the key a turn. The mechanism operated like a watchspring. When the key was wound tight, it was supposed to set off the demolition. He wound it once – nothing happened. Frantically, he wound it again – still with no success. The huddled soldiers and civilians waited endless minutes in the tunnel, still gasping, prone on the ground.

Friesenhahn now realized that the circuit was broken, and he would have to use alternative measures. First, he called on an emergency repair team to crawl out onto the bridge and fix the break in the circuit. This was a specially trained unit consisting of crack electricians who could spot where the trouble was and repair it quickly. As the group went to the entrance of the tunnel, several shells fell near by and small-arms fire came in more insistently. Desperation spread over the faces of the men, and Friesenhahn realized that it would be impossible for them to perform their mission in the short time remaining. Sterner and quicker measures were necessary. Friesenhahn called together all his noncommissioned officers at the tunnel entrance and asked for volunteers to go out and light the primer cord by hand. The primer cord had been attached to an emergency demolition charge, ready for just such a crisis. But there was a morale crisis among the noncommissioned officers. None stepped forward to volunteer for the job. To Friesenhahn, this was one of the biggest disappointments of his life. After what seemed like an eternity, Sergeant Faust finally said to Friesenhahn that he would do the job.

Faust made his way out of the tunnel and onto the bridge with great difficulty, for by now a large American force was lined up on the west bank, firing at everything that moved. The German railway engineers had placed the primer cord and the emergency demolition charge between 80 and 90 yards from the tunnel, at a point where they calculated the smallest amount of explosive would cause the maximum amount of damage. Friesenhahn was reasonably confident that if only Faust could light the primer cord the bridge would fall into the river. Then his confidence wavered as he suddenly recalled that the emergency demolition charge, which was originally supposed to contain 600 kilograms of Army explosive, actually contained only 300 kilograms of "Donerit," the less powerful industrial explosive, which had been delivered several hours before. He wondered whether it would be strong enough to wreck the bridge. As he watched Faust crawling out onto the bomb-battered structure, his confidence returned and he began to feel certain that even a small amount of explosive would be enough to deliver the fatal blow.

Too impatient to stay in the tunnel, Friesenhahn ran out and onto the bridge to get a closer look at what Faust was doing. Machine-gun fire forced him to drop into a shell crater for protection before he had gone very far. When he looked up he saw

Faust returning, and his first disheartening thought was that Faust had failed. But Friesenhahn had miscalculated the time needed for the primer cord to burn. Faust had done his job well. There was a sudden roar as timbers shot into the air, and the bridge seemed to rise from its foundations. All the Germans on the east side of the Rhine breathed a tremendous sigh of relief.

But they reacted too soon. A moment later, their relief turned to horror as they watched the bridge slowly settle back on its foundations.

It was still standing!

Fifteen

· · · · · ·

The Crossing of the Bridge

ON THE SURFACE, Karl Timmermann tried to treat his mission as if it were a big lark. This was part of his art of leadership. While giving orders to his three platoon leaders, he casually passed out some candy he had "liberated" in Remagen. "Here, try one of these Kraut rock candies, and don't break your teeth," he said with a flip to Forrest Miner, an assistant squad leader at the edge of the group.

"Now we're going to cross this bridge before –"

A deafening rumble and roar swallowed up the rest of Timmermann's sentence. The German Sergeant Faust had set off the emergency demolition two-thirds of the way across the bridge. Able Company watched in awe as the huge structure lifted up, and steel, timbers, dust and thick black smoke mixed in the air. Many of the G.I.'s threw themselves to the ground or buried their faces in their hands.

Everybody waited for Timmermann's reaction.

"Thank God, now we won't have to cross that damned thing," Mike Chinchar said fervently, trying to reassure himself.

Johnny Ayres fingered the two grenades hooked onto the rings of his pack suspenders, and nodded his head: "We wouldn't have had a chance."

But Timmermann, who had been trying to make out what was left of the bridge through the thick haze, yelled:

"Look – she's still standing!"

Most of the smoke and dust had cleared away, and the men followed their commander's gaze. The sight of the bridge still spanning the Rhine brought no cheers from the men. It was like an unwelcome specter. The suicide mission was on again.

A thousand feet away, the German soldiers were working frantically around the far end of the bridge. They looked as if they were going to make another attempt to blow the bridge.

"Maybe they're just teasing us to get us out there and then blow us all to kingdom come," Sabia said. "I tell ya it's a trap."

Timmermann's casual air had disappeared. He had thrown away his candy and the grin was gone from his face as he strode up to the bridge. He saw at one glance that although some big holes had been blown in the flooring of the bridge, the catwalks were clear for infantrymen. The Germans were still in a frenzy of activity on the other side and on the bridge itself.

Remagen Bridge showing damage from the German demolition attempts, taken from the east side of the Rhine. U.S. ARMY SIGNAL CORPS, NATIONAL ARCHIVES

He quickly circled his arm in the air to call his platoon leaders together. Other men clustered around, eager and apprehensive. "O.K., Jim, Mike and Joe, we'll cross the bridge – order of march, first platoon, third platoon and then second platoon."

There was a moment of silence.

Timmermann turned to Burrows, cupped his hand, and said in a low tone: "Jim, I want your platoon to bring up the rear so we have an officer in charge of the last platoon across." Then, in a louder tone which everybody could hear: "And when you get over, Jim, take your platoon up that high hill on the other side. You know, the old Fort Benning stuff: take the high ground and hold it?"

There was no sudden rush to cross the bridge. To the tired, dirty, unshaven men it looked like sudden death. Stomachs were queasy, not only from some wine discovered in Remagen, but from fear.

Timmermann moved tentatively up to the bridge, and started to wave his arm overhead in the traditional "Follow me" gesture. A chattering of machine guns from the towers made him duck. Jack Berry ran up to one of the General Pershing tanks, located Lieutenant Jack Grimball, and pointed at the towers.

Grimball did not hesitate. His Pershing let loose a blast.

Mike Chinchar, leader of the platoon ordered to spearhead the crossing, was knocked off his feet by the concussion. So was Dean Craig. Chinchar and Craig had their faces buried in the mud by the blast. Sabia was lifted off his feet, and shook his

Another view of the damaged Ludendorff Bridge, taken from the east side of the river. U.S. ARMY SIGNAL CORPS, NATIONAL ARCHIVES

head dazedly. Berry laughed uncontrollably as the trio staggered around, spitting out mud and trying to regain their equilibrium.

The tank shell opened a big crack in the tower, and the German machine-gun fire let up.

"Dammit, what's holdin' up the show? Now git goin'!" Timmermann yelled.

Big Tony Samele, who had been in the lead while the first platoon was cleaning out Remagen, turned to his platoon leader, Mike Chinchar: "C'mon, Mike, we'll just walk it across." At this point, the battalion commander, Major Murray Deevers, called out: "I'll see you on the other side and we'll all have a chicken dinner."

"Chicken dinner, my foot. I'm all chicken right now," one of the men in the first platoon shot back.

Major Deevers flushed. "Move on across," he yelled, sharply.

"I tell ya, I'm not goin' out there and get blown up," the G.I. answered. "No sir, major, you can court-martial and shoot me, but I ain't going out there on that bridge."

While Deevers was arguing, Lieutenant Timmermann was using more direct methods: "Get goin', you guys, git goin.'" He moved onto the bridge himself.

Chinchar shouted at Art Massie: "You leapfrog me up as far as that hole that's blown out." Massie had a quick and natural reaction: "I don't wanna but I will."

As they started out onto the bridge, suddenly the man who had been arguing with Major Deevers turned away from Deevers and joined the group from the first platoon which was moving across.

Timmermann's men had just started out onto the bridge when Lieutenant Mott and Sergeants Dorland and Reynolds of the engineers ran out to join them and started cutting wires connected to the demolition charges. The engineers were a doubly welcome sight, because the infantrymen had not expected them. When the big German emergency charge had gone off on the bridge Mott had decided that the main job of his engineers would be to locate and cut the wires to the other demolition charges. The three men joined Timmermann and his lead scouts just as they were starting across the bridge, and there was no time to coordinate any plans as the whole group surged forward.

The right side of the bridge was torn up by the German blasts, and so Chinchar's platoon started down the left catwalk. Here the men had some protection because most of the German rifle and machine-gun fire was coming from the stone tower on the far right end of the bridge. The fire had quieted down after Grimball's tank blast, but it started up again as the first infantrymen picked their way across.

When Chinchar's men were about a third of the way over, they came to a halt as the machine-gun fire intensified. The American tanks were still firing, but the German return fire from both the towers and the tunnel was growing stronger. Nobody dared move ahead.

From a half-submerged barge about two hundred yards upstream, the lead troops were getting more fire. It was not heavy and constant, but two snipers on the barge were beginning to zero in. There were no American tanks on the bridge, and so Timmermann ran back to yell to one of the General Sherman tanks at the bridge approach:

"How about putting something on that barge?"

The tank found the range and blasted the barge with its 75-millimeter gun until a white flag began to flutter.

"That's one thing they never taught us at Fort Knox," said a member of the tank crew later in reviewing his naval exploit.

Even with the barge menace removed, Timmermann faced a crisis. He ran forward to find that his old first platoon was frozen. The tank support was not silencing the opposition. The Germans were still running around on the far side of the river as though they were going to blow the bridge with the American troops on it. Timmermann waved for Sergeant DeLisio, leader of the third platoon.

"Joe, get your platoon up there and get these men off their tail," he yelled above the clatter of tank and machine-gun fire.

The little Bronx sergeant with the twitching mustache started weaving and bobbing across the bridge. One of the motionless figures hugging the flooring of the bridge grumbled as he passed:

"There goes a guy with more guts than sense."

If DeLisio heard him he gave no sign. Soon the rest of his platoon was starting over, and in a minute a few men from Burrows' second platoon had started also.

The reinforcements fired at the tunnel and the towers, and soon the enemy fire began to lessen.

U.S. Army War Office poster titled "Remagen Bridgehead: The U.S. Army in Action." U.S. ARMY SIGNAL
CORPS, NATIONAL ARCHIVES

Forrest Miner came up behind one of the men on the bridge and yelled:
"What's holding you guys up?"

"Don't you hear that machine-gun fire?"

"Fer cryin' out loud," Miner lied, "that's our own machine-gun fire coming from
behind us."

The man looked incredulous and then hobbled to his feet with a blank and resigned expression on his face. Above all the noise came Timmermann's constant:
"Git goin', git goin'." The company commander was everywhere, spurring, encouraging, and leading his men.

DeLisio worked his way up to the first man on the bridge, a third of the way across,
and shouted: "What's the trouble?"

"Trouble? Chrissakes can't you see all that sniper fire?"

"Why worry about a coupla snipers?" DeLisio laughed. "If this bridge blows up
we've got a whole battalion on it. Let's get off. C'mon, guys."

DeLisio, of course, was exaggerating—there wasn't a whole battalion on the bridge,
only part of A Company; but the psychology worked.

He helped uncork the attack. Other men with "more guts than sense" started to
get up and weave and bob behind him.

Sabia started to run, but the bridge turned into an endless treadmill. His leaden feet got heavier and heavier, and he felt as if he had been running for hours and getting nowhere.

Ayres, his grenades and canteen bobbing up and down, suddenly wished he had not consumed so much wine in Remagen, and he vomited on the bridge. Through a blown-out hole in the bridge flooring he saw the swift current below.

"If I fall," he asked himself, "will this pack drag me under?"

Across the river, a German train steamed into view, chugging south.

Colonel Engeman, back in Remagen with his tanks, spotted the train and joyfully exclaimed: "Hallelujah! I've always wanted to fire a tank at a locomotive." Four or five tanks opened up. The firebox of the engine exploded. German troops started pouring out of the train, and set up positions to fire at their tormenters on the bridge and in Remagen.

DeLisio waved back for his support squad, led by Joe Petrencsik and Alex Drabik. Then he edged forward. Heavy fire started to come down on the bridge – 20-millimeter shells from German anti-aircraft guns. Petrencsik with a sudden hunch yelled: "Duck!" DeLisio crouched, and something swooshed over his head and took a piece out of one of the stone towers.

In the middle of the bridge, Mott, Dorland and Reynolds found four packages of TNT, weighing 20 to 30 pounds each, tied to I-beams underneath the decking of the bridge. They climbed down and worked their wirecutters hot until the charges splashed into the Rhine. Above them they heard the heavy tramp of the infantrymen and the hoarse cry of Timmermann which everybody had now taken up: "Git goin'."

Back on the bridge, Dorland started to hack away at a heavy cable.

"Why don't you shoot it in two with your carbine?" Jack Berry asked.

Dorland put the muzzle up against the cable, and blasted it apart.

By this time DeLisio had traveled two-thirds of the way across the bridge. The little sergeant had a theory that if you advanced fast enough you wouldn't get hit, so instead of hugging the bridge when the Germans fired on him from the towers, he simply ran on until he got behind the towers on the German side of the bridge. DeLisio chortled to himself at his good luck, until he looked back and saw that the German fire from the towers was still pinning down the men who were supposed to be following him.

Somebody yelled:

"Who's gonna clean out that tower?"

DeLisio took the question as a challenge, and ran back to the tower where most of the fire was coming from.

He pushed aside a few bales of hay blocking the door to the tower. Just as he started into the door, a stray bullet went into the stone wall and ricocheted off. Sabia came up and yelled: "You're hit, Joe."

"You're crazy, Sabia. I don't feel nothin' at all."

Sabia insisted: "I saw that bullet, I tell ya I seen it go right through ya."

DeLisio ran his hands quickly around his field jacket, and finding no blood he brushed Sabia away and went on up into the tower.

Chinchar, Samele, and Massie then went up into the left tower. Everybody else moved forward. Many of them recalled what Nelson Wegener, DeLisio's old platoon sergeant, used to say after nearly every battle: "Guinea, you're one of the luckiest men alive. I dunno how you do it, but you always seem to get out of the toughest scrapes."

DeLisio started running up the circular staircase. There were three floors in the tower, and he couldn't take anything for granted. He heard machine-gun fire above him, and then it suddenly stopped. Had the Germans heard him coming, and was he heading into a trap?

He slapped open a steel door with the heel of his hand and burst in on three German soldiers. They were bending over a machine gun, as though it were jammed. There was an agonizing second as the three men jerked their heads around. DeLisio pumped out a couple of shots with his carbine, firing from the hip.

"Hände hoch!" he yelled.

The three Germans wheeled around with their hands in the air. DeLisio motioned them to one side with his carbine, and seizing the gun they had been using he hurled it out of the window. Men starting across the bridge saw the gun plummet from the tower and began to move with more confidence.

In his pidgin German and his sign language, DeLisio tried to find out if there were any more soldiers left in the tower. His captives assured him that there weren't. But DeLisio was skeptical and he motioned for them to precede him up the stairs.

On the top floor of the tower, DeLisio pushed the three Germans into a room, where he found a German lieutenant and his orderly. The lieutenant dived for the corner of the room, but DeLisio stopped him with a couple of shots. He took away the lieutenant's Walther pistol. Then he marched all five prisoners down the stairs and told them to proceed unescorted over the bridge to Remagen. They were the first in a long parade of German prisoners taken near the bridge.

Over in the left tower, Chinchar, Samele and Massie also tossed a German machine gun out the window and captured one cowering soldier. The flushing of the towers cost all of those involved the honor of being the first across the Rhine.

Alex Drabik, one of DeLisio's assistant squad leaders, had not seen him go into the tower and started looking for his platoon leader. He asked several people on the bridge, but nobody seemed to know. He made up his mind that there was only one thing to do.

"Let's go!" he shouted. "DeLisio must be over there on the other side all alone."

Drabik took off for the east bank, weaving and wobbling. Just before he got across the bridge he jounced so much that he lost his helmet. He did not stop to pick it up but kept running at top speed until he became the first soldier to cross the Rhine.

At Drabik's heels came the Minnesota plasterer named Marvin Jensen, repeating: "Holy crap, do you think we'll make it, do you think we'll make it?"

Pvt. Alex Drabik of Toledo, Ohio. Drabik was the first soldier to cross the Remagen Bridge. U.S. ARMY
SIGNAL CORPS, NATIONAL ARCHIVES

Drabik was the first man over, followed closely by Jensen, Samele, DeLisio, Chinchar, Massie, Sabia, a Missourian named Martin Reed and a North Carolinian named
Joseph Peoples. A few seconds later Karl Timmermann, the first officer over, set
foot on the German side of the Rhine.

Sixteen
· · · · · ·

From Toehold to Foothold

ONCE OVER THE BRIDGE Drabik wheeled to the left, still looking for DeLisio, and raced about two hundred yards up the river road. The rest of his squad followed close behind, and he hastily set up a skirmish line in a series of bomb craters to ward off a possible German counterthrust.

The bridge itself was still a big question mark for the Americans. Every man that crossed it wondered if the Germans had yet played their final card. Were they saving up a more devastating stroke that would at any moment topple the entire structure into the Rhine? The three engineers, Mott, Dorland and Reynolds, methodically searched for the master switch that controlled the German demolitions. Near the eastern end of the bridge, Dorland finally located the box that housed the switch, went to work on the heavy wires leading from it, and blasted them apart with a few rounds from his carbine. A few minutes later, the three engineers came upon a large unexploded 500 to 600 pound charge with its fuse cap blown. Mott and his men examined it closely and found it correctly wired and prepared for detonation. Cutting all attached wires, they made it harmless.

At the Remagen end of the bridge, Colonel Engeman, Captain Soumas, and Lieutenant Miller drove their men hard to clear the way for tanks and vehicles. While Mott and his two sergeants were ripping out demolition wires and determining whether the bridge could hold traffic, other engineers checked the approaches for mines and pondered the problem of filling up the tremendous crater at the bridge approach. Miller finally called up Sergeant Swayne, whose tank was equipped with a blade to operate like a bulldozer, and Swayne began pushing dirt and debris into the big hole.

On the east bank DeLisio, who had stepped off the bridge shortly after Drabik, had already been sent by Timmermann on another trouble-shooting assignment. With four of his best men, the little sergeant crept forward to investigate the menacing railroad tunnel at the end of the bridge. None of the Americans knew how strong a force the Germans had hidden in the blackness of the tunnel. All they knew was that it gave the enemy excellent cover and concealment and that from it the occupants had ideal observation over the entire length of the bridge.

The five men moved forward cautiously, hugging the ground as shots rang out of the dark. When they reached the entrance, DeLisio fired two shots into the tunnel,

The railroad tunnel on east end of bridge was a strong German defensive point. U.S. ARMY SIGNAL CORPS,
NATIONAL ARCHIVES

and several German engineers quickly ran out, hands high above their heads, as if they had been eagerly awaiting this chance to give themselves up. Misled by the easy capture of this handful of the enemy, DeLisio failed to realize that there was a much stronger force deep in the tunnel. Moving his prisoners back, he reported to Timmermann that the tunnel looked clear and then joined Drabik along the river road.

Inside the tunnel, Major Scheller and Captain Bratge had received word shortly before four o'clock that the Americans had crossed the bridge. The news spread immediately through the milling throng of soldiers and civilians, and it became almost impossible to maintain even a semblance of order. Tank shells were bursting inside the tunnel, rifle fire was ricocheting off the walls, and three railroad tank cars were dripping gasoline that formed pools of potential destruction at the feet of the miserable tunnel occupants. Panic-stricken civilians were clawing at the soldiers to stop resistance. Except for the few prudent engineers near the entrance who had made the most of their opportunity to surrender to DeLisio's patrol, few of the terrified Germans were aware even that five Americans had come and gone.

By a little after four o'clock Timmermann had only about 120 men on the east bank. As an experienced infantryman he had recognized immediately from the other side of the river that the Erpeler Ley, the highest point in the immediate area, had to be taken fast. Summoning Lieutenant Burrows, he ordered him to take the second platoon up the precipitous slope. The heights of the Erpeler Ley, as well as the tunneled depths, had become crucial.

Burrows later said: "Taking Remagen and crossing the bridge were a breeze compared with climbing that hill." The lower slope was very steep, and the face of the cliff was covered with loose rock. Footing was slippery, and several men were severely injured when they fell. About halfway to the summit the Americans began receiving 20-millimeter fire. The trees were leafless, and there was little underbrush in which to hide. Silhouetted against the face of the black cliff, the climbing men were easy targets for the German anti-aircraft gunners. The Erpeler Ley quickly became known as Flak Hill.

At first the fire seemed to come from the west bank, from the heights near the Waldburg Hotel where Sergeant Rothe's men from the bridge security company had been cut off by the rapid American advance. Colonel Engeman sent one of his light tank platoons, under Lieutenant Demetri Paris, to clean out the pocket on the Waldburg Hill. But the anti-aircraft fire continued with such intensity that Burrows' men soon became convinced that it was coming from the northern part of the bridgehead. Some of them crawled around the nose of the bluff to the right to get out of the line of fire. Others slid or rolled to the base of the cliff.

Burrows' casualties mounted. His platoon sergeant, Bill Shultz, was severely wounded in the leg by a 20-millimeter shellburst. Ralph Munch and Frankie Marek took refuge in a small craterlike depression, and Munch had just moved to another spot when a mortar shell burst close to Marek and sent a piece of shrapnel through him below his lungs. Those men who finally managed to reach the top saw only a few small sheds across a field about a hundred yards away and a handful of German soldiers wandering around unconcernedly. Jim Cardinale, one of the American machine gunners, called excitedly, "Come on, lemme paste those guys but good."

"Shut up or we'll shoot you by God," one of the other men threatened in low but urgent tones. "We'll shoot you and push you off the cliff—you want to give our position away?"

Cardinale calmed down, and the Americans atop the cliff began a period of cautious and worried waiting. They could see numerous German infantrymen and vehicles in neighboring towns. At the base of the hill and along the side the firing got heavier. The enemy seemed to be moving in for a counterattack.

The advance guard of the Remagen crossing was in a precarious position. With no weapons more powerful than light machine guns, Timmermann called for his anti-tank platoon under Lieutenant Dave Gardner to come to the east bank, instructing them to bring as many of their .50-caliber machine guns as they could and employ them on ground mounts covering the roads into the bridgehead. Gardner's men also brought over four rocket launchers and set them up in pairs with the machine guns.

Timmermann then appealed for more men, more weapons and more support. The battalion commander, Major Deevers, sent over Lieutenant Bill McMaster's C Company, followed by Lieutenant Jack Liedike's B Company about half-past four. Their arrival eased the situation, but the battalion was still woefully weak and too strung out to present a very firm defense against a counterattack. Had German tanks struck at the flimsy American force between four and five o'clock, the Remagen bridgehead would certainly have been wiped out.

This possibility troubled Timmermann a great deal as he took stock of his thin line of men. It also troubled the men, and weighed heavily on the minds of the B and C Company reinforcements that came across the bridge. Everybody was either asking about the arrival of American tanks or fearing the arrival of German tanks. The sound of German vehicles came from neighboring villages. Patrols on the edge of the bridgehead confirmed the suspicion that German forces were moving up for a counterattack.

On the Remagen bank Lieutenant Mott and armored engineers were doing everything possible to make the bridge serviceable for tank traffic. Makeshift repairs were made in the shattered planking, but it soon became clear that the bridge would not hold tanks before dark.

The officers and men on the east bank chafed at the delay. They knew that infantry alone would never be able to hang on to their slim toehold. Runners started back across the bridge with urgent requests for help. Not long before dusk, the sight of these runners caused a flurry of uneasy excitement. The backfire of German vehicles in the distance started more rumors that Tiger tanks were moving toward the bridge. Along thousands of yards of thinly held front the troops were so widely scattered that many of them lost contact. Small groups drifted back across the bridge. In the space of an hour parts of the three companies on the east bank slipped back to Remagen in the confusion and disorganization.

But the majority of the 27th Armored Infantry Battalion held on. Among those who remained were many who looked about for fellow Americans without seeing any; and the story later spread that only a few men had held the east bank of the Rhine on the night of March 7. Actually, the reinforcement of the bridgehead was resumed at dusk, and from then on throughout the night an almost steady stream of men crossed the bridge to bolster the defenses on the east bank.

Between four and five o'clock in the afternoon of March 7, just when Timmermann and his men were most vulnerable to counterattack, the Germans inside the tunnel had virtually got out of hand. Major Scheller, as the senior officer, instructed Captain Bratge to form assault detachments for the purpose of launching a counterattack; but discipline had vanished, and Bratge's efforts to bring order out of chaos were fruitless. Major Scheller repeatedly tried to establish contact with higher headquarters and report the failure to blow the bridge and the possible entrapment and elimination of the German forces in the bridgehead. Desperate at his failure in this, Scheller finally seized a bicycle and, without notifying Bratge, pedaled off to report in person.

Shortly after, Bratge ordered his adjutant, Lieutenant Siegel, to burn all classified documents. Despite the loud protests of the civilians, who feared the consequences of a fire in the gasoline-soaked enclosure, the order was carried out. Still unaware that Scheller had left the tunnel, Bratge then gave the following instructions to one of his noncommissioned officers: "You know the situation here. Try to get away from here and make every attempt to get in touch with higher headquarters. Inform them that the demolition of the bridge was unsuccessful and that the Americans have crossed the bridge."

The messenger found a motorcycle and wheeled it out of the tunnel. He mounted it and started down the road, traveling south. At least fifty American soldiers must have spotted him at the same instant. His camouflaged uniform blended with the landscape, but there was no hiding the staccato blasts from his exhaust. Johnny Ayres, a rifleman in Company A, took aim and pumped out three shots, but the cyclist with his head down kept on going. All along the hillside the American troops started winging shots in his direction. They seemed to sense that his mission was of special importance. A machine gun finally cut him down. The cycle turned over onto its saddle, the wheels churning the air and the backfiring motor making it jump around. The rider lay dead at the side of the road.

Inside the tunnel, Bratge had been looking in vain for Scheller. At twenty minutes before five he assumed command of the troops. After several more futile attempts to organize assault detachments, he ordered all military personnel to withdraw from the rear exit. To make sure that nobody stayed in the tunnel, Bratge and Friesenhahn started walking from the entrance and swept everyone toward the exit.

When the first German soldiers came out into daylight, hand grenades and machine-gun fire drove them back. Timmermann had detailed a squad to cover the tunnel exit. At five o'clock in the afternoon Bratge and Friesenhahn rallied their forces for one last attempt to break out of the tunnel. One man and a child were wounded trying to escape and panic again broke out among the civilians. Timmermann's men held their ground. They did not know how many German soldiers were left in the tunnel, and they had no intention of letting them come out to see how few Americans were blocking the exit.

At twelve minutes past five, Captain Bratge called together all the remaining officers – including Captain Friesenhahn and three lieutenants. He straightened up and addressed them crisply and formally:

"Gentlemen, Major Scheller and two other officers have absented themselves from the bridgehead for reasons unknown to me. I have again assumed the position of combat commander. In view of the situation which confronts me, I consider myself unable to bear further responsibility for the continuation of the fighting as combat commander. In accordance with the applicable Hitler order, I therefore ask: Who among you is prepared to take over as combat commander? All military personnel will be subordinated to the one who volunteers for the job."

Captain Bratge paused, and glanced around for a sign of response. Not a person moved. There was a stony silence.

Bratge, like a geometry teacher moving on to the next phase of the problem, intoned:

"Therefore, gentlemen, it becomes my duty to call for a volunteer for the job among the enlisted –"

He got no further. In the middle of the sentence, he glanced out of the tunnel exit and saw a white flag flapping in the breeze. Some German soldiers and civilians were already starting to leave. Helmets of the American soldiers seemed to be everywhere. With cocked guns, they were shouting to the Germans to raise their hands. The shooting had stopped.

Captain Bratge had lost his audience. For the record, even though nobody was listening or paying the slightest attention, he pointed to the tunnel exit, raised his voice and shouted:

"Let me say just one more thing. The white flag was raised against our will. To continue fighting now would constitute a brazen violation of the Geneva Convention and would make us responsible for the death of innocent women and children."

Now he sharpened his voice into a command: "For this reason I order that all fighting cease immediately! Please disable your weapons, and, soldiers, be the last to leave the tunnel."

The time was half past five. Stretcher-bearers picked up Sergeant Rothe and the other wounded, filed out of the tunnel, and climbed a long ladder against the wall of the railroad embankment. Captain Friesenhahn, looking around as he marched through Erpel into captivity, muttered over and over again: "How did they do it? How did those Yanks get from the bridge to the exit of the tunnel so fast?"

By the time Bratge, Friesenhahn, and their men had been marched to the bridge, the confusion in the American ranks had been dispelled. Forces were now pouring

German prisoners captured on the Remagen Bridge. U.S. ARMY SIGNAL CORPS. NATIONAL ARCHIVES

over the bridge, and the men eagerly took up their positions, encouraged by the sight of the big group of German prisoners being marched back.

Friesenhahn, the grizzled fifty-year-old veteran of many battles in World War I, marveled at the youth and spirit of the American soldiers. In Timmermann, he saw a company commander who was less than half his age. He looked in amazement as the wounded Americans from Burrows' platoon and the Battle of Flak Hill were brought to the bridge. Four of his own soldiers promptly picked up the stretcher bearing the first wounded American and started back across the bridge. An American medic helped carry the stretcher bearing the wounded Sergeant Rothe.

This brief exhibit of the compassion of all men for the less fortunate ceased abruptly when the stretcher-bearers were fired on from the neighboring town of Kasbach by German soldiers. One of the German soldiers carrying the wounded American doubled up and fell on the bridge, shot through the stomach. The Americans interpreted the shooting as revenge by SS troops trying to punish German troops who had been so "cowardly" as to surrender. The Germans interpreted it as the indiscriminate firing of German troops onto the bridge when they unmistakably saw American helmets and uniforms crossing over to the east bank. Whatever it was, it sharpened the bitterness and determination of the men who crossed the bridge.

Tank dozer manned by Lawrence H. Swayne, Clemon Knapp, Melvin E. Baker, Fred Lovely and James E. Thomas to fill in the 30-foot crater gouged by the German demolition at the approach to the Remagen Bridge.

Crossing the bridge as a prisoner, Captain Bratge encountered Lieutenant Timmermann. He had several suitcases full of personal items cached away in one of the stone towers, and he requested permission to carry them or to have someone carry them for him as he went into captivity. Timmermann looked at him, glanced at the shabbily clad German prisoners who were crossing the bridge with him, and then at the American wounded who were being carried back. Although Bratge's request had been made in German, and Timmermann spoke fluent German, he looked at Bratge coldly and answered in English: "No, take what you've got in your hand and git goin.'"

Seventeen
· · · · · · · ·

Reinforcements of the Bridgehead

AT A QUARTER TO FIVE in the afternoon of March 7, Colonel Engeman radioed to General Hoge: "Bridge intact. Am pushing doughs to other side. What are your plans? Advise as soon as possible." Hoge had long been well aware that the fate of the bridgehead depended on the reaction of higher headquarters. The slender infantry force beyond the Rhine needed rapid reinforcement if it was to survive the next few crucial hours, and the decision to furnish such reinforcement had to come from Hoge's superiors. As Hoge drove back to his C.P. in Birresdorf to report to his division commander, General Leonard, that the bridge had been captured, he held in his hand the division order (which had come down through First Army) to push south and concentrate on linking up with General Patton's army before crossing the Rhine. Hoge knew he had violated the order by insisting that everything in sight be pushed across the bridge. He still felt that, although he might lose a battalion, it would be worth it. His first order of business therefore was to get the order "clarified."

General Leonard had spent most of the day with the south column of his division, which was occupied in driving south to and across the Ahr River. Pleased with Combat Command A's sweep across the Ahr, he drove into Birresdorf in midafternoon to find out how General Hoge's Combat Command B was progressing. Just as the command car came up to the C.P., Hoge strode out to meet it.

"Well, we got the bridge," he said without elaboration.

Leonard said, with a touch of facetiousness and mock severity: "That's a hell of a note. Now we've got a bull by the tail, and caused a lot of trouble. But let's push it, and then put it up to Corps."

With these few words from his division commander, Hoge knew at once that his calculated gamble would pay off. That Leonard was prepared to fight to see that the men east of the Rhine were quickly reinforced was proved by his next order.

"Captain Alexander," he said to his aide, "shoot back to Stadt Mechenheim and tell Johnson that we have the Remagen Bridge, and find out from Corps if we can get out of this business of pushing south to join Patton."

Alexander covered in record time the seven miles to the 9th Armored Division C.P. in Stadt Mechenheim—the town from which Engeman's task force had jumped off that very morning. It took him only a few minutes to tell Colonel Harry Johnson, the division chief of staff, about the coup at Remagen, and Johnson picked up the phone at 4:30 to tell the news to III Corps. General Millikin, the corps commander, was out with the 78th Division, but Colonel James H. Phillips, the Corps Chief of Staff, knew how he would react. Without even delaying to check with his corps commander, Phillips instructed the 9th Armored Division to exploit the bridgehead at Remagen as far as possible and to use Combat Command A to hold what had already been gained in the push to the south. He said he would see to it that 9th Armored was relieved of its mission to the south.

Phillips then put in a quick call to General Millikin to let him know the situation, while the Corps G-3 (Operations Officer) Colonel Mewshaw, telephoned the word to First Army. General Hodges, First Army Commander, and General Thorsen, First Army G-3, then cleared with General Bradley at Twelfth Army Group, and at 6:45 called back, confirming the decision to exploit the bridge seizure. At 8:15, the First Army relieved the Corps of its mission of pushing south.

According to General Bradley's memoirs, *A Soldier's Story*, he was at his command post on the evening of March 7, 1945, with Major General Harold R. ("Pink") Bull, the SHAEF Operations Officer (G-3), when the telephone rang and the First Army Commander (General Hodges) reported the capture of the Remagen bridge. The following account is taken verbatim from *A Soldier's Story*, pages 510-513:

> "Brad," Courtney [Hodges] called, with more composure than the good news warranted, "Brad, we've gotten a bridge."
> "A bridge? You mean you've got one intact on the Rhine?"
> "Yep, Leonard nabbed the one at Remagen before they blew it up —"
> "Hot dog, Courtney," I said, "this will bust him wide open. Are you getting your stuff across?"
> "Just as fast as we can push it over," he said. "Tubby's got the navy moving in now with a ferry service and I'm having the engineers throw a couple of spare pontoon bridges across to the bridgehead."
> I pulled the long lead wire from my phone over toward the map-board. "Shove everything you can across it, Courtney," I said, "and button the bridgehead up tightly. It'll probably take the other fellow a couple of days to pull enough stuff together to hit you."
> I hung up on Hodges, turned on Bull, and thumped him on the shoulder. "There goes your ball game, Pink," I grinned. "Courtney's gotten across the Rhine on a bridge."
> Bull blinked back through his rimless glasses. He sat down before the map and shrugged his shoulders. "Sure, you've got a bridge, Brad, but what good is it going to do you? You're not going anywhere down there at Remagen. It just doesn't fit into the plan."
> "Plan — hell," I retorted. "A bridge is a bridge and mighty damned good anywhere across the Rhine." . . .
> "What in hell do you want us to do," I asked him, "pull back and blow it up?" Bull did not answer.
> I phoned Eisenhower at Reims to confirm the order I had given Hodges. Ike was delighted with news of the bridge. "Hold on to it, Brad," he said. "Get across with whatever you need — but make certain you hold that bridgehead."

After dinner that evening we returned to the office. Although news of the bridgehead had been greeted as a victory by my staff, Bull did not brighten. To him, Remagen was nothing more than an unwelcome intruder in the neatly ordered SHAEF plan. . . .

"But you know our plans for the Rhine crossing," he said, referring to Monty's prospective assault, and now you're trying to change them."

"Change, hell, Pink," I spoke curtly for by now I was growing impatient. "We're not trying to change a thing. But now that we've had a break on the bridge, I want to take advantage of it."

Bull, however, could not believe that I did not seek a diversion of forces from Monty. "Ike's heart is in your sector," he explained, "but right now his mind is up north." By then it was after midnight; I gave up and went to bed.

The Bradley-Bull discussion later gave rise to an anonymous poem which circulated after the seizure of the Remagen Bridge. The poem was entitled "Accident in the Allied Camp (after Robert Browning)" and went as follows:

You know Remagen Bridge was seized
    A week or two ago
The High Command was hardly pleased,
    It almost wrecked the show.
The bridge they thought as good as blown
    When Ike's assault began;
Allied Headquarters had their own
    Supreme strategic plan.

They said they scarcely would expect
    An independent line,
Although their plan did not neglect
    The crossing of the Rhine.
Remagen Bridge should have been wrecked
    According to design
For things in warfare are not done
    On this haphazard line.

SHAEF courier galloped to the ridge
    Where Hoge with all his troop
Stood looking on Remagen Bridge,
    And cried, "Regroup, regroup!
The spearheads that advance too far
    Imperil all the flank
Blow yonder bridge while yet you are
    Upon the western bank!

"The whole concerted war machine
    Together must advance,
You dare not take an unforeseen
    And accidental chance.
The Field Commander must not flout
    The Allies' master plan;

SHAEF will arrange a news blackout—
    Retire now while you can!"

Oh, then the eagle eye flashed fire
    Above the scene of strife
And General Hoge barked: "Retire?
    No, not on your sweet life!
Great snakes! I've crossed the Rhine," he cried.
    "There lies our new bridgehead,"
And sinking at the General's side,
    The man from SHAEF fell dead.

According to General Eisenhower in *Crusade in Europe*, pages 379-380, the following occurred:

> It happened that a SHAEF staff officer was in Bradley's headquarters when the news arrived, and a discussion at once took place as to the amount of force that should be pushed across the bridge. If the bridgehead force was too small it would be destroyed through a quick concentration of German strength on the east side of the river. On the other hand, Bradley realized that if he threw a large force across he might interfere with further development of my basic plan. Bradley instantly telephoned me.
>
> I was at dinner in my Reims headquarters with the corps and division commanders of the American airborne forces when Bradley's call came through. When he reported that we had a permanent bridge across the Rhine I could scarcely believe my ears. He and I had frequently discussed such a development as a remote possibility but never as a well-founded hope.
>
> I fairly shouted into the telephone: "How much have you got in that vicinity that you can throw across the river?"
>
> He said, "I have more than four divisions but I called you to make sure that pushing them over would not interfere with your plans."
>
> I replied, "Well, Brad, we expected to have that many divisions tied up around Cologne and now those are free. Go ahead and shove over at least five divisions instantly, and anything else that is necessary to make certain of our hold."
>
> His answer came over the telephone with a distinct tone of glee: "That's exactly what I wanted to do but the question had been raised here about conflict with your plans, and I wanted to check with you."
>
> That was one of my happy moments of the war.

Captain Harry C. Butcher, General Eisenhower's naval aide, recalls in *My Three Years With Eisenhower* (page 768) that the general also told General Bradley over the phone something like this: "To hell with the planners. Sure, go on, Brad, and I'll give you everything we got to hold that bridgehead. We'll make good use of it even if the terrain isn't too good."

In and around Remagen, very few people went to bed at all on the night of March 7.

Up and down the chain of command, commanders scraped together all possible troops and equipment to pour into the bridgehead. This was no easy task. The entire

American anti-aircraft artilleryman defending Remagen Bridge against attacking German planes.
U.S. ARMY SIGNAL CORPS, NATIONAL ARCHIVES

effort of the First Army was pointed south to join Third Army west of the Rhine. The road net eastward into Remagen was poor to begin with, and the increased load of troops and vehicles jammed it. The signal communications of the Army were headed south as were the main portions of the Army, Corps and division artillery.

When informed of the seizure of the bridge, General Millikin found that his infantry divisions (the 9th and 78th) were engaged in securing vital objectives, as was the rest of the 9th Armored Division. He made immediate plans to motorize one infantry regiment each from the 9th and 78th in order to speed them to the bridgehead. Two divisions were added to the Corps to take over the previous missions of the 9th Infantry and the 9th Armored, allowing the latter to concentrate on defending and expanding the bridgehead.

By half an hour before midnight, one 4.5-inch-gun battalion, one 155-millimeter-gun battalion and one 8-inch howitzer battalion were in position around the bridgehead. A curtain of interdictory fire was placed around the troops across the Rhine. Air cover was flown on a continuous basis, even though the German Luftwaffe did not start attacking the bridge until the following day. Light and heavy anti-aircraft units rumbled down to Remagen and soon began setting up around the bridge. By three o'clock

Despite the incoming artillery, German bombs and other distractions, an anti-aircraft gunner takes time out for a haircut on the banks of the Rhine. The Ludendorff Bridge in the background collapsed two hours after this photo was taken on March 17, 1945. U.S. ARMY SIGNAL CORPS, NATIONAL ARCHIVES

in the morning of March 8, the 482nd Anti-Aircraft Artillery Automatic Weapons Battalion was on its way to defend the area.

At the bridge, the armored engineers, under the capable direction of Lieutenant Hugh Mott continued to work at top speed to make the bridge ready to take vehicles. General Hoge had authorized the use of lumber from Remagen houses if necessary. Finally, just before midnight Mott gave the signal to Colonel Engeman that he could try to send his tanks over. By this time, the hard-pressed infantry on the other side of the Rhine had already repulsed several small-scale counterattacks of platoon size, and they were getting jittery about spending the night in such precarious positions without tank support.

Engeman quickly assembled his company commanders. He selected Captain Soumas' A Company as the first tank unit to cross the bridge, and Soumas singled out Lieutenant Miller's platoon of General Shermans to spearhead the move. Knowing that Miller had been in the habit of riding in the lead tank of his platoon, Engeman said, "Miller, you'd better let one of your tanks go out in front of you." Miller decided to ignore this suggestion, since it was not stated very directly; but there must have

American engineers repairing damage to Remagen Bridge. U.S. ARMY SIGNAL CORPS, NATIONAL ARCHIVES

been a betraying look on his face, for Engeman raised his voice to say: "Miller, that's an order that you'll have one of your tanks go out in front of yours. I'll not have one of my officers lost first crack out of the box. You're going to have to control those tanks and take them over."

Lieutenant Miller said to the tank commander of his Number 2 tank, Sergeant Goodson: "Speedy, I've got the toughest order to give you that I've ever given. You and I are going to have to change places tonight." Goodson nodded, hopped into his tank, and gunned the motor.

The moonless night was black and rainy. Engineers had strung white tapes roughly along the bridge, and tried to rope off the big holes in the planking. Goodson's massive tank lumbered onto the bridge, followed at a fifteen-foot interval by Miller's tank. The thirty-five-ton monsters lurched forward. Miller talked Goodson along through his intercom radio. "Take it easy, Speedy. . . . Don't get too far out front, now. . . . Can you see the white tape? . . . Have you got any idea how far in front of me you are?"

Goodson laughed easily. "Did you hear that bump?" "Yah," Miller said nervously.

"That was me you hit, lieutenant. Now take it easy yourself."

The tanks made their way across the rest of the bridge without incident. Four tanks in Miller's platoon (all but the tankdozer) took up positions east of the Rhine, followed by five tanks from another platoon in Soumas' company.

Engeman said to Major Deevers, "I sure wish we could get some tank destroyers over there too." Deevers' reply was: "I'll get 'em over there if I have to pull them over by hand."

The tank destroyer is not as heavy as a tank, and not as much trouble was anticipated in getting across the bridge. So the first destroyer started out a little faster than its fatter cousins the General Shermans. Nothing marred its journey until, three-quarters of the way across, it came to a point where the German emergency demolition had torn a great hole in the flooring. The right tread of the destroyer fell into the hole. The crew, unhurt, climbed out into the black night to find out what had happened. They were appalled to find the destroyer hanging on its side, precariously balanced over the Rhine. Engineers moved up to help right the vehicle, which blocked the entire bridge so that only foot soldiers could pass. Using crowbars, pushing and pulling with other vehicles, trying to jack up the suspended destroyer, the sweating engineers labored to get the destroyer out of the hole. After several hours of futile effort, they decided to try pushing the tank destroyer into the Rhine. This attempt failed as well—although the destroyer seemed to be balanced and hanging by a thread, it could not be budged. It was 5:30 in the morning before the balky vehicle was dislodged and towed away to make room for the traffic that had piled up behind.

As soon as the tank destroyer had been cleared from the bridge, additional troops and vehicles started across. The 1st battalion of the 310th Regiment of the 78th Division, with instructions to "cross the bridge, turn left and start fighting" was the first non-9th Armored Division unit to cross.

The night of March 7-8 was long and miserable for the American troops east of the Rhine. The nine tanks that had managed to cross had to be distributed along the 3,500-yard frontage of the bridgehead. Lacking enough infantry support, they were especially vulnerable in the darkness, which allowed enemy foot soldiers to approach undetected and fire rocket launchers at close range.

The Germans launched several determined counterattacks during the night, endeavoring to get close enough to the bridge to blow it up. In the confusion, Miller's tank was separated both from the other tanks and from the few infantrymen that were supporting him. In his isolated position he beat off several German sallies only by firing his machine guns blindly at wraithlike targets and in some instances by dropping hand grenades out of his tank turret on desperate enemy counterattackers who had eluded his machine-gun fire. Miller finally radioed back to Colonel Engeman for help, stressing the seriousness of the German counterattacks which were being launched against his unsupported position. Engeman's reply burned into his mind: "Hold your place until the last tank is shot out from under you."

Miraculously, the men in the bridgehead held on through the night, and at 5:30

in the morning, when the tank destroyer blocking traffic over the bridge was dislodged, the crisis passed. Reinforcements streamed onto the east bank to join the tankers and the infantrymen who had survived the dark hours. The Remagen bridge still stood firm, and the territory wrested from the enemy by foot soldiers like Timmermann and tankmen like Miller was no longer in danger of recapture.

In the twenty-four hours following the capture of the Ludendorff Bridge, the Americans had moved the following troops across the bridge:

27th Armored Infantry Battalion, 9th Armored Division
52nd Armored Infantry Battalion, 9th Armored Division
14th Tank Battalion, 9th Armored Division
47th Infantry Regiment, 9th Infantry Division
1st Battalion of 60th Infantry Regiment, 9th Infantry Division
311th Infantry Regiment, 78th Infantry Division
1st and 2nd Infantry Battalions of 310th Infantry Regiment, 78th Infantry Division
Company C of 656th Tank Destroyer Battalion
Troop C of 89th Reconnaissance Squadron
One platoon of Company B, 9th Armored Engineer Battalion
One and a half batteries of 482nd Anti-Aircraft Artillery Battalion

This gave the American forces in the bridgehead a total strength of close to 8,000 men – a remarkable feat in rapid movement – in the first twenty-four hours after the bridge was captured. On subsequent days, the rest of the 9th Infantry, 9th Armored, and 78th Infantry divisions and the 99th Infantry Division took over the bridgehead. The 78th Division generally occupied the northern sector, the 9th Infantry the center and the 99th Infantry the southern sector. The most savage fighting in the bridgehead was in the center, and the 47th Infantry Regiment bore the full brunt of the German counterattacks.

The first suggestion of morning light was appearing in Remagen on March 8 as Lt. Col. Lewis E. Maness led his 2nd battalion of the 47th Infantry Regiment over the bridge. From that point throughout the next two weeks his troops and the rest of the 47th Regiment fought one of the bloodiest battles in 9th Division history, in holding the center of the bridgehead against repeated 9th and 11th Panzer Division attempts to smash toward the Ludendorff Bridge. The men of the leading battalion drew their inspiration from their commander, 24-year-old "Chip" Maness, an ROTC graduate of Clemson in South Carolina. Starting as a company commander in the battles against Rommel's Afrika Korps in 1943, Maness had quickly shown his qualities of leadership at El Guettar, in the fighting around St. Lo, and on Hamich Ridge in the Hürtgen Forest.

Commenting on the 9th Division's exploits in the Remagen Bridgehead, the Division Chief of Staff, Colonel William C. Westmoreland, said in 1945: "There is an engineering parallel between the Remagen bridgehead and the construction of a bridge. An arch is the strongest type of bridge; pressure can be applied at any point, and

Starting the treadway bridge, downstream (north) of the Ludendorff Bridge. U.S. ARMY SIGNAL CORPS, NATIONAL ARCHIVES

the arch will withstand the pressure as long as the keystone is intact. If the keystone is pulled out, the arch will crumble. In the Remagen bridgehead, the 47th Infantry Regiment was the keystone of the arch. They provided depth and strength to the bridgehead. When the bridgehead was established, there were some who advocated an elongation of the bridgehead along the banks of the Rhine, as this was the path of least resistance. The enemy did not bother the river banks, but concentrated his attacks against a strengthening of the arch in the center." Colonel Westmoreland's phrase, "keystone of the arch" was used in conferring the Presidential Unit Citation on the 47th Infantry Regiment for its part in holding and expanding the bridgehead.

Because of the high priority for moving combat troops into the bridgehead and the great damage to the flooring of the Ludendorff Bridge, it was marked for one-way traffic going east. All available engineer troops and bridging equipment were rushed to Remagen to start round-the-clock construction of emergency pontoon and treadway bridges, as well as to operate tank and vehicle ferries and DUKWs to carry back the wounded to the west side of the Rhine.

On March 10, the 51st Engineer Combat Battalion and the 291st Engineer Com-

Completed treadway bridge at Remagen. The dramatic story of the construction of this bridge is chronicled in the exciting book by the commanding officer of the 291st Engineer Combat Battalion, Lt. Col. David E. Pergrin, First Across the Rhine. U.S. ARMY SIGNAL CORPS, NATIONAL ARCHIVES

bat Battalion started the harrowing work of constructing a heavy pontoon bridge and a treadway bridge, one to the north and one to the south of the railroad bridge. The men had to work under observed artillery fire delivered from the hills on the east side of the Rhine, and it also became evident that there were artillery observers with radios in Remagen who were helping direct artillery fire onto the bridges under construction. Furthermore, the German plane attacks were aimed at the temporary bridges as well as the railroad bridge.

Both units suffered heavy casualties in the back-breaking task of building the bridges under fire. The treadway bridge, built by Lt. Col. David E. Pergrin's 291st Engineer Combat Battalion, took 32½ hours to construct. The 51st Engineer Combat Battalion, led by Lt. Col. Harvey Fraser and Major Robert Yates, finished its heavy pontoon bridge in 29½ hours.

Tank ferry pressed into service. Three ferry crossings supplemented the crossings provided by the pontoon and treadway bridges. U.S. ARMY SIGNAL CORPS, NATIONAL ARCHIVES

At the bridge site, the military police became heroes within a few minutes of their arrival. When artillery shells and bombs were dropping in to blanket the whole area, traffic became hopelessly congested as men hopped from their vehicles to take cover. Through it all, the M.P.'s stayed out in the open, yanking men out of ditches, spurring vehicles onward, and convincing those who approached the bridge that the quickest way to avoid artillery and bombs was to get across the bridge in a hurry. Many military policemen were killed and injured in their exposed positions on the Remagen side of the bridge. As a result of their action, the Military Police Platoon of the 9th Infantry Division was awarded one of the rare Presidential Unit Citations given to an M.P. unit.

By a week following the capture of the Ludendorff Bridge, the Americans had massed 25,000 combat troops in the small bridgehead area. Despite desperate efforts to wipe out the bridgehead "at all costs," the Germans during the first week of expansion of the bridgehead were able to move in no more than 20,000 front-line combat troops.

At seven o'clock on the morning of March 8, one of the first jeeps driven across the bridge was manned by Chaplain William T. Gibble. At the entrance to the tunnel Chaplain Gibble stopped his jeep and set up a simple field altar. Not many soldiers could get out of their foxholes to participate in this first service east of the Rhine, but those who did gave quiet thanks to God for the miracle of Remagen.

Eighteen
. . . .

The Germans Lash Back at Remagen

BECAUSE NOBODY ON EITHER the American or the German side dreamed that a bridge would be taken intact at Remagen, there was neither an American plan to exploit the sudden success nor a German plan to rush reinforcements to plug the hole in their front.

Because of Hitler's adamant order to hold the Siegfried Line to the last man and not to pull back to the defense line of the Rhine, the Germans were without organized reserves immediately available to throw against the first American troops crossing the bridge. Not until two or three days after the bridge was captured were they able to organize a counterattack and move in fresh combat troops. Meanwhile, they fought savagely against the bridgehead with service troops and whatever combat troops could be flagged down in their flight across the Rhine.

Up and down the Rhine, the Germans had some service troops to help guard bridges, operate ferries, act as traffic guides and round up stragglers. These men had neither the skill nor the determination needed to recapture an objective as important as the Remagen bridge. Furthermore, German divisions were still trying to get across the Rhine to avoid capture, and the service troops were sorely needed for their assigned missions of keeping the other bridges and the ferries in working order.

The news of the debacle at Remagen spread slowly throughout the dazed German command. Major August Kraft, the battalion commander of the engineers at Remagen, had his headquarters at Sayn, about twenty-five miles to the south. His battalion was spread out along a forty-mile front from Remagen to Koblenz, and his task was to maintain and operate five bridges and numerous ferries up and down the Rhine. One of these bridges was the Ludendorff Bridge at Remagen. Kraft's mission had nothing to do with the conduct of tactical operations at the bridges; he was merely to supervise the units of his battalion in carrying out their engineering missions. Captain Friesenhahn's company had been in direct charge of demolition operations at the Ludendorff Bridge, and other units under Kraft's control were stationed at the other bridges in his sector. He had visited the bridge on the night before it was captured, and had satisfied himself that the demolition charges were properly placed underneath the bridge. Also, he had checked the ignition circuit and found it in working order. So he was very familiar with arrangements at the bridge.

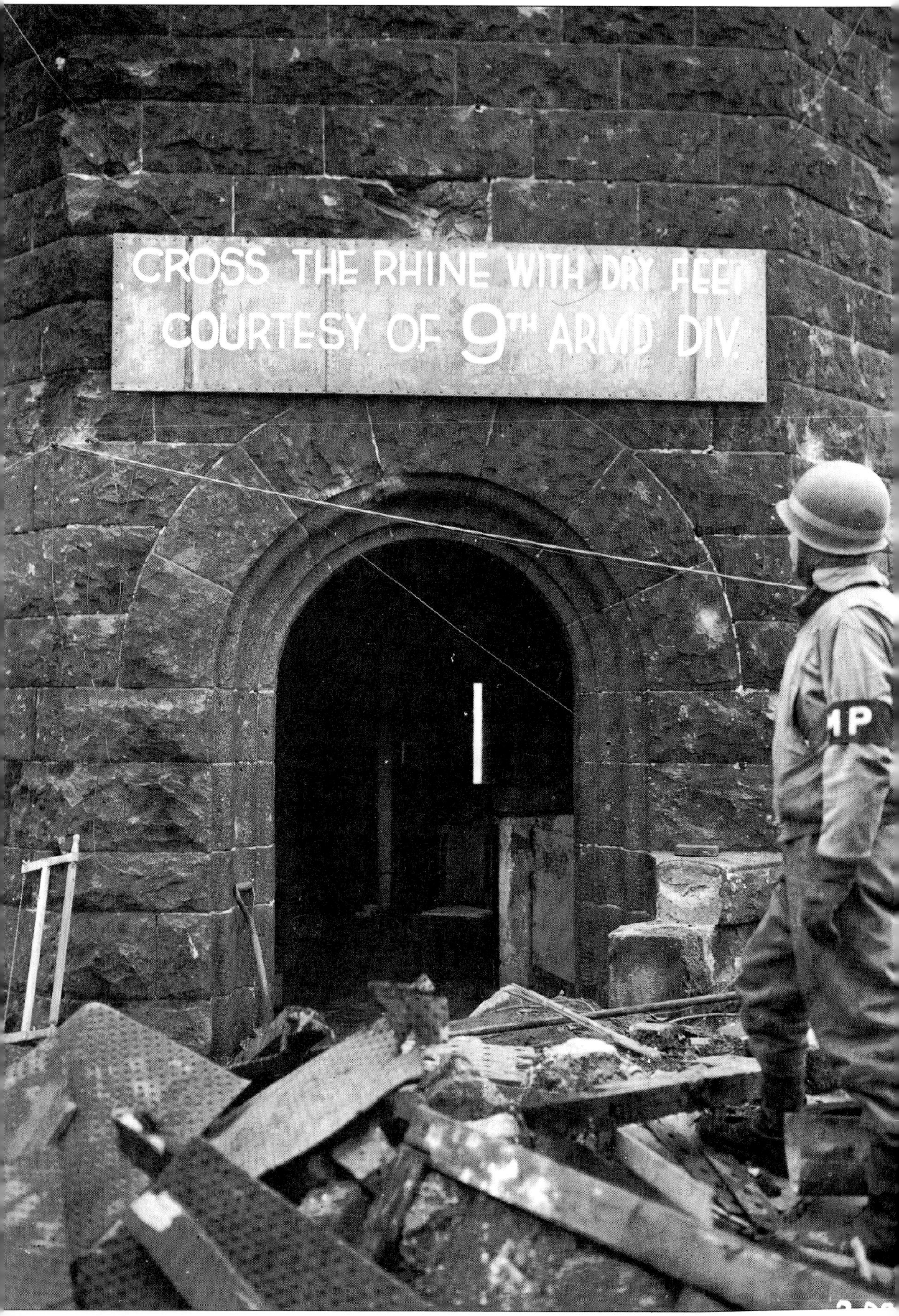
CROSS THE RHINE WITH DRY FEET
COURTESY OF 9TH ARMD DIV.
MP

Major Herbert Strobel had arrived in the Remagen sector only on March 2, when he was assigned to command a conglomeration called the "51st Motorized Engineer Regimental Staff" with headquarters at Rheinbrohl, five miles closer to Remagen than Kraft's headquarters. Major Strobel was the regimental commander and Kraft's superior.

About nine o'clock on the evening of March 7, Strobel first heard about the capture of the bridge. The delay was due to the fact that telephone and radio communication from the bridge had been cut off, and several messengers trying to get out of Remagen had been killed. All personnel in Remagen had been captured, and such news of the event as Major Strobel had he had gathered from civilians and from soldiers who had had some view from above Remagen of what happened. He telephoned to Kraft immediately.

Kraft agreed that a counterattack was necessary to recapture and destroy the bridge. As battalion commander, he felt he should lead the attack, but he pointed out that he had only twenty men. He could not launch an effective attack until he had been reinforced. Strobel, five miles closer to the bridge, then decided to lead the attack himself. He asked Kraft to supply a demolition expert and 1,000 kilograms of explosives (about a ton) within an hour, and he directed Major Kraft to make an immediate, personal inspection of the other bridges in his zone. Then Major Strobel hung up and, in the sixty minutes left, set about gathering the makeshift force he would lead against the bridge.

At precisely ten o'clock a truck rumbled up to Kraft's battalion headquarters, twenty miles from Remagen, quickly picked up the ton of explosives and the expert to detonate them and set out for the bridge. By that time Major Strobel had rounded up about a hundred engineers and anti-aircraft men for his counterattack. They engaged in a fierce, local struggle with the first Americans to cross the bridge, and just before dawn a handful with the explosives actually managed to reach the bridge. American troops from the 78th Infantry Division captured them before they could place the explosives, and when dawn broke Strobel withdrew and the last of the German attackers were captured.

Meanwhile, the German army telephone lines were burning with furiously urgent messages. Virtually every battle commander in the German army was on the move on that night, complicating the problem of making and carrying out quick decisions. In a highly fluid situation the major links in the chain of command operated poorly or not at all.

On March 6, the eve of Remagen, Adolf Hitler had spent six and one-half hours— from 3 to 9:30 p.m.—haranguing von Rundstedt's Chief of Staff, General Siegfried Westphal, on the shortcomings of the German commanders in the west. Westphal's chief, von Rundstedt, had been speaking his mind a little too often, and Hitler did not dare to call the old master himself on the carpet. So der Führer heaped his in-

AT LEFT: *The famous sign placed on Remagen Bridge after its capture on March 7, 1945. The sign is now in the Patton Museum at Fort Knox, Ky.* U.S. ARMY SIGNAL CORPS, NATIONAL ARCHIVES

dignities on Westphal, and discovered that the steely-eyed general fought him toe to toe. This infuriated Hitler. He was also incensed at a remark by von Rundstedt that the Siegfried Line was not all that it was cracked up to be. Von Rundstedt had been openly critical of the Hitler command that all troops stay in the West Wall fortifications and not yield an inch of ground. Hitler stormed at General Westphal:

"Would the German troops prefer to leave their defenses and go out and die in the open fields?"

General Westphal replied that it did not make sense for troops to remain in their fortified positions once the were cut off and outflanked. Enraged, Hitler pounded the table and said that the Allies were trembling in their boots as they faced the fortifications.

Back at his headquarters commanding the whole Western front from near Bad Nauheim, von Rundstedt thoughtfully reflected on the deteriorating course of events. He realized that his days as commander in chief of the western front were numbered. Toward the end of February, the Allied radio had broadcast a propaganda message asserting that the westem powers would accept German surrender from only one person: Field Marshal von Rundstedt. The message came to Hitler's attention. When von Rundstedt was told of the message he said resignedly to his chief of staff: "Now I shall not be staying here much longer."

This was the back-drop for Remagen. Hitler was in even more of a rage than usual. There was an open rift between him and von Rundstedt. And as General Westphal drove back from Berlin to von Rundstedt's headquarters, he was smarting under Hitler's sarcasm. On the way to Bad Nauheim, he learned of the debacle at Remagen. He tried to reach Field Marshal Model—the head of Army Group B, and next in command—but Model himself was on the move and did not learn of the fall of Remagen and the bridge until late that night.

Von Rundstedt's Operations Officer, General Zimmermann, heard about the Remagen incident in a very indirect way. He was talking with one of his anti-aircraft commanders near Koblenz when he heard about the bridge purely by chance. Immediately, he tried to reach Model. Surely the master of the Ardennes would know what to do. But Model could not be found; his headquarters were moving, and he himself was at the front at what he considered to be a more important point, riding up and down to encourage, improvise, lead, and squeeze the last ounce of effort from the exhausted German front-line army.

Frantically, General Zimmermann cranked his field telephone and tried to reach someone in command. Purely by accident, he at last made contact with Model's operations officer, Colonel Reichhelm, only to discover that Reichhelm was out of communication with his staff and units. For all practical purposes, Model's staff was leaderless and helpless with its head absent. In this crucial situation, some of the officers in von Rundstedt's headquarters had to step in and bypass the intervening headquarters until Model had the reins firmly in hand the next day. As a result, little was done to organize a quick and heavy counterattack on the night of March 7. About all that von Rundstedt's headquarters could do was to order that all forces available at the bridge site be concentrated in an effort to recapture the bridge. The Luftwaffe was then notified that if the bridge at Remagen could not be recaptured it was to be destroyed.

Inside Model's headquarters, the reaction to Remagen was peculiar. At first the report of the loss struck the headquarters, to quote the chief of staff, "like a bolt from the blue." It had been believed that the American forces would mop up west of the Rhine before attempting a crossing. Hence, the first crossing at Remagen did not seem particularly dangerous. The American forces east of the Rhine were described as being very weak, and it seemed certain that the small bridgehead would be wiped out within a few days.

Actually, Model's headquarters were more anxious about the situation south of Remagen, where the 4th Armored Division had knifed its way to the Rhine near Koblenz and was about to make contact with American troops in the north to cut off the last means of retreat of several German divisions west of the Rhine. Model's headquarters felt that the loss of these divisions would be even more disastrous than the loss of the Remagen Bridge.

The crafty Model sized up the situation more seriously on March 8. He ordered the 11th Panzer Division at Bonn to hold up a projected counterattack west of the Rhine, re-cross the river and sweep the east bank, then blow the bridge. This seemed like a fairly simple operation for a strong armored unit. It looked as if the abscess at Remagen would be cleaned out within a few days. The 11th Panzer Division had 4,000 men, 25 tanks and 18 artillery pieces available for the counterattack. Its presence immediately after the capture of the bridge might have collapsed the American bridgehead.

Yet what happened to the 11th Panzer Division was in a sense characteristic of the whole German army in the last stages of the war. The division first tried to collect enough gasoline to make the movement. The gasoline was difficult to get, and in some cases, vehicles had to be held up for several days. Then, the division tried to requisition both fuel and equipment from industrial plants in Düsseldorf and other sections of the Ruhr. This took up precious time. When the division started to move southward, the roads were clogged, and both its own vehicles and the vehicles ahead were repeatedly harassed by Allied air attacks. The division was low in morale to begin with, since it had been assigned so many different missions, and the orders and direction were changed so frequently, that the officers and men were numbed in their outlook. Not until the evening of March 8 could the forward elements of the 11th Panzer Division move southward, and the first portions of the division were not committed in the Remagen bridgehead until March 10.

Once the Strobel counterattack had failed on the night of March 7, the subsequent use of engineer troops to counterattack produced a veritable comedy of errors in the German command. On March 8, Major Strobel's head whirled as he listened to and tried to follow the orders of the various generals who strode into his command

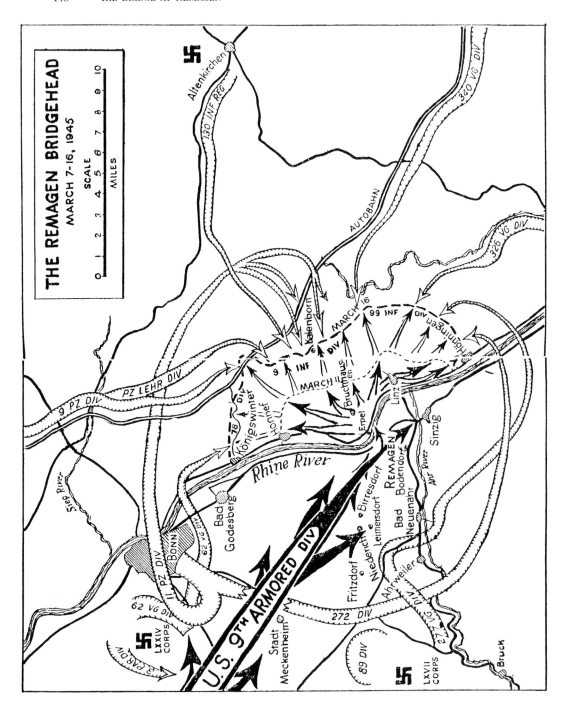

THE REMAGEN BRIDGEHEAD
MARCH 7-16, 1945

SCALE
0 1 2 3 4 5 6 7 8 9 10
MILES

post. First, there was a General Wirtz, Model's Army Group B Engineer Officer. Wirtz was interested in only one thing: that the engineers were providing enough ferrying facilities for the German troops who had to cross to the east bank of the Rhine. The ferries were any kind of boat, large or small, that could be commandeered for the mission. Private boat-owners freely gave up their river craft for this vast but fruitless Dunkerque. Opposed to General Wirtz was General von Berg, an officer responsible for building up the defenses in the Rhine area. Von Berg felt strongly that the engineers should be used as infantry to counterattack and wipe out the American bridgehead. Finally, there was General Janowski, who was also responsible for building up the defense along the Rhine; he took a position similar to General Wirtz's, insisting that engineer troops should be employed as engineers rather than as combat infantry.

At eight o'clock on the morning of March 8, General Wirtz arrived at Major Strobel's regimental headquarters to find out whether the regimental engineer troops were doing everything possible to get the 5th Panzer Army and other retreating German units across the Rhine. The retreat was in full cry, with the knowledge that the Americans were closing the vise on all German troops west of the Rhine. During the early days of March, the Americans captured 49,000 German prisoners in the Rhineland. Wirtz left Strobel's headquarters a few minutes after he arrived because of a message that American troops were advancing on Linz — a little town just south of Erpel on the east side of the Rhine within sight of the Remagen bridge. Dashing out of Strobel's headquarters, General Wirtz went to check on the combat situation in the vicinity of Linz.

About two hours later, at ten o'clock in the morning, General von Berg telephoned to Strobel's staff to use all the troops that could be scraped together for an attack on the expanding Remagen bridgehead. Strobel rushed what troops he had up to Hönningen, south of Linz and within striking distance of the bridgehead's southern-most point, even though this meant stripping his ferries of the personnel necessary to operate them.

But at one o'clock in the afternoon, General Wirtz encountered Major Strobel, heard his report on the action he had taken, and immediately countermanded von Berg's order. General Wirtz stormed that it was senseless to take urgently needed and highly trained engineer troops away from the ferries and use them for an infantry counterat-tack. In his eyes, von Berg's order was an irresponsible act that made no sense at a critical time when the ferries had to be in constant operation.

Now General Janowski arrived at regimental headquarters, and he complained bit-terly that his own engineer troops and staffs had been called off by Major Strobel. He said that his engineers had no business being siphoned off that way for use in tactical missions.

Wirtz left Strobel's headquarters, but Janowski was still there when von Berg arrived at three o'clock in the afternoon. When von Berg found that his order to use Strobel's engineers for a counterattack had not been carried out, he blew up with anger. A heated argument developed between von Berg and Janowski as to the proper use of the engineers. They finally agreed that since the engineers were already on the way to launch a counterattack they should continue their mission, but should pass under the command of the 403rd Engineer Training Regiment—an entirely different unit from the regiment commanded by Major Strobel.

The net result of all this argument and snafu was that although some of the service troops close to the bridge were thrown into the action and forced the American troops to fight for every inch they gained, others were delayed and held for what were considered more important missions. In the first twenty-four hours after the American troops crossed the bridge, it is doubtful that the Germans had more than 3,000 fighting troops at the spot to counterattack. In the next few days, they were able to move up several divisions, but the Americans moved into the bridgehead so fast that the chances of a successful counterattack became dimmer with every passing hour.

On March 9 the German High Command had awakened sufficiently to the seriousness of the bridgehead threat to dispatch a single commander to take charge of throwing the Americans back to the west bank of the Rhine. The man chosen was General Fritz Bayerlein, commander of the Panzer Lehr Division which had fought in Normandy and the Battle of the Bulge. The Panzer Lehr Division itself was reduced to 300 men and 15 tanks, but Bayerlein had under his control the 4,000-man 11th Panzer Division (already starting to arrive), the 9th Panzer Division (with 600 men, 15 tanks and 12 artillery pieces), and the remnants of the 106th Panzer Brigade with 100 men and 5 tanks.

Bayerlein was a strikingly sharp, frank and able general who was a master of tank warfare. He had fought in Poland and France and had been Rommel's Chief of Staff in the Afrika Corps in 1943. His jet-black, straight-combed hair and piercing eyes were familiar sights on the battlefield, and he rarely had to issue an order a second time to give it emphasis. He had had happier days, however. He was rather disgusted with the "rubbish" which he had to use at this stage of the war and he yearned for the days of old when he could weed out and select crack troops who were to comprise his fast-moving Panzer Lehr Division.

On March 9, Model and Bayerlein met to map out their strategy for eliminating the bridgehead. The two commanders eyed each other with some suspicion. Although Model was a field marshal and Bayerlein a mere lieutenant general, Model knew that Bayerlein was inclined to be acid in his comments. He had such combat experience that he could afford to be critical. Just before the Battle of the Bulge, Bayerlein had asked Model if he could get his Panzer Lehr Division pulled back in order to get fresh replacements and to reorganize and re-equip the division. Model had suggested tartly that Bayerlein ought to reorganize in the front line as he had discovered was necessary in Russia. Bayerlein looked him coldly in the eye and said if that was the way the German army had operated in Russia it evidently had not been too successful. The two men shared a mutual respect but also a mutual hatred.

Bayerlein presented to Model his plan to attack through the middle of the bridgehead to split it in two and then roll it up either to the north or to the south, depending on which direction seemed to produce the better results. The big attack was planned for dusk of March 10 with the approximately 10,000 combat troops then expected to be available. Model vetoed this plan because it appeared the southern sector of the bridgehead was being threatened by an American tank attack, and Bayerlein's forces were rushed there in an attempt to put out the fire.

In point of fact, almost the entire defense of the bridgehead could be explained in terms of small groups of infantry and tanks rushing to put out fires. The Germans were very adroit in slowing down the Americans and keeping them from breaking out into the clear for ten days. However, they scored only local and temporary successes in their efforts to reduce the bridgehead or to push close enough to destroy the railroad bridge or the pontoon bridges the American engineers had installed.

The capture of Remagen Bridge was the occasion for the removal of Field Marshal von Rundstedt as Commander in Chief of the western forces, although Hitler had for other reasons already become disenchanted with von Rundstedt. On March 8 Field Marshal Kesselring was summoned from Italy, and he arrived in Berlin about noon on March 9 to report to Hitler. There he was informed that he would take over. Hitler gave him a long briefing on the military situation and stated that the fall of Remagen had finally necessitated a change of command in the west. He felt that there was still time to refit the exhausted units on the western front, but that Remagen was the most vulnerable spot; and it was urgent to restore the situation there.

Kesselring left Berlin on the evening of March 9, and then conferred on March 10 with General Schmidt, who commanded the Luftwaffe in the west. He stressed to Schmidt that air attacks should be concentrated on the Remagen Bridge and the temporary pontoon and treadway bridges.

Then on March 11 Kesselring called a conference at Field Marshal Model's Army Group B headquarters. Bayerlein and other commanders attended, and when Bayerlein outlined his plan of attack against the bridgehead, Kesselring was furious to discover it had not yet been executed as planned. Model explained the difficulties in obtaining troops, supplies and gasoline. Bayerlein correctly pointed out that every time he readied his troops for an offensive the news was flashed that the Americans had captured the area from which the Germans had hoped to jump off on their attack.

The German air attacks against Remagen Bridge and the bridgehead area represented the last gasp of Hermann Göring's Luftwaffe.

March 8, a cold, rainy day with low overcast, was a very poor flying day, but the Germans sent out ten aircraft, eight of which were Stukas. They claimed two hits on the bridge. By the afternoon of March 8, the American 482nd Anti-Aircraft Battalion had three batteries in the bridgehead area, with three platoons on each side of the Rhine. The 413th Anti-Aircraft Battalion with 90-millimeter guns then moved in on the west bank. These were the first of a heavy concentration of American anti-aircraft forces that helped protect the bridge area. It was in fact the heaviest concentration of anti-aircraft troops and guns in the war.

German bombs attacking Remagen Bridge cause geysers in the Rhine. U.S. ARMY SIGNAL CORPS, NATIONAL ARCHIVES

The high point of the anti-aircraft defense of the bridge area occurred on March 15, when the Germans sent twenty-one fast bombers in an effort to knock out the bridge. According to official German records available after the war, the anti-aircraft shot down sixteen of them. This was too costly a price for the fast-dwindling Luftwaffe to pay.

Frustrated in the attempt to wipe out the bridgehead by tank-infantry attacks, or to knock out the bridge from the air, Hitler ordered that swimmers be dispatched to destroy the bridge. The German Navy had a specially trained group of determined young men, none over twenty-nine years of age, who had undergone their conditioning at a large indoor swimming pool in Vienna. On March 11, Lieutenant Schreiber was ordered by phone from Berlin to fly six of his best men to Frankfurt and thence proceed to the Remagen area. They drove to a point ten miles above Remagen, so that they could get the advantage of the fast Rhine current in floating downstream to their objective. But they met repeated difficulties with muddy roads, traffic jams, and the advancing Americans who were pushing the bridgehead outward every hour.

On March 16, the men received an urgent message from Model's headquarters that they had to take immediate action against the Remagen Bridge at all costs. So they donned their rubber shirts, trousers, gloves and shoes, and rubber flippers (duck feet). This skin-tight uniform was covered with a rubberized canvas union suit, which in turn was covered by a grey-blue jacket soaked in a chemical compound that gave

German saboteurs captured attempting to destroy Remagen Bridge. U.S. ARMY SIGNAL CORPS, NATIONAL ARCHIVES

off heat when soaked in water. Each man carried an oxygen mask across his chest, and a breathing apparatus to breathe under water. In good conditions, the mask enabled a swimmer to stay under water about an hour. Each man had four packages of Plastit, a pliable plastic explosive compound, weighing nearly seven pounds each. The packages were tied to an empty five-gallon oil can to give them buoyancy, and had time devices which enabled the swimmers to attach the explosive charges to cables or bridge supports and then presumably escape before they were detonated. The swimmers carried powerful pliers to cut their way through nets or other river obstructions. They also had light signals which they shot off at intervals to keep track of each other's progress.

When the intrepid swimmers tried to take to the water on the night of March 16 they discovered their assembly area was already under American artillery fire. After a couple of false starts, they postponed their trip until the next day, and entered the

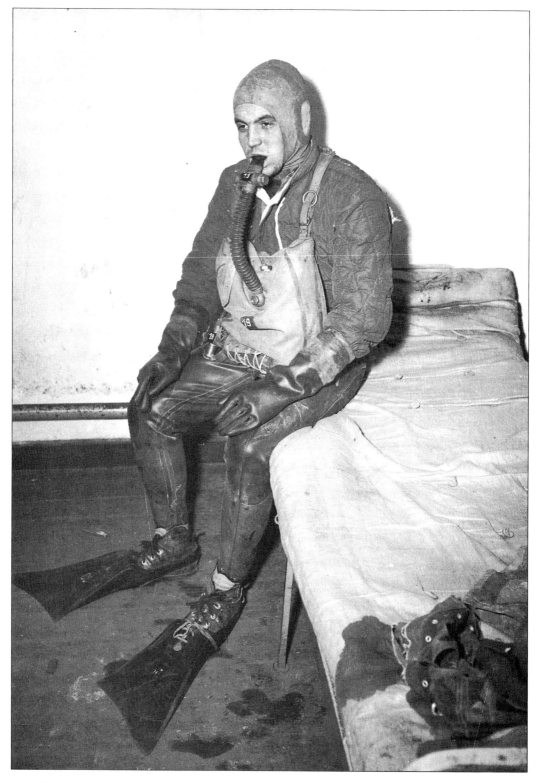

German "gam swimmer" captured when attempting underwater attack on Remagen Bridge. U.S. ARMY
SIGNAL CORPS, NATIONAL ARCHIVES

Rhine at 7:15 P.M. on March 17. Shortly before departing they learned that the Remagen railroad bridge had collapsed a few hours before, but they nevertheless kept on in an effort to destroy the pontoon and treadway bridges.

Lieutenant Schreiber got into trouble soon after they started when he tore his rubber swimming suit. The weight of his wet clothing hindered his progress, and the cold water gave him leg cramps. Still, he pressed onward. A few miles above Remagen some of the group were spotted by defending troops along the river banks, and heavy firing broke out along both banks. Responding to the cries of one of his wounded enlisted men, Lieutenant Schreiber swam over and was captured. One by one the other members of the game swimming troop were taken prisoner.

One of the main reasons why the swimmers failed in their mission was that their presence was detected by blinding searchlights which brought every object in the river into sharp focus. These searchlights were mounted on tanks and were used for the first time at Remagen.

The story of the searchlight tanks was filled with cloak-and-dagger mystery, and the veil of secrecy was not lifted until after the war. The tanks had been first developed by the British late in 1942 and adapted by the Armored Force at Fort Knox in 1943. An armor-protected searchlight was mounted on a medium tank in such a way as to throw a blinding light to a range of 800 yards, and to conceal accompanying tanks and friendly infantry. Six tank battalions and supporting troops were trained with these tanks at Fort Knox, and later in the California desert. Each soldier participating in the project had to sign a solemn oath of secrecy, and the trainees were never allowed off the post except in groups. When they visited their families with strange friends, many families assumed their sons were under arrest.

In August, 1944, General Eisenhower ordered that the searchlight tanks should not be used in action within twenty miles of forward positions without prior SHAEF approval. This was the ultimate in security, for the tanks were never tested in combat. Their value in defending the Remagen area was demonstrated in the capture of the German swimmers, who testified that they believed they would have succeeded had it not been for the blinding lights.

Further to discourage swimmers, depth charges were dropped regularly every five minutes from the bridge area. Aside from the one incident when the swimmers were captured, the American defenders had no trouble with attack from the water.

Hitler tried two other weapons on the bridge: a tremendous 17-centimeter railroad gun, and V-2 rockets. The railroad gun was drawn up on the southeastern edge of the bridgehead and caused many a G.I. to shudder as its heavy missiles gouged holes west of the Rhine. Its greatest damage was done in the town of Remagen, and the combat troops east of the Rhine in the bridgehead were relatively well protected by the steep Erpeler Ley. Hitler was sure that his V-2s would cauterize the whole bridgehead area, and on March 16 he notified General Bayerlein that, regardless of what would happen to the civilian population, he was determined to wipe out the bridgehead by saturating it with V-2s. Bayerlein commented that when the troops

Patrols along banks of Rhine on constant lookout for German saboteurs.

Powerful searchlights aid night defense of both the Ludendorff railroad bridge and the temporary pontoon and treadway bridges. U.S. ARMY SIGNAL CORPS, NATIONAL ARCHIVES

heard of Hitler's fantastic plan to use a highly inaccurate weapon as a tactical weapon close to the front lines, "the knowledge of this possibility did not increase the German soldiers' will to resist on that particular piece of ground."

The counterattacking forces faced a difficult task from the beginning. Once again, the breaks favored the Americans as the Germans became tangled in their own feet. But there was a clear explanation why the Americans held the bridgehead – they were able to move larger forces quickly with superiority in the air, and they held on and fought doggedly forward until they broke out of the bridgehead.

From the German standpoint, Field Marshal Kesselring gives a fair summary of the German counterattacks:

> The gravest danger lay in the fact that Remagen required an increasing flow of reinforcements and by itself almost swallowed up the replacements and supplies fed to C.-in-C. West., magnetically attracting everything right and left. This made the regrouping, resting and refurbishing of the other Army Groups more difficult, if not impracticable. In fact, the first counter-measures against the first enemy forces to cross the Rhine had not been taken with the uncompromising fierceness which might have ensured a swift and relatively easy restoration of the line, and the fate of the whole Rhine front hung on our wiping out or containing the bridgehead.

V-2 of the type fired at Remagen Bridge. COURTESY U.S. ARMY MISSILE COMMAND

Nineteen
· · · · · · ·

Death of the Bridge

SHORTLY AFTER THREE O'CLOCK on the afternoon of March 17, with a sickening roar of torn steel, the bridge at Remagen collapsed and fell into the Rhine. Within a few seconds, the massive Ludendorff Bridge, which the Germans could not destroy and the Americans could not repair, was gone. Though unexpected, the fall of the bridge should not have been surprising. The miracle was that, battered and maimed, it had stood so long.

The emergency demolition on March 7 had so shattered the upstream truss that the tremendous weight of the entire bridge had to be borne by only the downstream truss. This was a tremendous burden for one side of the bridge to bear, a bridge that had already been weakened by Allied bombings and had been knocked out several times by direct hits.

As soon as the bridge was captured, the heavy tread of infantry combat boots started beating its tom-tom on the bridge flooring. The combat engineers moved in with planks and hammers, hastily getting the flooring ready for tanks and other vehicles. The "repairs," which took place on the battered bridge in the early hours when it was first in American hands, were designed only to make the bridge passable for vehicular traffic. They did nothing to strengthen it, and in fact weakened it by adding a load of planking as an additional weight for it to sustain. A four-inch flooring, fifteen feet wide, over the 515-foot center span of the bridge added a dead load of approximately fifty tons.

Starting shortly before midnight on March 7, tanks, tank destroyers, jeeps, armored cars, guns, trucks, and half-tracks jerked and pounded their way across the bridge, straining the downstream supports and subjecting them to a twisting action never contemplated in the construction. From that time on, there was an almost continuous flow of heavy one-way traffic eastward across the bridge.

On March 8, the first of over 600 German artillery shells whistled in and exploded near the bridge. The enemy artillery barrages continued in rising crescendo. The height of the Erpeler Ley made it difficult for shells coming from the east to hit the bridge, but their explosions near the structure shook the ground and literally shivered the timbers. When larger projectiles from German railway guns boomed in, the bridge swayed precariously.

Then came the desperate attempts of Hermann Göring's Luftwaffe, winging up the Rhine to drop bomb loads at the bridge, geysering the Rhine, shaking the ground, but not quite knocking out the bridge.

In the spring of 1954, a German couple looked down on the ruins of the Remagen bridge from atop the Erpeler Ley, and the man said to his wife: "There the first Americans crossed the Rhine on a bridge and a few days later our Luftwaffe destroyed the bridge." Hermann Göring started this legend. In July of 1945, in his prison château in Mondorf, Luxembourg, a svelte and shrinking Göring proudly related how his powerful Luftwaffe had destroyed the bridge. He was told at first gently, then firmly, with documents and photographs, that those who had been at the Remagen bridge were positive that no German bomb had destroyed the bridge. He was adamant. "They proved it. They brought me aerial photos to prove it. The Luftwaffe destroyed your bridge," he insisted. The facts made no impression on him. He refused to be budged. And his legend lived long after he swallowed his cyanide capsule. Be that as it may, the Luftwaffe did set up some earth tremors which certainly did nothing to strengthen the bridge even if they did not destroy it.

The attacks of Hermann Göring's planes, including the first appearance of jet planes in the war, prompted the concentration of 50 per cent more anti-aircraft batteries than the American forces had at the Normandy beachheads. It is difficult to judge which shook the bridge the more: German artillery shells landing close by, or American anti-aircraft guns firing at the Luftwaffe. Wild and joyful bursts of fire belched from the ack-ack whenever a plane came into view, and the ground trembled some more. Soon, larger and longer-range artillery pieces wheeled into position near the bridge and whenever they boomed out their message of death the bridge shivered.

Within 2,000 yards of the bridge, a number of eight-inch American howitzers were thundering their fire out against the enemy. These big eight-inchers spewed out a total of 1,087 rounds, each one of which set up ground tremors, in the days while the bridge was in American hands.

All through the period when the bridge was in use, from March 7 to March 12, heavy traffic passed across. On March 12, recognizing the seriously weakened condition of the bridge, the Americans closed it for repairs. By that time a pontoon and treadway bridge close by made use of the original structure less vital. Yet the closing of the bridge for repairs did not relieve it of shock action. The engineers moved in with their heavy equipment. Lieutenant Hugh Mott, one of the engineers who first rushed onto the bridge to remove the demolitions on March 7, relates that he watched with some awe as those repairing the bridge "hacked at the loose supports, moved things around with cranes, clipped off bolts with their blow torches, and hammered and pounded from morning to night and then pounded some more after dark." Sipping champagne across the river in Erpel, Mott had full confidence that his fellow engineers knew what they were doing. "But they sure used a lot of heavy equipment, and they really hammered the bridge blue in the face," he recalled.

At 4 A.M. on March 8, C Company of the 9th Armored Engineer Battalion took

Round-the-clock efforts to repair the wounded bridge. U.S. ARMY SIGNAL CORPS, NATIONAL ARCHIVES

over the task of bridge maintenance and repair. On the morning of March 10, this responsibility passed to the 276th Engineer Combat Battalion. Both of these units worked on repairing the bridge while under very heavy artillery fire and air bombings.

Air compressors, electric welders, cranes and trucks moved back and forth over the injured structure, and while they were stationary they operated on the bridge flooring and supports. Naturally, they set up more vibrations, even though their object was to strengthen the bridge. Yet the repair work had proceeded very far, and informed observers believe that with twenty-four hours more time the engineers would have been able to repair the bridge sufficiently for it to remain standing. The flooring of the deck had been repaired, several floor members had been replaced, and a number of "stringers" supporting the bridge had been spliced together. The big item yet to be repaired was the truss at the point where the biggest German demolition had gone off, two-thirds of the way across the bridge on the right (south) side.

In order to repair this truss, all day long on March 16 a heavy crane had tried unsuccessfully to line up one of the broken chords with a cable stretched across both sides of the far end of the bridge. The clamps slipped when the engineers tried to take up on the cable, and the heavy crane remained on the bridge at just about its weakest point.

A security blackout hushed up the news of still another possible threat to the bridge – German V-2 bombs. The V-2's were a far more deadly form of the "pilotless aircraft" which had pestered London ever since the invasion of Normandy. The "buzz-bomb," or V-1, packed less of a punch, traveled more slowly, and always gave an advance warning. The V-2 announced its presence with a sudden rush of air, and exploded with no further warning.

After losing the Remagen Bridge, the Germans started firing V-2's at it from an area northwest of Bellendoorn, Holland. They fired about eleven rounds, several of which landed in the Rhine not far from the bridge. One round wrecked a building close to the Apollinaris Church in Remagen. The closest hit landed at 9:30 on the morning of March 12, in the backyard of a house belonging to a farmer named Herman Joseph Lange and his wife, Marion. A dozen American soldiers were billeted in the Lange house, about three hundred yards from the bridge, when the bomb struck and three of them were killed instantly. "One of them was a student from Chicago," related Frau Lange. "He wanted us to visit him after all this was over. He wasn't a fighting man. He was the kind of a boy who loved all people and won our hearts in two days. He was the kind of person who could build up friendship with the German people after the fighting stopped. But they carried out his body before I even found out his name."

Swallowed up in the V-2 crater were eight cows, two horses, two calves, three sheep, and three goats belonging to the Langes. Five or six pigs survived the blast, albeit in a dazed condition, and Frau Lange submitted that this might provide some medical clue of possible value to those investigating atomic blasts. The family dog disappeared, but limped home several weeks later. It never recovered completely from the experience.

Perhaps the bridge never recovered either. This is not to conclude that the V-2's were the straw which broke the camel's back. But it is a fact that eleven rounds of this extremely powerful explosive fell in the Remagen area, the last on the morning of March 17, several hours before the bridge collapsed. These heavy blasts undoubtedly contributed to the downfall of the bridge, although they were by no means the primary cause.

About two hundred men, principally engineers, and their equipment were working on the Ludendorff Bridge on the afternoon of March 17. Just before two o'clock, Captain Francis Goodwin, an engineer combat supply officer, walked into the railroad tunnel to investigate some German water supply equipment he had seen at the far end. Finding himself without a flashlight and unable to borrow one, Goodwin walked back onto the railroad bridge to see if he could borrow a light. As he walked across the bridge he made a mental note of how much lumber would be needed to complete the flooring and treading. He passed a squad of men policing up the odd pieces of lumber and loading them onto a 2½-ton truck. He watched them for a moment as they stacked the heavier 6×6 timbers along the sides of the bridge. He stopped briefly to talk with Major Carr, the commander of the 1058th Port Construction and Repair detachment, who did not have very long to live, and asked how long it would take to plank over the gap blown by the German demolition. Carr estimated that he could repair the gap in one more day but that it would take a month to completely repair all of the damaged parts of the bridge.

Captain Goodwin strolled across to the Remagen side of the bridge. He paused and asked one of the welders whether he had enough gas for cutting and welding. The welder assured him that the supply was adequate. The captain stopped by the crane which was trying to straighten out one of the members in the truss by tightening a cable, and he questioned the sergeant in charge about what he was attempting to do. Everything appeared to be in order. Captain Goodwin walked off the bridge at 2:45 P.M. The bridge still had fifteen minutes of life, and nothing unusual appeared to his practiced engineering eye.

At the time Captain Goodwin was leaving the bridge, Lieutenant Colonel Clayton A. Rust, the commanding officer of the 276th Engineer Combat Battalion – one of the two units of engineers working on bridge repair – was talking with a fellow officer near the center of the bridge. Rust and his battalion staff officer were walking toward the Erpel side of the bridge to inspect the progress of the work, which was concentrated two-thirds of the way across the bridge. Suddenly, about three o'clock, Colonel Rust heard a sharp riflelike report. It sounded like a rivet head being sheared off. He looked up and saw one of the hangers slowly break loose and dangle from the bridge. Then came another sharp report from behind him to the left. Another rivet had sheared off. Both of these noises came too quickly on top of each other for the colonel to shout any warning. The entire deck of the bridge started to tremble. Colonel Rust began to hear frantic cries from the men on the bridge as they dropped their tools and lumber and started to run. The whole deck was vibrating and dust was rising from the surface. Instinctively, he knew that the time was short, that everybody on the bridge was aware that it was colllapsing, and that it was every man for himself. He started to run toward the Remagen side of the bridge and in a few seconds found himself running uphill as the center span collapsed. Then the water of the Rhine swirled around his knees and in an instant he was engulfed. He had no sensation of falling, but the weight of one of the girders soon pinioned him under water. How long he was held under, Colonel Rust does not know, but suddenly his trap was sprang and he rose to the surface just as he felt his lungs would burst. Evidently another falling girder had jarred loose or jacked up the girder which had pinned him, thus reprieving him from almost certain death. The current then swept him down to the treadway bridge, where he was pulled from the Rhine, badly shaken but not seriously hurt.

"No one alive can say why the bridge collapsed," Colonel Rust said later. "The bridge was rotten throughout, many members not cut had internal fractures from our own bombing, German artillery, and from the German demolitions. The bridge was extremely weak. The upstream truss was actually useless. The entire load of traffic, equipment and dead load were supported by the good downstream truss. . . . It is

Ludendorff Bridge collapsed into the Rhine River on March 17, 1945. U.S. ARMY SIGNAL CORPS, NATIONAL ARCHIVES

my opinion as an engineer the collapse occurred as the result of vibrations caused by numerous possible sources, i.e., air compressors, one crane, a few trucks, several electric arc welders, hammering, and finally, but important, the not insignificant concussion of heavy artillery recently emplaced in the town of Remagen. . . . I believe that, as the vibration continued, the condition of the previously buckled top chord was aggravated to such an extent that it buckled completely under a load which of course it was not designed to carry."

The engineers of the 276th Engineer Combat Battalion and the 1058th Port Construction and Repair detachment lost 7 killed, 18 missing whose bodies were never recovered and 3 who subsequently died of wounds—a total of 28 who gave up their lives; 63 others working on the bridge were injured when thrown into the icy waters of the Rhine by the sudden collapse.

Scenes from the collapse of the Ludendorff railroad bridge, March 17, 1945. U.S. ARMY SIGNAL CORPS, NATIONAL ARCHIVES

A few minutes after the collapse of the bridge Army engineers rushed to rescue survivors. U.S. ARMY SIGNAL CORPS, NATIONAL ARCHIVES

Army medics removed the body of a soldier from the wreckage of the bridge.

U.S. First Army soldiers on east bank strip for the rescue of a soldier who is clinging to debris in the river.

The 51st Engineer Combat Battalion's bridge over the Rhine River, built while under German fire. The bridge was just upstream from the Ludendorff Bridge. COURTESY BARRY W. FOWLE, U.S. ARMY CORPS OF ENGINEERS

Twenty

· · · · ·

The Hitler Firing Squad

WHEN HITLER HEARD THE NEWS about the capture of the Remagen bridge, his anguished rage knew no bounds. He forthwith fired his western front commander, the aging Field Marshal von Rundstedt, and sent out a hurry call for Field Marshal Kesselring to leave his command in Italy and take charge of all operations in the west. Less than forty-eight hours after Timmermann's men had made their crossing of the Rhine, Hitler was haranguing Kesselring in Berlin, fuming that Remagen was just as dangerous as the bridgehead the Allies had made at Normandy and that those guilty should be punished. The slogan, "Wheels Must Roll for Victory," plastered on so many billboards in the Third Reich, had in practice been replaced by that brutal parody, "Heads Must Roll for Victory."

Before Hitler had set up any machinery to seek out and execute the Remagen "culprits," lower commanders were scurrying around to find scapegoats. General von Bothmer, the commandant of Bonn and Remagen, was sentenced to five years' imprisonment for his role in the loss of the bridge. To Hitler, this sentence was a light tap on the wrist; even the "suicide" of von Bothmer failed to satisfy der Führer's demand that there be a public blood-letting to set an example to the army commanders, the troops, and the people.

Hitler then decided to set up a drumhead court-martial which would act quickly to execute those he felt were responsible for the treachery at Remagen. He telephoned to Major General Rudolf Hübner, who was then commanding a Volksgrenadier division on the Russian front, and ordered him to hasten to Berlin to set up the court martial.

The confidential efficiency report on General Hübner remarked, significantly, that he had "an unhealthy ambition which influences the effectiveness of his thinking." In spite of, or perhaps because of, this trait, Hübner rose fast in the German Army. As a regimental commander, he not only had a good battle record but endeared himself to the high Nazis by making a number of recommendations on how the armed forces in the field could be infused with more of the Nazi spirit. Hitler personally had seen some of his reports, and had brought him to Berlin once before to help develop a corps of National Socialist "guidance officers." Hübner also gave Nazi propaganda lectures at various headquarters; one of the lectures was described by a high-ranking

German staff officer as "an oily and cunning threat against all officers who furthered ideas that were not 100 per cent consistent with the official party line."

Hübner received his divisional command on the Oder front in January, 1945, and shortly thereafter Hitler visited him at some length in the field. This was an unusual honor for Hübner, for Hitler rarely left his headquarters after being injured on July 20, 1944, in the bombing attempt on his life. The two men hit it off beautifully. Hübner said in later years that he immediately "succumbed to the demoniac power of this man. I was an absolute follower of Hitler. I had complete confidence in him and believed that he was Germany's savior." For his part, Hitler found an army man who considered Nazi loyalty the most important factor in military strategy. So Hitler did not have to look far when he sought a man who would exact swift penalties for the Remagen debacle.

Hübner arrived in Berlin on March 10 for his conference with Hitler. He found Hitler bitter and vindictive, although at the same time persuasively factual when he talked about Remagen. Hitler reviewed developments in both theaters of war, pointing out that there would inevitably come a break between the Anglo-Americans and the Russians which would save Germany. He argued that if the Germans could hold the Rhine front they still might have a chance to win the war, but this could be only if lack of discipline and cowardice were stamped out ruthlessly. To accomplish this all-important objective, he explained, he was setting up a special court martial and giving General Hübner the high and patriotic mission of presiding over the court. Hitler alternately flattered Hübner and fired his ambition. He went on to talk for half an hour about the duties of the special court-martial. The first case to be tried was that of the culprits at Remagen Bridge. Hitler launched into a loud tirade against the guilty ones who were responsible for the loss of the bridge, which he described as a national disaster and a military catastrophe of the first order. When Hübner left the conference his blood was stirring with indignation against the traitors of Remagen.

Two other army officers were assigned to the special court martial, Lieutenant Colonels Paul Penth and Anton Ehrnsperger. None of the three officers had any legal training. The composition of the court reflected Hitler's profound distrust of jurists and the rules by which they bound themselves. Although the code of German military law was quite explicit in the procedure and jurisdiction of courts martial, the Hitler tribunal was bound by none of these regulations. It was also unique among trial bodies in that it had its own execution squad which traveled along behind the court during its deliberations, simply waiting for the opportunity to do its duty when the guilty ones had been designated.

General Hübner dominated the three-man court. Penth and Ehrnsperger followed his lead in all matters connected with the work of the court. The two lieutenant colonels knew that Hübner would never have countenanced any serious opposition and that he could have summarily replaced either of them at the slightest provocation. Penth was an even more rabid Nazi than Hübner, and he was convinced that he also was performing a high patriotic mission by rooting out cowardice and lack of discipline through fire and the sword. He had distinguished himself in combat as an engineer officer, and had served in the Army Personnel Office. Ehrnsperger, though sufficiently impressed by National Socialist thought to believe Hitler a genius, was not a member of the Nazi party and did not go about his job on the court martial with the same point of view as the other two members. He was the junior member of the court, and was considerably younger than the other two. Although, as the trials progressed, he developed some reservations about the way the court was operating, he felt himself too young to argue with his superiors and fanatically convinced colleagues.

On the evening of March 10, the members of the special court began their rounds. They called first at Kesselring's headquarters. Kesselring's eyes blazed with anger as he told Hübner that the Remagen affair was a filthy business and that it might result in the collapse of the whole western front. Early the next morning the trio proceeded to the headquarters of Field Marshal Model, commander of Army Group B.

The brilliant, quick-tongued Model had already formed his own opinions about who was to blame for the Remagen affair, and he did not relish having an outside court martial turn up evidence that he should find himself. In his many trips to his corps and army command posts, Model kept an eye out for possible culprits. On one of these trips, on March 10, he discovered the unfortunate Major Scheller, just reporting back to his LXVII Corps command post at Altwied. Model and Hitzfeld asked Scheller to tell them in detail just what had happened at Remagen. Scheller described, step by step, his arduous trip to Remagen during the rainy night of March 6, and the harrowing events at the bridge on March 7.

"But why did you leave the bridge?" Model asked sharply.

"I grabbed a bicycle, and went to try and get help," Scheller answered, still confident.

"Why didn't you telephone for help, or at least organize a counterattack?" Model persisted. Scheller's voice now quavered a little.

"The telephone was out, and I thought it was important that higher headquarters get news of the situation."

Model looked at Scheller with some scorn, and then rasped at him:

"Why did it take three days for you to get back here from Remagen? Why did you desert your unit?" This was more than an implication. Scheller winced as he replied, and his answer sounded lame, even to himself:

"Herr Feldmarschall, I was commandeered to hold a road block. Then when I tried to get back to my corps, it had moved its command post. I did my best."

At this point, Model interrupted and, according to General Hitzfeld, "seized Scheller's shoulder in a rather despicable manner and shouted: 'Here we have one who is guilty.'"

Model also had his men out hunting up other officers—somehow nobody higher than a major turned up—who could be charged with responsibility for the events at Remagen. He told the members of his staff that he wanted these men prosecuted quickly and energetically. He said pointedly that if they did not proceed with the proper energy the whole headquarters would suffer in the eyes of Hitler. They all understood that their necks depended on sticking together and finding culprits who were neither directly on the Army Group B staff nor favorites around the headquarters.

When the special court arrived in the zone of Army B, Field Marshal Model was asked to assign to it an officer who could help in resolving any legal questions. Model detailed his own Army Group legal officer, Colonel Felix Janert, for the task. It was a difficult job for Janert to perform, because he had to keep Model informed and satisfied, and he also had to serve General Hübner without being a full member of the court and without being able to influence Hübner's actions. Whatever reservations he had about the court's methods of procedure Janert could not express openly, lest he run the risk of being accused of sabotage and being executed himself.

One of the first things Colonel Janert asked General Hübner was whether he should supply members of the special court with the military justice code and the war-time regulations on military criminal procedure. Hübner dismissed the suggestion, expressing the opinion that only the Führer's order was necessary as a guide to the special court martial, and that the court martial was not to be bound at all by the wartime regulations on military criminal procedure. He also waved aside suggestions that defense counsel be supplied for those accused.

The court first interviewed general officers who had been in charge of the engineers or defense troops in the area. They talked with Lieutenant General Botsch, who had authority over tactical operations at Remagen from March 1 until eight P.M. on March 6, when he had been given command of a corps; General Janowski, in command of engineer operations in the Remagen sector; General Wirtz, the Engineer Officer of Army Group B; and General von Berg, who had commanded the Wehrkreis in the Remagen area. These officers were quizzed about the chain of command, and the names of all subordinate officers who had anything to do with Remagen. For a while the finger of suspicion pointed at one general officer, General von Kortzfleisch, head of the Rhine Defense Sector, because he had not taken all possible measures to recapture the bridge. The court and General von Kortzfleisch agreed that he had a valid excuse, however: his orders, transmitted to him by radio, had been all too brief, they had not mentioned the units under his control, communications had been disrupted, and he had received his orders too late to enable him to counter-attack. Explanations just as valid as these fell on very deaf ears when presented by lower-ranking officers who were dragged before the court martial.

For a brief time on the morning of March 11, the jurists examined witnesses and assembled evidence. Besides questioning Scheller, they concentrated their fire on the two engineer majors, Herbert Strobel and August Kraft, and an anti-aircraft lieutenant, Karl Heinz Peters. The court began to develop the theory that Strobel, commander of an engineer regimental staff charged with responsibility for protecting river crossings in a wide area along the Rhine, should have led a counterattack once the bridge was lost. On each of three interviews he had with the members of the court, Strobel became more agitated, and before he left his command post for the last meeting with the court-martial Strobel remarked to his adjutant that "they are trying very hard to find a culprit." Strobel commented that if the court tried to accuse him, he would speak out and tell them that if Hitler knew how his generals were shirking their responsibility, and if he knew all about their actions and their conflicting orders, there would be plenty of sudden changes. He asked one of his staff to prepare a report on why the demolitions had not destroyed the bridge at Remagen, and he took this report with him when he appeared for interrogation on March 11. Although he was agitated by the unfair way in which the court appeared to be questioning him, he was confident that he would emerge with a clean bill of health. He was an energetic officer according to all those who knew him, thorough, loyal and very able.

Major Kraft, commander of the engineer battalion whose troops were at the Remagen Bridge, was even more confident that he would prove his innocence. He was a very quiet and modest officer, almost to the point of being inarticulate, but extremely conscientious and indefatigable in everything he attempted. He was fifty-four years old at the time of the Remagen episode and could look back with some pride on his civilian and military career. He had won an Iron Cross, First Class, during World War I, and had established a distinguished record as a civil servant in the postal service. Those who did not know Kraft well termed him "mousy" because he was inclined to be self-effacing and at times appeared to be indolent. His superiors quickly learned that they could get ahead by standing on his shoulders, because he would go to any lengths in order to get a job done well. His subordinates loved and admired him for his willingness to fight for their rights and shoulder the blame for their mistakes.

After one trip to visit the court-martial, Kraft returned to tell his adjutant that "everything was in order and the matter was settled." On the morning that he left his command post to be tried, he casually told his staff that he would be back at noon. He told his driver the same thing.

Scheller, somewhat shaken by the denunciatory remarks of Model, nevertheless was firmly resolved to fight for his innocence. The events at Remagen and the encounter with Model were enough to break most men, but Scheller had pride and determination and he hoped he could convince the court martial that he had done everything that could be expected.

Lieutenant Karl Heinz Peters, a young and impressionable regular officer of the anti-aircraft branch of the Air Force, had been entrusted with great responsibility for an officer of his age in being given command of the experimental anti-aircraft battery equipped with the super-secret new rocket launchers. Of all the officers who stood trial, Peters was the most pessimistic about the results. He felt that he had done something wrong, and his youth did not help his bearing before the court martial.

At four o'clock on the afternoon of March 11 the court martial convened in the house of a farmer named Eschemann in the little town of Rimbach, some thirty miles east of the Rhine. Hübner, Penth and Ehrnsperger sat on a couch in the sitting room. Above them hung a framed canvas on which was inscribed this motto in big black letters: "If God be for us, who can be against us?" Janert, Model's legal representative, sat in a lone chair to the side. There was no recorder. No one else was present in the room. Guards stood outside the door to make sure the proceedings were carried on in private.

General Hübner asked Janert to prepare a written indictment against each of the accused officers, setting forth the crimes of which he was accused. He quickly cleared his throat, swore in the other judges, and announced that the special court martial would proceed to the first case, that of Captain Willi Bratge. Bratge was tried in absentia, and no witness or other individual appeared to defend him. The judges discussed the evidence they had gathered from eyewitnesses and from staff officers who had made inquiries about developments at the bridge. Bratge was accused of not having given the order to blow the bridge at the proper time, despite the fact that he was the responsible combat commander. There was some evidence that Bratge had delayed issuing the demolition order, despite the insistence of Captain Friesenhahn, the engineer commander at the bridge. He was also accused of having withdrawn into the railroad tunnel instead of fighting the bridge crossing as hard as he might have, and was reproached for not launching a stronger counterattack. Finally, he was accused of surrendering the German troops in the tunnel without resisting as long as he might have. These charges were quickly disposed of, and the court martial voted to sentence Bratge to death in absentia, despite the comments of the legal counsel, Janert. Janert carefully expressed the opinion that it was not legal to sentence Bratge to death since he was not present to defend himself, but the other judges on the court ignored this argument. Janert felt that it was not worthwhile pressing his opinion very hard, because Bratge was absent and it would not be possible to carry out the death sentence. He felt that there would be time later, if Bratge reappeared, to have a fuller trial. Janert concluded that Bratge was being sentenced to death in order to make a deeper impression of the seriousness of the Remagen affair, and to serve as propaganda.

The irascible General Hübner then summoned Major Scheller to appear before the court martial. The door of the sitting room opened, and Scheller was prodded slightly by two noncoms who told him that he was wanted inside. The tall, young officer slowly and stiffly walked up in front of his accusers. His pale, intelligent face revealed the strain of the past week's developments. Hübner, in the center of the couch, rustled a few papers on a small table in front of him, but did not consult the papers as he thundered his accusations at Scheller. Where was he when it was time to blow the bridge? Why hadn't he seen to it that it was blown up promptly? Why had he disappeared when the crucial moment came to blow the bridge? Was he hiding in the railroad tunnel? Where had he gone after the Americans crossed the bridge? Wasn't he responsible as the officer in command for launching an immediate counterattack? If he had left to get help, why had it taken him three days to get back to corps headquarters? What proof could he offer, at this very minute, that he had not been acting negligently, and in a cowardly fashion. In fact, was he not guilty of high treason by his actions? As Scheller became more and more rattled, Hübner's stream of questions quickly merged into high-pitched denunciations.

Scheller looked around desperately at the others in the room. Penth, at Hübner's right, sat stolid, barely flicking an eyelash. His lips were pressed tightly together. He calmly took off his glasses and polished them. When he put them on again they gave him a look of serenity. Ehrnsperger, to Hübner's left, looked eager and interested, but did not open his mouth. Janert, off to one side, seemed to be trying to cover up whatever he was thinking. In his Bavarian dialect, Scheller tried to penetrate the unfriendly atmosphere. He carefully explained that he had assumed command of the bridge only a very short time before the American troops came. He stressed that the bridge had been seized so rapidly he had not even had time to figure out the complicated command channels through which he had to operate. Elaborating on this point, he testified that no one, in the few hours available, could have familiarized himself with all the technical details of how the bridge was to be blown up. Furthermore, he added, he simply didn't have enough troops for an effective counterattack. He had begun to build up a fairly convincing case of the complexities of the situation at Remagen when Hübner cut him short with the thunderous accusation that his cowardice and treachery had enabled the enemies of the Reich to breach the Rhine.

As Janert listened to Hübner's diatribe, he thought back to a conversation he had had with Model about Scheller. After hearing an account of Scheller's actions, the field marshal had commented: "Well, as commanding officer at the bridge, he was responsible for demolishing the bridge in good time, wasn't he? And if he failed to do that, it's a capital offense and the death sentence is surely justified." Janert knew that Model had talked to Hübner about Scheller, and he recognized that Hübner was impatiently moving toward the inevitable verdict.

Hübner had indeed got "the word" from Model in no uncertain terms. As his voice rose to a new crescendo, his denunciation was intensified with contempt for Scheller. After all, wasn't this the officer that Model told him had made false reports to his corps commander about what happened at Remagen? And hadn't General Hitzfeld, the corps commander, even recommended Scheller for a high decoration after hearing these absurd stories? Hübner became more violent. He upbraided and abused Scheller for having the gall to defend his actions. (Later, Hübner said in a sworn statement: "I am unable to say how long the trial against Scheller lasted, nor could I say how many times Scheller was heard. I admit, however, that I addressed Scheller roughly and angrily during the trial. I was injured several times on my head so that my slight irritability is attributed to that. These injuries were apparently the reason for my impulsive and precipitate behavior.")

Penth joined briefly in the denunciation of Scheller. He pointed out that Scheller had been guilty of gross negligence in failing to take decisive action when the Americans first approached the bridge. Furthermore, he continued smoothly, Scheller had shown his complete wretchedness and cowardice by his performance after the Americans crossed. Then came Penth's most scathing comments: "One could really expect from a general staff officer some understanding, willingness to command and resolution. Instead of reorganizing the confused troops into a defensive force, he left the leadership to an infantry lieutenant of his division and asserted that he had to go to the rear area in order to report the incident. He thus got out of his responsibilities through his unbelievable cowardice."

Hübner screamed at the thoroughly cowed Scheller, "Do you admit your cowardice and your guilt?"

Scheller resignedly mumbled in the affirmative as he was led from the room.

It took very little deliberation for the court to decide Scheller's fate. The words of Model had made the death sentence virtually mandatory. Scheller's defense that he had been unfamiliar with the situation, that he could not get proper orientation during the period of extreme confusion, that he did not know the chain of command or the technical details of how the bridge was to be demolished, and that there were hardly enough German troops to recapture the bridge – none of these points made any impression on the judges. The legal representative, Janert, tried to criticize Scheller in less stringent terms by pointing out that his role at Remagen had been hazy and questionable, that he had neglected certain obvious things, and that he was unequal to the tasks which had been imposed on him. Janert tried to imply that although Scheller was guilty of negligence, his guilt was insufficient to justify a death sentence. Of course, Janert could not press this line of reasoning very strongly – the intention of the court had been too obvious from the start. Almost perfunctorily, the court pronounced Scheller's death sentence.

Hardly had the sentence been pronounced when General Hübner ordered Lieutenant Karl Heinz Peters brought in. To the three judges, the case of Lieutenant Peters was even more cut and dried. They all felt that it deserved little of their time. "We can make this short," General Hübner said.

Peters was shaking slightly when he entered the room to stand before the court. A regular officer still in his early twenties, he seemed even younger as he reddened and shifted from foot to foot before the terrifying glances of the judges. Not a word was spoken for a minute or two.

Peters tried to run through his story in his mind as he waited for the judges to speak. He had been in command of an anti-aircraft battery, equipped with a new and top-secret weapon (Flakwerfer 44) – a series of rocket-launchers which could hurl shells at enemy planes at a high rate of speed and with phenomenal accuracy. Because of the highly classified nature of this weapon, Peters knew that it should be destroyed if there were danger that it might fall into Allied hands. On the day the Americans had captured the Remagen Bridge, Peters had most of his battery deployed on the west bank of the Rhine. As the American forces approached and their guns boomed in the distance, he started to move his battery across the bridge. Traffic was congested, progress was slow, communications were poor, and some of the younger men in his battery kept drifting away. He lost much precious time trying to keep them together. Unnerved by the magnitude of his task, and appalled by the confusion, he vainly ran back and forth across the bridge in his efforts to maintain control. He had waited before ordering any of his top-secret weapons to be blown up, because he wanted to save them if he possibly could. The instructions he issued to his battery were therefore to destroy them only if they could not be taken across the Rhine. In trying to stay with his main body of men and weapons, Peters was on the east side of the Rhine when he discovered that the time had passed when he could safely go back to the west bank to find out if there were any stragglers or weapons left. So he could not prove definitely that the rocket launchers had all been destroyed, even though he had left orders to that effect. Once across the Rhine, Peters started his depleted battery on a road march eastward to Weimar, where the technical service of this experimental new battery, the Inspector of Anti-Aircraft Artillery, was located. Only then did he discover that some of his weapons were unaccounted for. He confidently assumed that they had been destroyed as per his orders.

Peters had little chance to tell his story or to justify his actions. His thoughts were interrupted by a rasping, almost snarling accusation by General Hübner: "You are guilty of high treason and deserve to be shot for your cowardice!" Peters gasped. This was not a question, although General Hübner seemed to demand some kind of answer. Peters mumbled, "Yes, sir." The words escaped unconsciously. He had meant only to indicate that he had heard Hübner's stunning words; he had not intended to express agreement. But Hübner warmed up to his task:

"Oh, so you admit your guilt, do you, young man? You admit you let one of our greatest military secrets fall into enemy hands? You admit that you did not destroy these precious rocket-launchers which der Führer planned as one of the secret weapons which would throw back the Americans?"

Hübner's voice rose as before in thunderous denunciation. Peters shrank under the wordy barrage. Janert, the legal expert, was astounded. Hübner had in front of him numerous notes and legal papers on Peters, including the record of a court martial charge by the Division of Anti-Aircraft Artillery, but he mentioned none of these. Nor did he even take the trouble to read or prefer a charge against Peters. (Hübner and his associates vehemently denied that they acted arbitrarily, but he later said in a sworn statement: "I do not remember the details of the trial. I do know though that we were all horrified as to what a disappointing officer he was. It is therefore possible that his hearing was very short, since the question of guilt was very obvious.")

Hübner impatiently and abruptly brought the farce to a close by issuing a stark sentence of death by shooting. This caused the other judges to lean forward slightly, but they made no objection. The trembling young Peters, speechless, was taken by the arm, and he stumbled toward the exit. Hübner shot one more sarcastic barb at him before he left the room: "You are a coward, and you deserve to be shot to death. You admit that, don't you?"

"Yes, I must admit that," Peters said almost inaudibly as he went out the door.

Penth later insisted that the trial had really lasted more than a few minutes. "It may be true," claimed Penth, "that Hübner addressed the defendant violently. It is also true that Hübner cast strong reproaches upon him. But I do not remember that Hübner insulted Peters or called any of the other defendants 'swine.' It is out of the question that such strong language was used."

After the trial of Scheller and Peters, the two officers were taken under heavy military guard to the home of Heinrich Ochsenbrücher, also in Rimbach. One of the Ochsenbrücher daughters, Mrs. Minna Bitzer, prepared a simple meal for the two officers and persuaded the guards to allow the condemned men to eat. On the morning of March 12 about ten o'clock, a farmer from Rimbach named Wilhelm Schumacher, who was tending his fields outside of town, looked up from his work to see a squad of ten soldiers leading a German officer into the woods several hundred yards away. The procession sloshed through huge puddles of water left by several days of rain. The officer's hands were handcuffed behind his back. Schumacher recognized the insignia of the soldiers as from the Grossdeutschland Division. All of them carried rifles.

Several orders were barked shortly after the soldiers entered the woods. Then Schumacher heard a volley. Not long afterward, the soldiers marched out of the woods. Later that day another squad of soldiers appeared with a second officer, handcuffed in the same way. The volley of shots rang out again, signaling the death of the second of the two officers condemned by the court-martial. They were both shot in the back of the neck.

The men who paid the extreme penalty were not accorded the services of a chaplain in their last hours. They received thirty minutes in which to write to their families and then were taken out to be executed. The bodies were looted, and the letters to their families were burned. The squad of executioners threw several spadefuls of earth over the corpses and marched away, leaving them only a few inches under the surface of the ground.

On the day that Scheller and Peters were sentenced to be shot to death, Major Herbert Strobel and Major August Kraft were summoned from their posts and ordered to report to an unnamed headquarters in Oberirsen, a little town rear Rimbach in the Westerwald. Between eight and nine o'clock that evening, Heinrich Schmidt, a rugged farmer in his mid-fifties, answered a knock on his door to find a group of soldiers asking for quarters for Strobel and Kraft. Although some military personnel were already staying at Schmidt's house, he made one room available for the two German majors. They spent the night at Herr Schmidt's without guard.

After Kraft and Strobel had got settled, Herr Schmidt came to their room and talked with them for several hours. They told him that they had been ordered to report to headquarters at Oberirsen, but they did not know the reason. They appeared calm and confident in their conversation with him, which ranged over many subjects, including a review of the desperate situation which Germany was facing on all fronts of war. As they talked, Mrs. Schmidt served coffee and food to the visiting officers, who were very appreciative of these courtesies. About midnight they went to sleep, and the house was quiet throughout the night.

On the following morning, Majors Kraft and Strobel reported to Field Marshal

Model's headquarters in the Pick Restaurant in Oberirsen. The court martial got under way in the Pick Restaurant just about the same time that the firing squad was doing its work in Rimbach.

As Kraft and Strobel prepared to face the court on the morning of March 12, their consciences were clear. Blissfully unaware of the kind of trial that awaited them, they were confident that an objective review of their relationships to the loss of the Remagen Bridge would absolve them of any blame.

Strobel entered the judgment chamber first. He was met almost immediately by a barrage of questions in an accusatory tone. General Hübner and his colleagues on the court berated him mercilessly on a number of counts: Why had he remained at his regimental command post on the night of March 7? Why hadn't he gone to the bridge personally? Why hadn't he succeeded if he was really trying to launch a counter-attack to blow up the bridge? Why hadn't he pursued a more determined counterattack on the next day? To these questions, Strobel could only reply that he had taken a big risk on the night of March 7 by starting the counterattack even though this conflicted with his assigned mission of manning and protecting the Rhine ferries; that the darkness of the night had made it difficult for an organized counterattack to get through and blow up the bridge; that strong American forces had checked his attempt at the break of dawn on March 8; that he had had no artillery and tanks necessary for a successful counterattack; that he had been caught between the conflicting orders of Wirtz, von Berg, and Janowski.

To these protestations by Major Strobel, Hübner, Penth and Ehrnsperger reacted with scoffing and jeering. They termed him a coward for sticking to his command post. They blamed him personally for the failure of the counterattack. Strobel's defense, which on paper seemed quite strong, collapsed in the face of these prejudged conclusions. He threw up his hands and resigned himself to his fate.

Some years later, Count von Schwerin, who had been a panzer division and corps commander on the western front, investigated the circumstances of the trial and the sentences imposed. Writing an opinion for the court at Koblenz which was investigating the war guilt of Hübner, Penth and Ehrnsperger, von Schwerin had this to say about Strobel's role at Remagen:

"Major Strobel cannot be blamed for not having proceeded personally to the bridge. On the evening of March 7 he and his staff had the more pressing mission of concentrating their forces and launching the attack. On March 8 his time during the forenoon was fully taken up, under most confusing circumstances, by his efforts to protect himself against contradictory and, in some cases, impracticable orders. Major Strobel was the engineer commander and was responsible for the crossing operation of an entire army over the Rhine in the face of hotly pursuing enemy forces. More importance certainly must be attached to the missions he had to perform here than to the requirement that he should have been at the bridge personally, where he could not, in practice, have changed the situation anyway. There is a possibility that, on the whole, he was not active enough. However, this would not justify the imposition of the death sentence and his immediate execution. A crime meriting the death penalty would have been evident only if Strobel had, with criminal intent, withheld the forces available to him or had refused to carry out orders. Neither of these two circumstances existed."

Proceeding with its mission of selecting heads to roll, the court turned next to Major Kraft. The quiet, almost impassive fifty-four-year-old Kraft was completely shattered by the charges hurled at him by Hübner and the two other members of the court. He considered the accusations as gross insults to his loyalty. Disgusted by the whole proceeding, he chose not to dignify the charges by answering them. Kraft tried to do only one thing: to put in a strong plea for his subordinate, Captain Friesenhahn, even though he knew that Friesenhahn was an American prisoner and could not be tried in person. Unable to speak effectively, reluctant to try to defend himself when others' lives were at stake, and revolted by the indecency of the trial, Kraft made little attempt to justify his own actions. The louder Hübner screamed at him, the more reticent Kraft became, until he finally acknowledged – preserving his dignity to the last – that he was anxious to get the trial over with and would say he was guilty.

As almost an anticlimax, the court quickly acquitted Captain Friesenhahn in absentia. It is difficult to establish precisely why Bratge should have been sentenced to death and Friesenhahn acquitted. Friesenhahn, a World War I veteran, had been a member of the National Socialist Party since 1933. Bratge had also been a Nazi party member, but for a far shorter time. Both officers had had distinguished military records during World War II. Janert, the legal adviser to the court, asserts that he was able to intervene effectively in behalf of an acquittal for Friesenhahn. Perhaps the court was convinced by Major Kraft's statements that Friesenhahn had taken more active steps than Bratge to blow the bridge. Also, it may have been influenced by the fact that Bratge had surrendered his troops in the tunnel, although it is difficult to ascertain how the court could have received a factual report of the surrender at the time it passed judgment.

On the morning of March 13, Majors Strobel and Kraft were taken out to a wooded area near Oberirsen. Their hands were handcuffed behind their backs. They were shot to death through the backs of their necks. No chaplain was present. They were buried in less than a foot of soil where they fell. Only after Major Kraft's son, Günther, returned from the war did the two bodies receive decent burial in a Lutheran cemetery at Dirnbach.

Field Marshals Kesselring and Model then sent out a special teletype to all members of the armed forces, stating that "an important bridge across the Rhine has fallen into enemy hands without being damaged, despite the fact that all preparations for its demolition had been made. This has happened because the responsible leaders have abandoned the bridgehead. They have acted in an irresponsible and cowardly way. The five guilty officers were condemned to death by court martial, one of them, a captain, in absentia. The sentence was executed against three majors and one first lieutenant. The above information is to be communicated to all troops as rapidly as possible and should be considered as a warning to everyone. Who does not live in honor will die in shame." This was followed by a communiqué in which the names of the executed officers were made public.

Twenty-one
. . . .

Facts and Fiction

HITLER'S TRAVELING COURT, complete with firing squad, had done its job. Five culprits had been selected. The four in German hands had died, and the fifth was a prisoner of the Americans. Even the Germans, however, must have had doubts as to whether justice had indeed been done. Scapegoats had been needed – and supplied. But the truth as to what had really brought on the Remagen debacle was too elusive to grasp so soon after the event. Even years later, although the evidence points to some definite conclusions, parts of the story are still untold, and conjecture must fill in the gaps.

Shortly after the event, many newspapers carried accounts quoting Sergeant Joseph DeLisio to the effect that he had captured a German engineer captain who was supposed to have blown the bridge but was found drunk. Questioned about the newspaper stories later, DeLisio commented that they were accurate except for these details: (1) the officer was a lieutenant instead of a captain; (2) the officer, although an engineer, had no assigned responsibility for blowing the bridge; (3) the officer was seized in a cellar in Remagen, on the west side of the river, and was not near the bridge at the time of his capture; (4) the German officer never laid claim to having anything to do with the bridge, but was apparently one of a group assigned to defend Remagen and was only easing the pain of impending capture through a little imbibing. Other reports of the drunkenness of German officers and soldiers appear to have even less relationship to the facts.

More plausible, perhaps, are the accounts which relate to possible sabotage of the demolitions, either by the regular German troops, by civilians in Remagen, or by some of the foreign workmen in Remagen and near the bridge. Sensational writers in German pictorial weekly magazines have written lurid stories of German officers at Remagen who "sold out" to the Americans for bags of gold, sabotaging the demolition charges to prevent the bridge from being destroyed.

One tale – that Major Scheller was such a traitor – is a patent falsehood. In the first place, there is no contemporary record or reliable postwar recollection that any American officer or agent dealt with any German officer or agent about sabotaging the Remagen bridge. Any American agent interested in making such a deal would have selected a bridge at a point where the Americans really wanted to cross – such as Cologne or opposite the Ruhr. Had an American agent succeeded in making a deal, he certainly would have informed the advancing American troops so that they could take advantage of it and converge on the Remagen bridge. The 9th Armored Division approached gingerly, and the sight of the bridge still standing came as a complete surprise. From Major Scheller's standpoint, if he had indeed intended to betray his cause to the Americans he would probably have contrived to get himself captured by the Americans. For Scheller to make such a deal with the enemy and then to show up at corps headquarters, he would have had to be wholly lacking in intelligence, and the record shows that he was not a stupid man.

Among other military personnel at the Remagen bridge, however, the facts about sabotage are somewhat less clear. There is, for example, the story told by Private Karl Hennige, a member of Captain Friesenhahn's engineer company. Hennige, born in Alsace, veteran of the First World War, was forty-eight years old at the time of Remagen. He was inducted into the German army in 1940 at Metz, was assigned later to Captain Friesenhahn's engineer company, and contrived to have his wife take up residence in the town of Remagen. As the Allies approached, Mrs. Hennige urged her husband to surrender at the earliest possible moment. He evidently had even better ideas—or so he claimed when interrogated after his capture by a Mobile Field Interrogation Unit of General Bradley's headquarters. Although he had joined the German army in 1940 in order to escape forced labor or deportation, he had been a French citizen by reason of his residence in Lorraine after World War I, and his sympathies were French.

Hennige claimed that he was the last German soldier to cross the Remagen bridge to the east bank prior to the crossing of the American troops. He was about two-thirds of the way across when, about two P.M., heavy American machine gun fire forced him to drop onto his stomach temporarily for protection. Close enough to touch were two cables that connected with the main demolition charge and also the emergency fuse. Using two five-centimeter mortar shells which he had with him, Hennige's statement continued, he smashed the fuse band and then cut the cable with his pocketknife. After he had cut the wires, he ran to the east side of the river and took shelter in the railroad tunnel.

If Hennige's story was true, he had cut the demolition cable more than an hour before Captain Friesenhahn unsuccessfully turned the plunger to try and set off the main demolition. But the German officers at the Remagen Bridge claim that the circuit was tested and found to work as late at 3:12 P.M., an hour after Hennige says he cut the cable. Whose account can be accepted? Hennige supplies no details on how he managed to cut the cable under the eyes of the watchful guards; on the other hand, those who deny the Hennige version supply no details which prove conclusively that the circuit was sound when tested at 3:12 P.M. Captain Friesenhahn, who was interrogated immediately after Hennige, scoffed at Hennige's story, pointing out that the demolition cable was imbedded in a strong pipe, which could not possibly have been cut by knife.

A somewhat more detailed account was given to the American authorities in March, 1945, by Stanislaus Sevinski, a Polish laborer. At the time American troops first crossed the Remagen Bridge, Sevinski was a member of "Construction Platoon Posen I," consisting of Polish and Russian laborers. The unit was stationed in Erpel, directly across the river from Remagen. On March 6, the day before the bridge was captured, Sevinski's account goes, he and the members of his platoon were ordered to install planking over the railroad tracks of the bridge to enable vehicles to cross. Once they finished the planking, late on March 6, they were not allowed to go onto the bridge again. Sevinski and his fellow members of the construction platoon lived in the railroad tunnel on the Erpel side of the river. They knew that the demolition wire ran from a generator in the railroad tunnel out to the explosive charges near the east pier of the bridge. They watched the demolitions being placed and prepared by Regular Army members of Captain Friesenhahn's engineer company.

According to Sevinski, the foreign workers in the railroad tunnel held a secret meeting and decided that they would do everything possible to preserve the bridge so that the attacking Americans could cross it. They selected a Polish worker, whose name Sevinski did not know, to cut the wire in the tunnel. (The wire was connected with the ignition switch, located right at the entrance to the tunnel. The ignition switch set off the demolition on the bridge itself.) In order to forestall detection by the German engineer demolition squad which checked the connection every few minutes, the Polish saboteur bound the ends of the cut wire together, thus preserving the taut appearance of the unimpaired connection. He did this in the darkness of the railroad tunnel, where there were no lights and there were no German soldiers watching him. Then, just before Captain Friesenhahn ordered all in the tunnel to lie down and cover their ears before the attempted blast, the Polish worker jerked the wires apart.

The compelling part of Sevinski's story is that his description of the planking of the bridge, the placement of the demolition charges, and the general timetable of events—all the way through his recollection of Captain Friesenhahn's order just before the attempted demolition—coincides precisely with events as they actually developed. But did Sevinski's friend actually cut the wire? It is interesting that Sevinski did not claim this credit for himself in talking with the American troops, nor did he name the man who had performed this service. Thus he could not have told the story to get a reward for either himself or his unnamed associate, although he may have told it to become the center of attention.

Captain Bratge and Captain Friesenhahn both heatedly deny that there could have been any truth in Sevinski's account. They base their denial on these facts: (1) the demolition cable was carefully guarded at all times and could never have been cut under the noses of the guards; (2) the plunger for activating the demolition charges was *outside* the railroad tunnel, and the wire could never have been cut inside the tunnel. It is true, however, that the generator supplying power for the electric circuit was located inside the tunnel, and it is conceivable that the current may have been cut off. This Bratge and Friesenhahn also deny in the most strenuous terms, claim-

ing that if the circuit was in working order in the test three minutes before the attempted demolition, then the generator could have had nothing to do with the matter.

Unfortunately, Sevinski and his associates in "Construction Platoon Posen I" have
melted into obscurity, and with them any opportunity to check further. After a brief
moment of triumph when they lorded it over their former captors, looted the stores
of Remagen, and drank up the stocks of champagne and wine in the town, they stayed
around briefly to cheer their American liberators. The Americans used them as in-
terpreters, and the Poles and Russians proceeded to even old scores with the Remagen
civilians, who in turn did everything possible to make their life uncomfortable. Finally,
tiring of their new role as oppressors, they started to slip out of town and move back
toward the east, leaving behind no address or record by which they could be traced
in case the fortunes of war changed once again.

Still another provocative clue may be found in a statement by Sergeant Gustav
Vogel, a noncommissioned officer in Captain Friesenhahn's engineer company.
Sergeant Vogel, who came from Vienna, was known to be opposed to the Nazi régime,
but there is no evidence that he belonged to any group that wanted to prevent the
destruction of the bridge. Captured by the first American troops who crossed the
bridge on March 7, Vogel said nothing to his interrogators about sabotage but made
some harsh remarks about Captain Bratge, who he claimed spent his time in the
tunnel while Captain Friesenhahn was trying in vain to secure the order to blow the
bridge. On the morning of March 7, Vogel told his Remagen girl friend that she need
not have any concern about the Ludendorff Bridge, for there was no danger that it
would be demolished. Vogel confidently went on to tell her that the bridge would
remain standing even if the bridge commander had to be killed. After the dramatic
events of the afternoon of March 7, the girl recalled vividly what Vogel had told her,
and she repeated it. But Vogel never revealed his source of information, did not indicate that he would do anything about preserving the bridge, and perhaps made
the remark merely to allay the fears of his frightened girl friend.

The late Dr. Gustav Zeck, who was the official historian of the city of Remagen
for many years, prepared an account entitled "The Last Weeks of the War in Remagen,"
in the course of which he scouted the possibility of sabotage: "It is quite certain, and
this has been supported by conversations with many eyewitnesses, that more than
a few military personnel—especially members of the bridge maintenance company—
were against the Nazi regime and objected to its desire to prolong the war. It is possible
that this may have resulted in some concerted action. Having talked to many members
of the bridge maintenance company, I am convinced that many know more than they
are willing to tell about certain actions. Since they will not talk, it is impossible to
secure clarity about developments, and without clarity every investigator is reduced to
probabilities. Therefore the question must be phrased: Is the possibility of sabotage such
that sabotage is also probable?" Dr. Zeck, after reviewing the evidence, concluded that
despite the reluctance of many members of the bridge maintenance company to talk
about the matter in detail, it was "highly improbable" that sabotage actually occurred.

In company with Captains Bratge and Friesenhahn, Manfred Michler (the German writer who has done more than any other single person to investigate and publicize the events at Remagen), and every German officer up to and including Field Marshal Kesselring, Dr. Zeck believed that the cable to the main demolition charge was severed by a lucky hit from an American tank firing on the bridge. These authorities agree that the lucky hit was scored in the three minutes between the last time the circuit was tested, 3:12 P.M., and the time Captain Friesenhahn unsuccessfully attempted to set off the demolition by turning the plunger. Since III Corps had ordered no artillery fire on the bridge except time fire or pozit fuse, if such a shell landed it must have come from a tank because American tanks *were* firing onto the bridge.

It may be that the Germans find the tank shell theory attractive because it refutes the possibility of sabotage. "Sabotage" is a dirty word, and the patriotic German finds distasteful the notion that it could take place in such a situation. There was no opportunity for the Germans to investigate with any care why the charge did not go off, and they can depend only on two points made by Captain Friesenhahn. The German captain states that he was thrown to the flooring of the bridge by an exploding shell as he was rushing back to the Erpel side of the Rhine after having exploded the preliminary demolition on the Remagen side of the bridge. When returning as a prisoner of war, according to Friesenhahn, he saw a yard-wide gap in the pipe whose jagged edges seemed to indicate that the pipe had been shattered by a shell.

No Americans corroborated Captain Friesenhahn's story. They made no thorough, or even cursory, investigation at the time. They did not measure the gap in the pipe, nor examine the edges, nor try to ascertain whether a tank shell had actually caused the gap. The reason for this lack of interest was twofold: the first troops on the bridge were mainly interested in cleaning off the demolitions and not in analyzing why they did not detonate; second, it seemed somewhat pointless to conduct a post mortem when they were still in the midst of a fight.

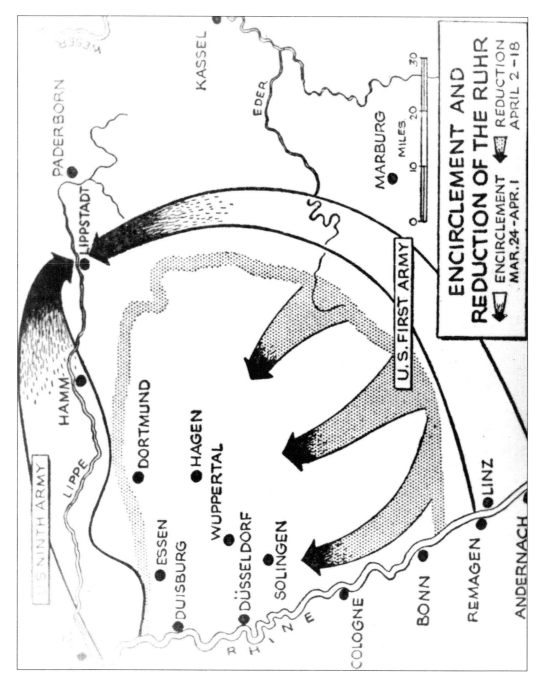

Surprise capture of the Remagen Bridge enabled American forces to encircle 300,000 German troops in the Ruhr, thereby shortening the war in Europe, which ended on May 8, 1945.

Twenty-two

The Significance of Remagen Bridge

FOR ALMOST THREE WEEKS after the capture of the Remagen bridge, American troops fought bitterly in the woods and gullies of the Westerwald. They inched forward, expanding the bridgehead hour by hour, pushing laboriously to the east, to the north and to the south. Not until March 16, when American forces reached the Bonn-Limburg autobahn, seven miles east of the Rhine, did they have the maneuver space in which to fan out. For the infantry and tankmen who slugged it out in the bridgehead, for the military police and anti-aircraft men who were strafed at the Rhine crossings by attacking planes, and for the engineers who struggled in the face of air and artillery fire to build pontoon and treadway bridges over the river, capture of the Remagen Bridge seemed to stiffen rather than weaken enemy resistance. To many of these men, it did not seem that crossing the bridge had accomplished much.

The capture of the Ludendorff Bridge materially hastened the ending of the war. It was an electrifying development at the moment, but it was followed a few weeks later by General Patton's sneak crossing of the Rhine south of Remagen at Oppenheim, and then by Field Marshal Montgomery's grand assault across the river south of Arnhem after extensive preparations and blasts on the trumpet.

One of Karl Timmermann's fellow townsmen from West Point, Nebraska, rumbled across a Rhine pontoon bridge with gasoline and supplies, several weeks after Timmermann's exploit. He commented that the Rhine seemed little wider than the Elkhorn back home and certainly not as wide as the Missouri River. He confidently told his friends that to cross a bridge like that was small potatoes. For years afterward, he spoke up in West Point American Legion meetings, in all the local bars, and at the corner drugstore, disparaging what Timmermann had done at Remagen.

The Germans had a far different reaction. In his conference with Field Marshal Kesselring two days after the capture of the Ludendorff Bridge, Hitler told him bluntly that the really vulnerable spot on the western front was Remagen, and that it was urgent to "restore" the situation there. Hitler took a personal hand in hurrying all available troops to reduce the Remagen bridgehead. The 11th Panzer Division wheeled southward from the Ruhr. The Panzer Lehr and 9th Panzer divisions followed, swallowing many gallons of precious, high-priority gasoline. Many other divisions and scraps of divisions joined in the frantic German fight to contain the bridgehead.

Field Marshal Model's Chief of Staff, Major General Carl Wagener, summed up the German view as follows: "The Remagen affair caused a great stir in the German Supreme Command. Remagen should have been considered a basis for termination of the war. Remagen created a dangerous and unpleasant abscess within the last German defenses, and it provided an ideal springboard for the coming offensive east of the Rhine. The Remagen bridgehead made the other crossings of the Rhine a much easier task for the enemy. Furthermore, it tired German forces which should have been resting to withstand the next major assault."

The Remagen bridgehead was vital in helping to form the southern and eastern pincers for the Allied troops that surrounded and trapped 300,000 German soldiers in the Ruhr.

As sorely needed German troops were thrown against the Remagen bridgehead, the resulting disorganization and weakening of defenses made it much easier for other American Rhine crossings to be made to the north and south of Remagen. Just as the loss of the bridge was a blow to German morale, so did it provide a strong boost to American and Allied morale. Not only did it make the end of the war seem close at hand, but it also emboldened the combat troops when they were confronted with chances to exploit opportunities. It underlined the fact that the German army's soft spots could be found through aggressive attacks, thereby spurring American forces to apply greater pressure.

After the war, General Eisenhower had this to say about the significance of the seizure of Remagen Bridge: "Broad success in war is usually foreseen by days or weeks, with the result that when it actually arrives higher commanders and staffs have discounted it and are immersed in plans for the future. This was completely unforeseen. We were across the Rhine, on a permanent bridge; the traditional defensive barrier to the heart of Germany was pierced. The final defeat of the enemy, which we had long calculated would be accomplished in the spring and summer campaigning of 1945, was suddenly now, in our minds, just around the corner." General Eisenhower's Chief of Staff, Lieutenant General Walter Bedell Smith, termed the Remagen Bridge "worth its weight in gold."

President Franklin D. Roosevelt, with only six weeks to live, shared the elation of the field commanders over the significance of Remagen. The victorious Army Chief of Staff, General George C. Marshall, had this appraisal to make:

> The prompt seizure and exploitation of the crossing demonstrated American initiative and adaptability at its best, from the daring action of the platoon leader to the Army commander who quickly directed all his moving columns. . . . The bridgehead provided a serious threat to the heart of Germany, a diversion of incalculable value. It became a springboard for the final offensive to come.

War correspondents on the scene added their eyewitness accounts on the significance of seeing American troops on the east bank of the Rhine. The Associated Press cabled on March 8: "The swift, sensational crossing was the biggest military triumph since the Normandy landings, and was a battle feat without parallel since Napoleon's conquering legions crossed the Rhine early in the last century." Hal Boyle wrote from the front that "with the exception of the great tank battle at El Alamein, probably no tank engagement in World War II will be remembered longer than the dashing coup which first put the American army across the Rhine at Remagen." He added that the crossing of the Rhine by the men "who knew there was strong likelihood the dynamite-laden bridge would blow up under them at any moment has saved the American nation 5,000 dead and 10,000 wounded."

"It was a moment for history," stated *Time* magazine.

The nation expressed its gratitude to the heroes of Remagen in numerous ways. Both the United States Senate and the House of Representatives interrupted their deliberations to cheer the news. In the House, a spirited debate took place as to which state could claim the first man to cross. Congressman Brooks Hays of Arkansas declared philosophically: "I am sure there will be glory enough for all."

All around the country, local civic and patriotic organizations honored the men who had wrought the miracle of Remagen. The feeling toward the Remagen heroes was perhaps best expressed in an editorial in the March 10, 1945, *New York Sun*, which concluded with these words:

> Great shifts in history often do hang upon the developments of minutes. Americans know, and the enemy has learned, that given the least opportunity, American soldiers are quick to seize any break and exploit it to the fullest. The men who, in the face of scattered fire and the great threat of the bridge blowing up under them, raced across and cut the wires have materially shortened a struggle in which every minute means lost lives. To all who utilized that ten minutes so advantageously goes the deepest gratitude this country can bestow.

Captain Karl Friesenhahn, the little German engineer who was in charge of the engineer company at Remagen in 1945, returned to Remagen in 1954. I saw him gaze over the ruins of the bridge, and he quietly asked what awards the American Army had given to Lieutenant Timmermann, Sergeant Drabik, Lieutenant Mott and the other first Americans who had crossed. When I told him that they had received Distinguished Service Crosses, Captain Friesenhahn replied with some feeling:

"They deserved them—and then some. They saw us trying to blow that bridge, and by all odds it should have blown up while they were crossing it. In my mind, they were the greatest heroes in the whole war."

Remagen heroes visit with President Dwight D. Eisenhower in the White House, Washington, D.C. From left, seated: George P. Soumas, Perry, Iowa; C. Windsor Miller, Silver Spring, Maryland; President Eisenhower; General Carl Spaatz (ret), U.S Air Force; Anthony March, Editor, The Army Times, Washington, D.C. From left, standing: William J. Goodson, Pendleton, Indiana; Michael Chinchar, Saddle River Township, N.J; Colonel Leonard E. Engeman, Redwood Falls, Minn; Lt. General John Leonard (ret), San Antonio, Texas; Alex Drabik, Toledo, Ohio; Anthony Samele, Bronx, New York; Joseph S. Petrencsik, Cleveland, Ohio; John Grimball, Columbia, South Carolina; Secretary of the Army Robert T. Stevens; SFC Joseph DeLisio, Bronx, New York; Major Hugh Mott NGUS (inactive), Nashville, Tenn; Major Emmet J. Burrows, NGUS (inactive) Hoboken, N.J; Eugene Dorland, Manhattan, Kansas; Dr. Ken Hechler, Historian of Remagen Bridge; Deputy Secretary of Defense, Robert Anderson. President Eisenhower invited the heroes of Remagen to the tenth anniversary of the capture of the Ludendorff Bridge, March 7, 1955

Postscript Written in 1957

TODAY AT REMAGEN, there are a few stone piers in the river and four brown stone towers on the river bank–all that remain of the Ludendorff Bridge. No effort has been made to rebuild it. The people of Remagen openly oppose a bridge at this point, not only because it destroys the sweeping vista up the Rhine, but because they say a bridge always invites bombings and battle in wartime. The citizens love the little ferry that gets buffeted by the current in its journey back and forth across the river.

Across the river from Remagen, the railroad tunnel where the last German defenders surrendered is now sealed up at one end. In the tunnel itself a Cologne firm is growing mushrooms. Huge piles of manure, necessary for the cultivation of mushrooms, are strewn around the spot where the Americans first set foot east of the Rhine. A sightseer walking in the streets of Remagen or at the site of the bridge would find no monument, no sign, no marker of any kind to indicate that a historic event occurred here. There are only weeds, old tin cans, and the leftovers from some old picnic lunches never cleaned up.

Not long after the bridge collapsed in 1945, the engineers erected a wooden plaque, listing the names of their comrades who had been swept or crushed to their death in the twisted girders of the falling bridge. The plaque was set up on one of the stone towers. Local residents say it has been missing for several years.

In 1954, when I brought Captain Willi Bratge back to the site of the Remagen Bridge, this former German officer, who had been sentenced to death for his part in the Remagen episode, expressed the hope that some day the American and German veterans of Remagen should meet there and clasp the hands of friendship. Captain Bratge mentioned his idea to several old soldiers in Remagen, who expressed fear that this would only serve to reopen old wounds. "But we can use this as a symbol," Captain Bratge said, "to express and demonstrate the friendship between America and Germany today, and also our human friendships as individuals. If we could only meet and shake hands at the very point where we shed our blood in 1945, I believe it would emphasize our feeling of good will, one toward another."

What has happened to those who fought at Remagen Bridge? On the German side, Captain Bratge still teaches school and lives quietly on the upper floor of the schoolhouse in a little town of 250 inhabitants near the East German border. Captain Friesenhahn lives in Koblenz, where he supervises an athletic club. Gerhard Rothe manages the Central Hotel in Remagen. Jacob Klebach still practices part-time carpentry in Remagen. Other members of the German infantry and engineer units which

Lt. Karl H. Timmermann, 27th Armored Inf. Bn, 9th Armored Div., U.S. First Army, awarded the Distinguished Service Cross by Maj. Gen. John W. Leonard, Commander of the 9th Armored Division, April 5, 1945. U.S. ARMY SIGNAL CORPS, NATIONAL ARCHIVES

fought at Remagen still live in the town. Dr. Hans Kemming is again bürgermeister of Remagen, after being replaced by the American forces when they arrived in 1945.

On the American side, the generals who participated in one way or another in the capture of the Remagen Bridge—Hoge, Leonard, Millikin, Hodges, Collins and Bradley—are living in retirement. Colonel James H. Phillips, who was III Corps Chief of Staff, is now a major general heading the Army Security Agency. Lieutenant Colonel Leonard Engeman, the 14th Tank Battalion Commander, and Lieutenant Colonel Norman B. Edwards of III Corps G-3 are both full colonels serving in Japan and Europe, respectively.

Major Murray Deevers, who commanded the 27th Armored Infantry Battalion, was killed in 1954 in a plane crash in Japan. One of the three courageous engineers who ripped out the demolition wires on the bridge, John A. Reynolds of Lincolnton, North Carolina, was killed by a sniper a little over a month after the Remagen crossing.

The first officer across the Rhine, Lieutenant Karl Timmermann, returned to his home town of West Point, Nebraska, to rejoin his wife and new daughter.

The first man to cross Remagen Bridge, Sgt. Alex Drabik (right), receiving Distinguished Service Cross from his 9th Armored Division Commander, Gen. Leonard. Sgt. Michael Chinchar, who also received the Distinguished Service Cross, is at center of the photo. U.S. ARMY SIGNAL CORPS, NATIONAL ARCHIVES

After several years as a civilian, Timmermann rejoined the Army in 1948 as a recruiter. He was sent to Korea in 1950 during hostilities, fought in the Inchon invasion, but cancer struck him down and he died in an Army hospital in Korea in 1951. West Point honored him with a special ceremony in 1995.

Sergeant Alex Drabik, the first man over the bridge, is now working as a butcher in Toledo, Ohio. Sergeant Joseph DeLisio reenlisted and fought in Korea. He married a beautiful Japanese girl and is now stationed in Japan as a Sergeant, First Class, Regular Army.

Captain George P. Soumas, commander of the first tank company to cross the bridge, is practicing law in Perry, Iowa, where he recently completed a second term as County Attorney. Lieutenant C. Windsor Miller, platoon leader of the first tank platoon to cross the bridge, is Vice President in charge of Mortgaging at the Thomas J. Fisher Realty Co. in Washington, D.C. Lieutenant John Grimball, who brought his tank platoon up to the Ludendorff Bridge and covered it with fire, is practicing law in Columbia, South Carolina, and is also a member of the South Carolina legislature.

Sergeant William J. Goodson, who commanded the first tank across the bridge, is making starter brushes for automobiles at the Delco-Remy plant at Anderson, Indiana.

Lieutenant Hugh Mott, one of the three engineers first on the bridge, is now City Treasurer of Nashville, Tennessee. Another engineer, Sergeant Eugene Dorland, is a stone mason in Manhattan, Kansas.

Lieutenant Emmet Burrows, who led the attack on the town of Remagen and was the second officer across the bridge, is office manager for a transport firm in Hoboken. Sergeant Joseph S. Petrencsik is employed by the Cleveland Welding Co. Sergeant Anthony Samele is a mail handler in the post office at Long Island City. Sergeant Michael Chinchar is a combination man for the Interchemical Corp., at Lodi, New Jersey.

On the tenth anniversary of the capture of Remagen Bridge, March 7, 1955, President Eisenhower assembled the commanders and Distinguished Service Cross winners at the White House for an anniversary celebration. President Eisenhower greeted the Remagen heroes with these words:

> Gentlemen, I have asked you to come here this morning because you know old soldiers' minds are bound to turn back once in a while to dramatic events of war – particularly of the kind that took place at the Remagen bridgehead.
>
> Now, of course, that was not the biggest battle that ever was, but for me it always typified one thing: the dash, the ingenuity, the readiness at the first opportunity that characterizes the American soldier.
>
> You men are only a typical group of the great forces that were in Europe, but it did seem to me that here, on the 10th anniversary of the day you went across the Rhine, you might not mind coming in and saying hello to the man who was responsible for directing this whole over-all strategy.
>
> I also brought with me General Spaatz. He typified the unity between the ground-air team on the battlefield that was responsible for victory.
>
> Now I must confess to you that I have done something on my own responsibility. I have organized here the Society of the Remagen Bridgehead. I have prepared for each of you a little certificate which I hope you will keep and retain as of some sentimental value. It is nothing except to say in my little way to you, and through you to all of the 9th Armored Division – and all of the whole Army, Navy and Air Force behind you that was responsible for this thing – my own personal thanks.
>
> Incidentally, one of these certificates is made out to all the officers and men of the 9th Armored Division, and General Leonard says he is going to send it down to Fort Knox as a memento.

Postscript Written in 1993

TODAY AT REMAGEN, the two stone piers which jutted out into the Rhine River for over 30 years after the capture of the Ludendorff Bridge, were removed in 1976. The piers were blasted out in order to make river navigation safer. No longer are mushrooms being grown in the old railroad tunnel on the east bank of the Rhine. The entire area on both sides of the Rhine has been cleaned up. A thriving museum has been built on the Remagen side of the river, with artifacts, books and photographs of the dramatic events of March 7, 1945.

Although Captains Bratge and Friesenhahn are gone, their spirits still remain. On March 7, 1985, many veterans of the epic Remagen battles, both German and American, reassembled in a moving ceremony labelled "Reconciliation at Remagen." Former adversaries embraced to the cheers of the crowds of onlookers. More elaborate ceremonies are planned for the 50th anniversary of the capture of the Remagen Bridge on March 7, 1995.

Many of the heroes of Remagen still survive. Gone are Grimball, Goodson, DeLisio, Petrencsik and others. Leonard Engeman lives in Nevada City, California. C. Windsor Miller has moved to Fairfield, Pennsylvania. Others have retired.

There is a new bürgermeister (mayor) in Remagen, named Hans Peter Kürten, who replaced Dr. Hans Kemming. Kürten sparked the establishment of the museum at the bridge, and played a leading role in organizing the 1985 reunion on the 40th anniversary of the capture of the bridge.

World-wide attention has been focused on the spectacular seizure of the Ludendorff Bridge on March 7, 1945. The U.S. Military Academy at West Point, N.Y.; Command and General Staff School at Leavenworth, Kansas; the Armored Center at Fort Knox, Ky.; and the Army Corps of Engineers at Fort Belvoir have all utilized the dramatic actions at Remagen as illustrations in training. A large number of television documentaries have been produced on the capture of the Remagen Bridge, including a series entitled "Twentieth Century," narrated by Walter Cronkite; "Battleline" produced by Sherman Grinberg; "The Big Picture" produced by the U.S. Army; a 25-minute training film produced by the Arts and Entertainment Network featuring the construction of the temporary bridges at Remagen and especially the treadway bridge built by Colonel David E. Pergrin's 291st Engineer Combat Battalion.

On May 5, 1987, the Army Corps of Engineers filmed a documentary on "The Bridges at Remagen," featuring construction of the pontoon and treadway bridges.

The original paperback publication of *The Bridge at Remagen* sold over 600,000 copies.

The following photographs were taken by C. Windsor Miller of Fairfield, Pa. He was a member of Company A, 14th Tank Bn., 9th Armored Division—the first tank company to cross the Rhine River at Remagen, Germany, March 7, 1945. These four photos were taken with a German Leica that Miller took from a surrendering German officer near the end of the war.

Column of German soldiers fleeing Russian troops in order to surrender to the Americans. Miller was ordered to take his platoon of five tanks and intercept a small group of stragglers and hold them until a truck could pick them up and take them to be processed. Final count was nearly 20,000. Near Carlsbad, Czechoslovakia, May 1945. COURTESY C. WINDSOR MILLER

A Company men playing volleyball. Tanks parked beyond fence in background. Burgunstadt, June 1945. COURTESY C. WINDSOR MILLER

A Company men and civilians leaving a church in Burgunstadt. A section of the church was set aside for Americans, who were not permitted to sit with Germans. The priest was German and could not give communion to Americans. COURTESY C. WINDSOR MILLER

A Company men performing maintenance on tanks and weapons. Tank on right was Lt. Miller's, tank on left believed to be Sgt. Goodson's. COURTESY C. WINDSOR MILLER

Ken Hechler and Alex Drabik (the first soldier to cross Remagen Bridge) leave the White House after presenting the first copy of the book The Bridge at Remagen *to President Dwight D. Eisenhower.*

Making The Movie: The Bridge at Remagen

Stars Caught in Russian Invasion Trap—
Their Cloak and Dagger Escape

REPRINTED FROM *TV and Movie Screen* MAGAZINE, JANUARY 1969

EDITOR'S NOTE: *West Virginia Congressman Ken Hechler, author of the best-seller,* The Bridge at Remagen, *is technical adviser to the David L. Wolper Production of the film based on his book. Congressman Hechler escaped from Czechoslovakia 12 hours before the recent Russian invasion, which temporarily halted filming near Prague. Stars of the cast were trapped by the Russian thrust, but managed to reach the Austrian border. The film will be completed in Hamburg, Germany, and at a location near the Pope's summer home outside of Rome, Italy.*

AT 5:30 A.M. on August 21st, Bradford Dillman knocked on Robert Vaughn's door at the Park Hotel in Prague, and in a matter-of-fact tone announced:

"Look out your window! The Russians have invaded Czechoslovakia."

Always a man with the cool response, Vaughn gazed in disbelief at the long-gunned tanks and armored cars in the square below, and then stated simply: "I would say that your appraisal is accurate."

Since June 6th, which was D-Day for the Normandy invasion of Europe by the Allies in World War II, Vaughn, Dillman, E. G. Marshall, Ben Gazzara and George Segal, along with scores of other actors, supported by hundreds of Czech extras, have been filming the first American picture to be made in Czechoslovakia. It may be the last, although the producer and cast feverishly hope not, for the Czechs have broken their backs to make this film a success.

When an American armored spearhead reached the heights above the Rhine River at Remagen, Germany, on March 7, 1945, an incredible sight unfolded far below: a bridge was still standing! While the German defenders frantically tried to blow up this last barrier to the heart of their homeland, a small group of infantry, tankers and engineers stormed across the bridge at Remagen to score the first military crossing of the Rhine since Napoleon. The exploit probably saved 10,000 lives and shortened the war in Europe by months: V-E Day followed two months after the Remagen Bridge was captured.

Major Barnes (Bradford Dillman, standing) tells his men that Able Company will lead the attack on the Remagen Bridge in The Bridge at Remagen.

Why make this movie in Czechoslovakia? For two years, David Wolper scoured the United States, Germany and the rest of Europe in search of a bridge and terrain similar to Remagen, where the Rhine cuts through a deep gorge. The original bridge at Remagen was destroyed in 1945 and never rebuilt, and filming on location was virtually impossible because of the heavy river traffic on the Rhine.

"We found a similar bridge at the little town of Davle, near Prague, and also got permission of the Czech authorities to stop the river traffic during filming. They even provided a ferry for the citizens to get back and forth across the Vlatava River," David Wolper explained.

The producers then sank millions of dollars into redesigning the bridge approaches and scenery to duplicate Remagen. Four huge stone towers were built of plaster. A complete church was constructed. About $150,000 was spent in blasting a 60-foot railroad tunnel in one hillside, for the Germans used the tunnel for their last-gasp defense. The highway bridge itself was then lifted and redesigned as a tracked railroad bridge, and later planked over—as the Americans did at Remagen. The art director, Alfred Sweeny, achieved a modern miracle by duplicating the scene at Remagen.

Robert Vaughn plays German Major Paul Kreuger in The Bridge at Remagen.

"More smoke! Dammit, I said more smoke!"

Fifteen times a day, the loud British bellow, punctuated with colorful profanity, dominates the set. John Guillermin, who directed *The Blue Max* and *Guns at Batasi*, is the London-born director of *The Bridge at Remagen*. Perfection with a loud voice are his watchwords. Dramatic realism with battle scenes are his forte. His task is made doubly difficult because his directions, liberally interspersed with juicy phrases, had to be translated into Czech for the many supporting native actors.

"This is the roughest, toughest, dirtiest film I've ever made," said George Segal, collapsing into a chair after one sequence. A man of tremendous physical energy, when Segal staggers into his hotel at 7 p.m. or later every night, his shoulders look a little bent, but he always smiles through the deep layer of grime and soot. Segal plays the role of *Lt. Hartman*, the American company commander who leads the first infantry across the bridge—despite his cynicism about the Army and his role in the war. He is a hero in spite of himself.

Brig. General Shinner (E. G. Marshall, right) tells Major Barnes (Bradford Dillman) to take the Remagen Bridge before it is destroyed in The Bridge at Remagen.

Look for a long cigar and a brown-knit cap, plus a scarf, and you can spot Ben Gazzara on the set. A lying, cheating, looting, stealing, unprincipled and independent character, Gazzara plays the role of *Sgt. Angelo*, in which he frequently clashes with *Lt. Hartman*. As a mark of his independence, Gazzara carries a looted German weapon with him throughout the film. E. G. Marshall has been assigned the task of portraying *General Shinner*, the American armored division commander.

For legal and dramatic reasons, the real-life characters who were at Remagen Bridge are not given the same names in the film.

Robert Vaughn scores a genuine dramatic triumph as the German *Major Paul Kreuger*, who is dispatched from higher headquarters to take command of the Remagen Bridge defense. Vaughn has cultivated an aristocratic German accent to make a convincing portrayal. To me, one of the spine-tingling high points of the film is provided in one simple line which Vaughn delivers in his own style. An infuriated Hitler sent out an execution squad when the Remagen Bridge failed to blow up. *Major Kreuger* is summarily tried and sentenced to death by a drum-head court-martial. As the fanatical Nazis lead him to his execution, American bombers appear overhead. "Enemy's?" asks someone.

Hechler with producer David Wolper.

Ken Hechler (left) with George Segal (center), who plays Lt. Hartman, and Ben Gazzara (right), who plays Sgt. Angelo.

"Who is the enemy?" *Major Kreuger* asks, somewhat cryptically.

Napoleon Solo had a bewildering series of narrow escapes in *The Man from U.N.C.L.E.* Robert Vaughn had several real ones in Czechoslovakia. When *Major Kreuger* is tied to the stake and executed by a firing squad, this sequence was filmed at the town of Duchov, some 60 miles north of Prague (where the great lover Casanova wrote his *Memoirs*). Always a stickler for realism, Director Guillermin had "squib charges" placed inside Vaughn's German uniform, so that the impact of the firing squad's bullets would show up clearly. The squib charges were made double strength, and they accidentally detonated against Vaughn's bare skin instead of merely ripping out of his uniform. The result was painful second degree burns on his chest.

It is probable that more explosives and dynamite are used in *The Bridge at Remagen* than any other war film yet made. Logan Z. Frazee and his two sons supervised the "special effects" in a remarkably realistic fashion. On the day I left Czechoslovakia, Logan Frazee was mixing some explosive which prematurely went off in his face and it was feared his eyesight would be impaired. At last report, however, his injuries were not serious.

Of course, none of these hazards were potentially as serious as the Russian invasion of Czechoslovakia which struck during the night of August 20-21. Czech members of the crew informed the Americans during the night of the impending danger. Even prior to the Russian invasion, the East German press had been clamoring that "busloads of American troops were arriving in Prague disguised as tourists, actors and film technicians." The charge was first made in May by the East German news agency, A.D.N., and again a few weeks before the Russian invasion by the East German newspaper *Neues Deutschland*. The latter even went so far as to claim there was a definite connection between an American arms cache of World War II vintage that had supposedly been discovered and the "arsenal" of weapons used in the filming of *The Bridge at Remagen*. The Russian satellites were charging that the movie was really some kind of a C.I.A. operation!

This may have been the reason why, when the Russians invaded Czechoslovakia, apparently the tanks, weapons and equipment used in the film were confiscated. It became impossible to continue in Czechoslovakia, and the cast made quick plans to evacuate.

Aided by the U.S. Embassy, the members of the cast piled into taxicabs and headed for the Austrian border. They encountered many menacing signs along the way, as refugees were fleeing and Russian tanks were moving to command every strategic crossroad in Czechoslovakia. Several of the cast and crew were of course apprehensive lest they be stopped, robbed, or have valuable camera equipment taken away from them. Fortunately, that portion of the film which had been completed between June 6 and the invasion had already been safely shipped out of the country.

In the mad confusion which followed the Russian invasion, the members of the cast milled around the International Hotel. Sleep was virtually impossible for the American citizens caught in the unexpected invasion trap. A number of wives and

The temporary bridge erected near Castel Gandolfo (the Pope's summer home) as final scenes were shot after Russians drove the movie company out of Czechoslovakia.

children accompanied their mates on what was to be a combination second honeymoon for some and a memorable family holiday for others.

The tenseness of the situation was heightened when someone recalled that the International Hotel was built under Stalin's regime, and was once used as barracks for Russian officers. Right behind the hotel is the Czech Army barracks, which added a touch of grim warlike realism as the stunned cast and crew caught sight of the Russian tanks which ringed the hotel.

In the cloak and dagger atmosphere of the fleeing film personnel, many left behind valuable personal belongings and movie equipment. Bob Vaughn, his personal secretary, Sharon Miller, told us, suffered the greatest loss. He left four suitcases and a steamer trunk behind, plus his notes for his Ph.D. dissertation. Fortunately, Sharon added, "I have sufficient copies of the notes at home."

"I just hope," Vaughn said, "that the American Embassy can recover all of my personal gear."

Since sleep was out of the question, Brad Dillman and his co-stars rehashed the events that led to their mad dash from the city encircled by tanks and guns. It was a Czech driver for the American film group who pounded on Dillman's door at the Park Hotel at 5 A.M. to alert him to the danger. Suddenly wide awake, Brad, as mentioned earlier, banged on Vaughn's door. They were the only members of the cast living at the Park Hotel, near the center of Prague. Within two hours they met 70-odd members of the *Remagen* crew at the International.

At the height of the confusion, Wolper, outwardly calm, began arrangements with

Congressman Ken Hechler on the movie set of The Bridge at Remagen.

our Embassy to rescue the Americans. It was like a scene from a movie as the motorcade moved out of the trouble zone. Some breathed a sigh of relief, others, with a strong sense of history in the making, left with reluctance.

Czechs, who had worked on the film, manned 20 taxis for the motorcade. In tow, with the fleeing Americans, was a 25-year-old waitress the Ben Gazzaras planned to hire as governess for their two children.

The motorcade arrived at the Austrian border about 7:30 P.M., just one hour before the exit to safety was sealed off.

"I know it sounds silly," Vaughn's lovely secretary sighed, "but the worst thing of all is that I feel like I've deserted the Czechs."

Vaughn, Segal and Dillman nodded in silent agreement.

Appendix

· · · · · · ·

In honor of their achievement in capturing the Remagen Bridge and exploiting the bridgehead east of the Rhine, a number of individual units were awarded Presidential Unit Citations. A list of the units which received these citations follows.

Combat Command B, 9th Armored Division, composed of the following units:

Headquarters and Headquarters Company;
27th Armored Infantry Battalion;
52d Armored Infantry Battalion;
1st Battalion, 310th Infantry Regiment;
14th Tank Battalion;
Company B, 9th Armored Engineer Battalion;
Troop C, 89th Cavalry Reconnaissance Squadron (Mechanized);
3d Platoon, Troop E, 89th Cavalry Reconnaissance Squadron (Mechanized);
1st Platoon, Company F, 89th Cavalry Reconnaissance Squadron (Mechanized);
Company B, 2d Medical Battalion;
Company C, 656th Tank Destroyer Battalion (SP);
2d Platoon, Reconnaissance Company, 656th Tank Destroyer Battalion (SP);
16th Armored Field Artillery Battalion;
400th Armored Field Artillery Battalion;
482d Antiaircraft Artillery Automatic Weapons Battalion (SP);
Detachment, Military Police Platoon;
Interrogation of Prisoners of War Team 106;
Detachment, Counter Intelligence Corps Team 509;
Ambulance Platoon, 423d Medical Collecting Company
276th Engineer Combat Battalion
Company C, 9th Armored Engineer Battalion, 9th Armored Division
9th Signal Company
94th Signal Battalion
The Military Police Platoon, 9th Infantry Division
3d Battalion, 310th Infantry Regiment
47th Infantry Regiment; with the following attached units:
84th Field Artillery Battalion;
Company B, 9th Medical Battalion;
Company B, 15th Engineer Battalion;
Company A, 746th Tank Battalion;
Company C, 899th Tank Destroyer Battalion

The following is a sample of the Presidential Unit Citation:

PRESIDENTIAL UNIT CITATION

GENERAL ORDERS   WAR DEPARTMENT
N. 72   Washington 25, D. C., 28 August 1945

* * * * * * * *

BATTLE HONORS.—As authorized by Executive Order 9396 (sec. I, WD Bul. 22, 1943), superseding Executive Order 9075 (sec. III, WD Bul. 11, 1942), the following unit is cited by the War Department under the provisions of section IV, WD Circular 333, 1943, in the name of the President of the United States as public evidence of deserved honor and distinction. The citation reads as follows:

Combat Command B, 9th Armored Division, composed of the following units:

Headquarters and Headquarters Company;
27th Armored Infantry Battalion;
52d Armored Infantry Battalion;
1st Battalion, 310th Infantry Regiment;
14th Tank Battalion;
Company B, 9th Armored Engineer Battalion;
Troop C, 89th Cavalry Reconnaissance Squadron
    (Mechanized);
3d Platoon, Troop E, 89th Cavalry Reconnaissance Squadron
    (Mechanized);
1st Platoon, Company F, 89th Cavalry Reconnaissance
    Squadron (Mechanized);
Company B, 2d Medical Battalion;
Company C, 656th Tank Destroyer Battalion (SP);
2d Platoon, Reconnaissance Company, 656th Tank Destroyer
    Battalion (SP);
16th Armored Field Artillery Battalion;
400th Armored Field Artillery Battalion;
482d Antiaircraft Artillery Automatic Weapons Battalion (SP);
Detachment, Military Police Platoon;
Interrogation of Prisoners of War Team 106;
Detachment, Counter Intelligence Corps Team 509;
Ambulance Platoon, 423d Medical Collecting Company,

is cited for outstanding performance of duty in action from 28 February to 9 March 1945 in Germany. On 28 February, *Combat Command B* launched an attack from the vicinity of Soller and less than twenty-four hours later crossed the Erft River at Derkum. Forcing the enemy into disorderly retreat, the unit headed southeast, reaching the heights west of Remagen on 7 March, where troops of the command could see the Ludendorff Bridge across the Rhine River with large numbers of German troops fleeing across it. At 1500 hours that day, a prisoner was captured who revealed that the bridge was mined for demolition and was to be destroyed at 1600 hours. At 1535 hours, one column of *Combat Company B* reached the western approach to the bridge. The span was still intact. Although the destruction of the bridge was imminent, American troops unhesitatingly rushed across the structure in the face of intense enemy automatic weapons fire. An explosion rocked the bridge but did not destroy it. Engineers scrambled down the abutments, cutting wires leading to other demolition charges and disposing of hundreds of pounds of explosives by hurling them into the river. Bulldozer tanks, working under heavy artillery and small-arms fire, filled craters at the bridge approach to permit vehicular passage. Upon reaching the opposite bank, troops of *Combat Command B* fought gallantly and cleared the surrounding high ground. Although the strength of the span was unknown, tank units rumbled across the bridge after dark and lent their support to foot troops. Antiaircraft artillery men deployed their weapons so skillfully that in the ensuing days numerous enemy airplanes were destroyed in vain attempts to destroy the bridge. The superb skill, daring, and esprit de corps displayed by each officer and man of *Combat Command B, 9th Armored Division*, in the dash to the Rhine, the capture of the Ludendorff Bridge, and the successful exploitation of this first bridgehead across Germany's formidable river barrier made an outstanding contribution to the defeat of the enemy.

* * * * * * * *

By order of the Secretary of War:

OFFICIAL: G. C. MARSHALL
  EDWARD F. WITSELL   -   *Chief of Staff*
  Major General
  Acting The Adjutant General

Individual Awards

DISTINGUISHED SERVICE CROSS

The Distinguished Service Cross is the highest award which is conferred only on members of the U.S. Army. It is second only to the Medal of Honor, which is also awarded to members of other branches of the service. The following officers and men of the 9th Armored Division were awarded Distinguished Service Crosses for their heroism at Remagen:

Sergeant Alex A. Drabik of Holland (Toledo), Ohio, squad leader of 3d platoon, Company A, 27th Armored Infantry Battalion. First man over the bridge.

Second Lieutenant Karl H. Timmermann of West Point, Nebraska, company commander of Company A, 27th Armored Infantry Battalion. First officer over the bridge.

Sergeant Joseph DeLisio of Bronx, New York, platoon leader of 3d platoon, Company A, 27th Armored Infantry Battalion. Cleaned out machine gun nest on bridge.

First Lieutenant Hugh B. Mott of Nashville, Tennessee, platoon leader in Company B, 9th Armored Engineer Battalion. Led engineers who ripped out demolition wires and cleared the bridge of explosives.

Sergeant Eugene Dorland of Manhattan, Kansas, Company B, 9th Armored Engineer Battalion. One of engineers who helped clear the bridge of explosives.

Sergeant John A. Reynolds of Lincolnton, North Carolina, Company B, 9th Armored Engineer Battalion. One of engineers who helped clear the bridge of explosives.

Captain George P. Soumas of Perry, Iowa, company commander of Company A, 14th Tank Battalion, the first tank company to cross the bridge.

First Lieutenant C. Windsor Miller of Silver Spring, Md., platoon leader in Company A, 14th Tank Battalion, the first tank platoon to cross the bridge.

Sergeant William J. Goodson of Pendleton, Indiana, Company A, 14th Tank Battalion. Tank commander of the first tank which crossed Remagen Bridge.

1st Lieutenant John Grimball of Columbia, South Carolina, platoon leader in Company A, 14th Tank Battalion. Head of first tank platoon to reach the bridge.

Sergeant Michael Chinchar of Saddle River Township, New Jersey, platoon leader of 1st platoon, Company A, 27th Armored Infantry Battalion. One of first group of infantrymen across the bridge.

Sergeant Joseph S. Petrencsik of Cleveland, Ohio, assistant squad leader in 3d platoon, Company A, 27th Armored Infantry Battalion. One of first group of infantrymen across the bridge.

Sergeant Anthony Samele of Bronx, New York, squad leader in 1st platoon, Company A, 27th Armored Infantry Battalion. Third man across the bridge.

The following is a sample of the citation for the Distinguished Service Cross:

HEADQUARTERS
FIRST UNITED STATES ARMY
APO 230

200.6—Timmermann, Karl H.   (A)
SUBJECT: Award of Distinguished Service Cross
TO: Second Lieutenant Karl H. Timmermann, 01311343,
        Infantry, United States Army.

Under the provisions of Army Regulations 600-45, as amended, you are awarded a Distinguished Service Cross for heroic achievement as set forth in the following:

CITATION

Second Lieutenant Karl H. Timmermann, 01311343, 27th Armored Infantry Battalion, United States Army. For extraordinary heroism in action against the enemy on 7 March 1945, in Germany. Upon reaching the Ludendorff railroad bridge across the

Rhine River, Second Lieutenant Timmermann, aware that the bridge was prepared for demolition, and in the face of heavy machine gun, small arms and direct 20mm gun fire, began a hazardous trip across the span. Although artillery shells and two explosions rocked the bridge, he continued his advance. Upon reaching the bridge towers on the far side, he cleared them of snipers and demolition crews. Still braving the intense machine gun and shell fire, he reached the eastern side of the river where he eliminated hostile snipers and gun crews from along the bank and on the face of the bluff overlooking the river. By his outstanding heroism and unflinching valor, Second Lieutenant Timmermann contributed materially to the establishment of the first bridgehead across the Rhine River. Entered military service from Nebraska.

COURTNEY H. HODGES
Lieutenant General, U.S. Army
Commanding

DISTINGUISHED SERVICE CROSSES AWARD
FOR EAST OF RHINE COMBAT

Warren S. Deyoe, 309th Infantry Regiment
Patsy Retort, 311th Infantry Regiment
Herbert J. Welch, Jr., 52d Armored Infantry Battalion

SILVER STAR

The following members of Company A, 27th Armored Infantry Battalion, were awarded Silver Stars for their action at Remagen Bridge on March 7, 1945:

Jack Berry	Philip J. Lawrence	Carl A. Parnell
Dean T. Craig	Martin J. Reed	Artis L. Massie
Marvin D. Jensen	John F. Ayres, Jr.	Joseph K. Peoples

The following members of Company A, 14th Tank Battalion, were awarded Silver Stars for their action at Remagen Bridge on March 7, 1945:

Robert A. Jones	William E. Richard	Lawrence H. Swayne
	Berthold Fried	

SILVER STARS AWARDED
FOR REMAGEN BRIDGEHEAD COMBAT

9th Armored Engineer Battalion

Ellis G. Fee	Lauren E. Little	Roy A. Kelly
Herbert C. Walker	Cecil W. Hanson	John P. Allen

III Corps

Paul Behee	Norman B. Edwards	Remington Orsinger
Philip R. Calder, Jr.	Paul V. Kane	Thomas J. Sharpe
George E. Dowling	F. Russel Lyons	

9th Armored Division Hq.

Walter Burnside	John E. Hyde	John D. Noell
Adna C. Hamilton	John W. Leonard	

*—Killed in Action

14th Tank Battalion, 9th Armored Division

Melvin E. Baker	Fred Lovely	James E. Thomas
Clemon Knapp	John L. McFarland	Meron J. Thompson

16th Armored Field Battalion, 9th Armored Division

Raymond W. Aakre	James A. Monat, Jr.	Harold S. Pivnick

27th Armored Infantry Battalion, 9th Armored Division

*Vaughn C. Butler

52d Armored Infantry Battalion, 9th Armored Division

*David D. Bryce	William G. Stampahar	Cleston F. Stevens
*Anton Drabiak		

60th Armored Infantry Battalion, 9th Armored Division

Clayton W. Barrett	Merton E. Lersner	George A. Smith
Howard G. Etter	Carl A. Nelson	William Q. Tripp
Joseph S. Goretski	James E. Schafer	Melville P. Wallace
Floyd D. Harder	William J. Sigman	Leon E. Williams

656th Tank Destroyer Battalion, 9th Armored Division

Michael J. Beckins	Herman Shook

482d Antiaircraft Battalion:

James B. French, Jr.	Isadore Marks

634th Antiaircraft Battalion

Edward R. Gover	Daniel A. Lotito	Ernest J. Richardson

51st Engineer Combat Battalion

Robert B. Yates

276th Engineer Combat Battalion

Herman L. Shapiro

291st Engineer Combat Battalion

Melvin E. Champion	Frank C. Dolcha	William H. Smith

552d Engineer Heavy Pontoon Battalion

William F. Tompkins

988th Engineer Treadway Bridge Company

Abden F. Gilbert	Omar D. Rodgerson

998th Engineer Treadway Bridge Company

George Barthel	Byron C. Isanhart	Howard L. Scott
Virgil A. Boley		

111th Engineer Combat Group

Harry W. Anderson

47th Infantry Regiment

Oreste Russo

*—Killed in Action

1150th Engineer Combat Group

Kenneth E. Fields

9th Infantry Division

Barend J. Albers, Jr.
Edward J. Barry
Herbert Blaker
Benjamin W. Blansit
Frank C. Blum
Joe A. Bolt
John H. Bonn
William C. Bowen, Jr.
William A. Brooks
John P. Buder
*Lee R. Burgess
Lester H. Burr
George E. Close
L. D. Cooper
Samuel R. Craddock
John A. Craun
Thomas J. Cunnea
James W. Davis
Loran Davis
Robert D. Decker
Joseph S. De Latte
James C. Driscoll
Daniel E. Duncan
Eugene L. Earle
George E. Fahrman, Jr.
Harold A. Fander
Raymond Feltner
Ray P. Firestone
Barney C. Fisher
John B. Gagnon, Jr.

Richard C. Gardner
Judson C. Gatch
Charles E. Gilliland
Charles D. Gooden
Preston O. Gordon
Thomas J. Hall, Jr.
John M. Hatfield
Kenneth W. Hill
James E. Horn
Andrew Hudak
Lewis D. Hudson
Irving C. Hughes, Jr.
John J. Janik
Karl P. Janes, Jr.
*John G. Keyser
Joseph W. Kilkenny
Paul P. Kizan
Sam A. Klein
Harold G. Leist
Alfred J. Levine
Francis D. Lyons
Terrence J. McCormick
John T. McCutcheon
Bernard E. McEntee
T. C. McFarland, Jr.
Henry McKenzie
George C. Marks
Currie P. Mombourquette

James W. Nolan
Aubrey C. Norcross
James H. O'Brien
John W. O'Connell
Alonzo T. Palmer, Jr.
William D. Parkhouse
Joseph Paskiewicz
Anthony J. Ponticello
*Nathan W. Pope
Leonard L. Pourchot
Thomas E. Rogers, Jr.
Alan R. Sawyer
Henry E. Scearce
Earl W. Schafer
Charles H. Scott
Herbert W. Sheidy
George D. Sillars
Albert Sokoloff
Frank N. Stacey
*Joseph S. Taubner
Joseph G. Tott
John J. Tunek
Lupe C. Valcazar
James L. Weaver
*Bernard L. Wolensky
Myron L. Wolfson
Donald M. Young
Orville C. Young, Jr.
Paul J. Yurik

78th Infantry Division

Dorian N. Begin
Robert J. Bigart
William F. Claiborne
Frank R. Comfort
William E. Copley
James A. Ferguson
William L. Floyd
Marvin G. Hendrix
Eldred M. Jordan
Donald L. Karch
Earl J. Kasten

Paul T. King
Michael J. Klinowski
Carl Kohl
John J. Kosak
Albin S. Kurdy
Dalton F. Lolley
Harry Lutz
Stanley Michinski
John H. Miller
Douglas A. Moore
George P. Mountain

William W. Nehuys
Lawrence S. Noyes
Verne J. Petersen
Leonard C. Prather, Jr.
William J. St. Hilaire
Edward L. Salsgiver
Clarence C. Sandusky
Elmer I. Schreke
James R. Upham
Franklin W. Van Buren
Lloyd A. Wingfield

99th Infantry Division

Eldon J. Bailey
Lee R. Bidwell
Millard W. Boucler
Clifford Bradford
John E. Brock
John R. Bullock
Bernard E. Cannon
*Robert M. Chandler
John W. Clites
Elmer T. Davis
David E. De Rose
*Robert C. Dillon
Robert J. Gallery
Earl B. Gibson, Jr.
James A. Graham
Frederick H. Grim

*Sherwood D. Henry
Glen R. Hileman
William F. Holcomb
Jerry W. Holloway
Henry S. Kupfer
Robert A. Lahay
Wesley B. Langholz
John H. Lanier
Charles M. Lindsay
*John H. Matthews, Jr.
James J. Morris
John D. O'Donnell
Egbert C. Oliver
Merle L. Otto
William G. Patterson

Joseph Pollock
Thomas W. Porter
John L. Quinn
Lewis H. Roosa
Andrew P. Sessions
Frank C. Smith
William R. Smith
Leo A. Solomon
Clyde A. Thomas
William A. Veech
*Frederick Wagner
Hartsell E. Wharton
Raymond J. Willaredt
Thomas H. Winchester
Archie S. Wing

—Killed in Action

LIST OF MEMBERS OF LEADING UNITS
CROSSING REMAGEN BRIDGE—March 7, 1945

Company A, 27th Armored Infantry Battalion

Peter Acosta
Gerald Adams
Roy W. Amick
John B. Anderson
William C. Ash
John F. Ayres, Jr.
John Azukas
Rudolf Bachmeyer
Paul L. Baker
Ronald G. Banta
Walter W. Barnes
William R. Barnes, Jr.
Thomas R. Barnett
Franklin D. Bates
James Bauer
Willie J. Bearden
Frank T. Bebber
Hal D. Beckham
Harry C. Bennett
*Herman J. Bernacki
Blaine E. Berosek
Garrett Berry
Jack Berry
Eldon F. Bieber
*Marius R. Bizier
Wayne Bothwell
Kenneth M. Braga
Nicholas Brdar
Fred Bridgett
Carlyle Brode
Ray W. Brown
Robert O. Bruegel
James A. Bullock
Wilson R. Burger
Emmet J. Burrows
Stanley B. Bush
James R. Cenerota
James Cardinale, Jr.
Ralph Chiccarelli
Russell H. Chilcoat
Michael Chinchar
Boyd R. Coffey
Thomas H. Cowick, Jr.
Dean T. Craig
Fred Crawford
Robert B. Crawford
Edward Czerwinski
Leonard J. Czyzewski
Jesse E. Daniels
Glennus E. Davis
Chester M. Dawson
Joseph DeLisio
Robert E. DeLong
Wayne D. DeTurk
John W. Dlugose
Constantine G. Dominick
Alex A. Drabik
Andrew P. Drake
James L. Droppleman
Phil Dunn
Walter J. Dunsmore
Carl L. Edwards
Richard W. Edwards
Charles A. Ellett
William J. Faloni

Norman J. Farry
Edward T. Fleischauer
Leo J. Flick
Noble K. Foster
Verlin A. Franke
*George M. Franklin
David O. Gardner
Alexander Giles
George V. Giles
Elmer J. Goehl
Anthony F. Goetz
Leo A. Gominiak
LeRoy J. Gorrell
Cecil Graves
Johnnie O. Grissom
Jack Grote
Joseph J. Gruttola
Arthur H. Gustafson
Pablo B. Gutierrez
Robert L. Hall
Richard W. Hansen
Roy L. Heaston
John H. Heitman
Lawrency J. Hennessey
Norman B. Henrichson
Francis D. Herman
Lyle R. Hess
*Willie D. Himes
Fred Horning
Clarence L. Huth
Ray H. Inman
Raymond W. Jackson
Cecil Jarvis
Clinton M. Jensen
Marvin D. Jensen
Elmer T. Johnson
Ronald F. Johnson
Edward Jundt
Eugene Kantorski
Jerry W. Katras
Marion N. Kelley
James G. Kennedy
Michael J. Kenny
Jack B. Kerce
Ray L. Kimsey
Jerry L. King
George R. Kirk
Albert Koestel
Albert V. Koon
Elmer Kost
Jack K. Kotlark
Charles D. Kreps
Frederick F. Kriner
Edward J. Kukielski
John F. Lafferty
Elliot E. Lang
Clifford E. Larrison
Helmer Larson
Richard H. Larson
Philip J. Lawrence
Robert C. Lindman
Elmer B. Lindsey
R. C. Lively
Vernon B. Lott
Hayward D. Luckett, Jr.

Edward H. Lucyk
William G. Luhr
Bernard D. Lyons
Kennon E. Lyons
William F. Macer
Louis J. Machen
Virgil O. Manuel
Frank J. Marek
Jewell W. Marshall
Harry E. Martin
Marion D. Martindale, Jr.
Artis L. Massie
August C. Matt
John J. McCarty
Charles E. McDowell
Jack W. McElroy
Joseph M. McFarland
Franklin P. Mendonca
Joseph C. Mendoza
Gaccarino Mercadante
Martin P. Meyers
Herman F. Michael
Onufry T. Migura
Forrest A. Miner
Gustave C. Mohr, Jr.
Ralph O. Munch
Chester A. E. Mundy
Elmer G. Munson
Elmer J. Mutchler
Irvin K. Nakielski
Simon Offenberg
Joseph D. O'Keefe
Steven C. Page
Charles F. Paukner
John Papushak
Carl A. Parnell
Almon Parson, Jr.
Robert G. Parsons
Daniel Patterson
LeRoy R. Patterson, **Jr.**
Joseph Pavich
Charles C. Payne, **Jr.**
Charles W. Penrod
Joseph K. Peoples
Joseph S. Petrencsik
Paul E. Petrosky, Jr.
Benjamin A. Phillips
Myron Plude
Stanley J. Pol
John M. Post
Paul Poszich
Herbert Prewitt
Ross L. Purdham
Louis F. Puzo
Martin J. Reed
Orin A. Reed
George J. Reese
*James J. Reilly
Andy Repko
Wilmer H. Reusink
Ismael A. Reynosa
Elmer C. Richards
Frank D. Richardson
Charles Rotert

*—Killed in Action

Norman Rubio
Edward Ruggiero
Mitchell Rundbaken
William C. Ruppert
John Rusakevich
Dominick M. Russo
Cornelius F. Ryan
Carmine J. Sabia
Anthony Samele
Jess R. Sanders
*Joseph J. Santomauro
Karl D. Saulpaw
Richard D. Schaeffer
John J. Schafer
Charles L. Schmidt
Herbert F. Schrecke
Airston T. Scott
Ralph Shackelford

Charles C. Shaffer
Gerald W. Sheffield
George O. Shipp
Harold E. Simmons
Carl H. Smith
George F. Smith
Hubert F. Smith
Richard E. Smith
Samuel Sommerfield
Clair H. Sowers
*Richard Sowka
Richard P. Stack
Marvin R. Staton
Sol Stern
Jay C. Swisher
Byron G. Tate
Marconi L. Taylor
Karl H. Timmermann

Raynold Topp
Joe J. Traska
Joseph P. A. Turgeon
Thomas P. Varner
Allen J. Viergutz
Joseph Vitczak
Henry Vogelstein
Albert A. Vogt
*Steve A. Vrona
Selden G. Wadkins
*Leo M. Walraven
Donald Ward
Herbert Wayne
Nelson L. Wegener
Francis White
Benjamin B. Williams
Thomas N. Williams
Robert O. Wirowek

Company A, 14th Tank Battalion

Tommy G. Akin
Robert L. Ashcraft
*Charles L. Auber
Melvin E. Baker
Eugene A. Ballew
Stanley Barszcz
Howard J. Best
Harold E. Blincoe
Smith W. Bowling
Earl R. Brooks
Kenneth O. Brown
Glen A. Brownlee
John T. Cagle, Jr.
Walter E. Cain
George F. Captain
Buy W. Caraway
*Pat W. Carter
*Rudolph F. Cerveny
Jack M. Connell
Lawrence C. Courier
Ivy R. Cow
William N. Culbertson
Frederick B. Curtis
Walter P. DeMarco
Thomas DiGrigorio
Charles L. Dickey
George R. Doering
Edmond J. Dupree
Jonathan R. Ellis
Ralph Engelman
Cecil E. Estes
Randle J. Floyd
Joseph Flynn
William A. Fox
Hubert D. Franklin
Berthold Fried
Herman A. Garavaglia
William J. Goodson
John Grimball
Raymond C. Gustafson
Melvin H. Gustwiller
Kenneth L. Hadley
Jarold F. Haines
Frank B. Halsell
John M. Hannan
George S. Herder
William H. Hess
*Fred E. Humphrey
Andrew L. Hunt
Harry Isaacs

James R. Jackson
John H. Jackson, Jr.
Robert F. Janes
Sam T. Jarrell
Elwood C. Jewell
Buren J. Johnson
Clifford A. Johnson
Glen A. Johnson
Robert A. Jones
*Chester Key
Clemon Knapp
Homer L. Knapp
Joseph Kuchel
John J. Kuhlman
Frank V. Lamphers
Trig L. Large
Charles A. Laws
Walter L. LeMaster
Lark H. Lester
Leonard Levine
George W. Littlejohn
Richard E. Lively
Fred Lovely
Anthony Mancini
John Marshall
Calvin C. Massingale
C. Windsor Miller
Hayden Millican, Jr.
Wallace J. Mills
William B. Mitchell, Jr.
Carl J. Moore
Charles M. Moore
Richard S. Moore
Alfred E. Morgan
*Sidney Moscovitz
William Moulton
*Henry C. Mounts
Ira L. Mullins
Lester L. Myhre
Bernard P. O'Daniel
Raymond E. Owens
Walter D. Paterson
Akie Patterson
Joseph J. Phillips
Fred E. Poeller, Jr.
Fred C. Raines, Jr.
Paul W. Reed
Roy Reed
William E. Richard
Zealand B. Rider

Jerome Ritterband
Darius S. Roark
Granger M. Roberson
Walter C. Rose
John I. Rounds
*Wilbur V. Rouse
Melvin J. Russell
LeRoy T. Ruth
Joe R. Ruzicka
Waldon Savage
George F. Schumacher
Ambrose A. Scott
Hyatt Shackleford
Howard B. Shaffer
Carl L. Shell
Walter E. Smalley, Jr.
George P. Soumas
James C. Stevens
Waymond E. Stiles
Donald R. Sucker
*Lawrence H. Swayne
John A. Sutton
Merschel J. Taylor
John Terman
*Richard H. Thessen
James E. Thomas
Harold L. Thompson
Lonnie Thompson
Christopher C. Trimble
Joseph E. Trujillo
Burton G. Tucker
George J. Tuma
Charles E. Tunis
Robert D. Utterback
Clarence C. Van Briesen
George A. Vario
Vincent Verducci
Jacob H. Verkennes
Paul Vitale
Joseph J. Vlach
Warren M. Voepel
John M. Volpe
Elgart L. Wahl
Morris C. Walden
Joseph Walker
Ray P. Walker
Thomas E. Ward
Everett Warner
Edwin M. Weaver
Oakley M. Weeks
Arnold Yoho

*—Killed in Action

Clement A. Wegman
Fred E. Weis
Allie C. Welch
John A. Whitehead

Clifford R. Whitener
Ernest E. Wills
William G. Wilson
Howard J. Woodard

Darrell Workman
•Adolph A. Young
James W. Zills, Sr.
Anthony Zinko

Company B, 9th Armored Engineer Battalion

Alfred J. Abrams
George W. Adams
Frank Andre
Walter F. Anttonen
Arthur R. Arnwine
Paschal J. Arseneau
Golden C. Arthur
Frederick J. Bath
Raymond J. Bedard
Seymour Bogen
Joseph A. Bolech
Russell B. Bragg
Howard F. Brown
Arthur L. Brumfield, Jr.
Earl K. Childres
Robert O. Chisolm
Joseph G. Chorbak
Coy F. Clark
Wilburn J. Coberley
Wiley R. Conerly
LaRue Confer
Robert D. Courtwright
Ralph E. Creemer
John M. Cuthbert
Frank Del Greco
Robert E. Dobson
Eugene Dorland
Joseph T. Druso
Alvin H. Ebarb
George A. Edgar
William E. Ellison
Harlan E. Elsea
Ralph F. Evans
Melvin E. Fanning
Dominick I. Fiorina
Benjamin P. Forrest
Amos Frick
Anthony J. Frisina
Albert Fuchs
Donald L. Gardner
•Edmund J. L. Gary
Joseph F. Gdovin
Walter C. Gorray
Jay H. Gorsuch
Marvin R. Guntley
Dale W. Gustin
Ragain Gyder
Herman W. Hahn
Harold R. Hamilton
Harold O. Hansen
Harry L. Hansen
•Richard W. Hansen
George T. Hardin
Lorenza A. Harrison
Joseph E. Hayden, Jr.
John J. Heine
J. D. Henderson
Melvin G. Highbarger
Gordon B. Hill
William H. Hoffman

Charles C. Huch
William W. Hundley
Donald C. Jasmer
Albert E. Jones
John L. Jones
Sumney W. Jones
Roy D. Johnson
Andrew Kamedy
Dale Keen
John T. Kennedy
Frank J. Kovach
Donald J. La Londe
David J. La Page
Bennie W. Larimer
Samuel J. Lemieux
Julius J. Lis
Jesse D. Littrell
Paul Lopez
Harry R. Loutsenhizer
Carl G. Luhr
Patsy A. Mainelli
Lunti N. Maki
Wendell Malcolm
Andrew J. Manganaro, Jr.
Elmer J. Massey
Wilfred T. Matthews
Frederick J. McMinds
Henry H. Meyer
James H. Meyers
Lewis M. Mies
Vincent J. Mileo
John B. Mitchell
Willie E. Moeckel
Clifford E. Monroe
Russell E. Moon
Herman E. Moss
Hugh B. Mott
John E. Moyto
Joseph Muniz
Walter J. Nagorka
Roy L. Nelley
Walter J. Nowicki
Nils B. Nyland
William F. O'Donnell
Clarence J. Okazaki
Clarence W. Peterson
Henry C. Phelps
Paul D. Phillips
Frank Piccirilli
Mitchell S. Pitman
Joseph H. Poganik
Joe B. Prestianni
Floyd H. Pritts
Carnnie L. Provau
Paul J. Rappold
Walter W. Reed
William D. Reichert
•John A. Reynolds

George E. Rice
Herbert L. Richerson
Glenn O. Rickard
Louis N. Rockafellow
Paul F. Rogers
Paul H. Rose
Conley L. Rowland
Nello R. Ruguone
Wilfred J. Rushia
Bernhard Rust
George B. Sanford
Ray W. Schroeder
Lawrence F. Schuler
Alvin Schultz
David W. Schwartzbeck
Robert M. Sedey
Alex Semryck
Harold Shapiro
James R. Sheldon
Wayne E. Shipton
Joseph M. Skurlock
Emery E. Smith
Frank Smith
Ralph L. Smith
Ollie Spellman
Philip H. Sporle
Victor E. Stachowski
Jamie G. Stokes
Charles E. Stuck
Benjamin Suchy
Arthur J. Szyminski
Tony C. Thompson, Jr.
Samuel M. Tomillo
•Carl F. Tubbs
Alton B. Tucker
Harry J. Tyson
John W. Ullrich
Anthony Valensky
Ernest L. Vornbrock
Charles K. Walker
James H. Waller
Samuel E. Warrington
Frank S. Warzeka
Harold E. Wasson
Edward G. Weaver, Jr.
Charles W. Weeks
Allie Whittington
Gordon Wilk
Lester B. Williams
Arthur A. Wilson
Roy W. Winkelmann
Roman A. Wisniewski
Frank R. Wojciechowski
Robert D. Woldt
Russell Wood
William J. Wood
Hiram Woods
William B. Wright
Everett Ziegler

•—Killed in Action

About the Author
· · · · · · · · · · · ·

On the day that the Remagen Bridge was captured, Ken Hechler was commanding a four-man team of combat historians near the town, and was on the bridge talking with the first men to cross, within a short time. After the war he returned to Germany to interview the officers and men of the German forces assigned for the defense and demolition of the bridge.

During and after World War II, Hechler served with the United States Government in various administrative positions in the Bureau of the Census, Office for Emergency Management and Bureau of the Budget. Starting as a draftee in 1942, he served as a private in the infantry, received his commission as a Second Lieutenant in the Armored Force, and then went overseas and was successively promoted to Major after service in the European Theater of Operations. He collected five battle stars and a Bronze Star.

Ken Hechler was born in Roslyn, New York, September 20, 1914, and his brother Charles Jr. still lives in Roslyn. He now makes his home in Huntington, West Virginia. In addition to serving as Secretary of State for West Virginia, he frequently is called on to talk to school, college and community groups about Remagen and many public issues.

Hechler has always been interested in writing and politics. At Columbia University, he received a Ph.D. in Political Science in 1940, and taught courses at Columbia College starting in 1937. In 1939, when Professor Raymond Moley, former Roosevelt brain-truster, went on leave from Barnard College, he asked Hechler to take over his key course in "Political Personalities." While at Columbia, Hechler also started doing writing and research for Judge Samuel I. Rosenman, another intimate and FDR speech-writer. This led to a fifteen-year association with Rosenman and assistance to him and President Roosevelt on the massive 13-volume *Public Papers and Addresses of Franklin D. Roosevelt*, annotated. In 1947 Hechler returned to teaching, taking a post at Princeton University. He stirred hundreds of Princetonians to become active in politics, and his unusual teaching methods* won special feature in *The Saturday Evening Post* and *Time* magazine. *Time* also broke the story that he was leaving teaching in 1949 for a while "in order to get a little closer to practical public affairs." He was unemployed for a month before getting the job he wanted—special assistant in charge of research at the White House, under President Truman. He stayed at the White House four years, accompanying President Truman throughout the country. Aside from general research and writing, his main job was to brief the President on the nature, background and outlook of every town he visited to make a "whistle-stop" speech.

---

*His most unique contribution to teaching was the installation of a telephone in the classroom, hooked up to an amplifier. This enabled him, after advance notice, to call up senators, governors and other political figures, and to carry on conversations related to the class assignment so the class could hear and get a more practical slant on what they were studying.

In 1953 Hechler became Associate Director of The American Political Science Association, where he developed the Congressional Internship Program, enabling young teachers and journalists to spend a year of practical work in congressional offices. In February 1956 he was appointed Research Director for Adlai E. Stevenson's campaign and traveled with Governor Stevenson throughout his primary and election campaigns. In February 1957 he returned to teaching, at Marshall College. During the summer of 1957 he was Administrative Aide to United States Senator John A. Carroll of Colorado.

Only one year after moving to West Virginia, in 1958 Hechler ran for and was elected to the U.S. House of Representatives. His victory was attributed to two causes: he enlisted the support of hundreds of high school and college students attracted to his ideals and program; and he distributed copies of *The Bridge at Remagen* as his principal campaign literature.

Congressman Hechler was the only Member of Congress to march with Martin Luther King at Selma, Alabama, in 1965. He soon became a champion of the health and safety of thousands of coal miners in his district. He led the fight to enact a stringent health and safety act in 1969. He was the first Congressman to introduce legislation to set a ceiling on the amount of coal dust allowed in the mines, and to compensate miners suffering from "black lung."

During his nine terms in Congress, national columnist Jack Anderson rated Hechler among the top twenty Members of Congress in "integrity and effectiveness." *Field and Stream* magazine pegged him among the top eight Congressmen in "understanding, commitment, extent of involvement in issues, and effectiveness in getting things done."

Ward Sinclair, while Washington Bureau Chief for the Louisville Courier Journal, wrote to Congressman Hechler: "I want you to know that no public official I've ever dealt with, no public figure, came close to making on me the impact you did. No figure ever gave me more hope than you did. No figure ever inspired me to keep plugging in my own small way than you did. No one. You don't have to be told of the similar impact you have had on thousands of other people like myself who believe somewhat in the wayward system, and have faith that man and his institutions will do the right thing if shown the light. You are one who carried the light high for all to see. . . ."

In 1976, while serving his ninth term in Congress, Hechler became disturbed by the millions of dollars being spent in the West Virginia gubernatorial campaign. At the last minute, he filed for Governor, resolving to accept no contributions from anyone. It was a poor and fateful decision, as voters questioned his quixotic effort to disrupt the well-financed race and give up a safe seat in Congress. He finished third in a field of eight.

For a period, he returned to teaching at Marshall University and the University of Charleston. In 1984, he ran for and was elected West Virginia's Secretary of State. He was re-elected in 1988 and 1992. His priorities have been to clean up elections, to curb excessive campaign expenditures, and to encourage more young people to participate in politics and the governmental process. He is currently serving his third term as Secretary of State.